Refugee and Immigrant Students

Achieving Equity in Education

A volume in
International Advances in Education: Global Initiatives for Equity and Social Justice
Elinor L. Brown, Rhonda Craven, and George McLean, *Series Editors*

Refugee and Immigrant Students

Achieving Equity in Education

edited by

Florence E. McCarthy
University of Western Sydney, Australia

Margaret H. Vickers
University of Western Sydney, Australia

INFORMATION AGE PUBLISHING, INC.
Charlotte, NC • www.infoagepub.com

Library of Congress Cataloging-in-Publication Data

Refugee and immigrant students : achieving equity in education / edited by
Florence E. McCarthy, Margaret H. Vickers.
    p. cm. – (International advances in education: global initiatives
for equity and social justice)
 Includes bibliographical references.
 ISBN 978-1-61735-840-1 (pbk.) – ISBN 978-1-61735-841-8 (hardcover) –
ISBN 978-1-61735-842-5 (ebook) 1. Refugees–Education. 2.
Immigrants–Education. 3. Educational equalization. I. McCarthy, Florence
E. II. Vickers, Margaret H. (Margaret Helen), 1945-
 LC3715.R43 2012
 371.826'912–dc23

                                                    2012016428

CONTENTS

PART I

PEDAGOGICAL INITIATIVES ADDRESSING ISSUES
OF EDUCATIONAL EQUITY FOR IMMIGRANTS AND REFUGEES

PART II

REFUGEE AND IMMIGRANT SCHOOL–COMMUNITY PARTNERSHIPS

PART III

SYSTEMIC ISSUES AND POLICIES FOR REFUGEE
AND IMMIGRANT EDUCATIONAL EQUITY

ACKNOWLEDGEMENTS

The focus of this book is on educational equity issues affecting immigrants and refugees around the world. Given that prior publications have given greater coverage to immigrant issues, the emphasis in this volume is on the complexities of delivering educational equity for refugees, no matter where they live. In creating this book, scholars whose research focuses on refugee education were invited to submit chapters, and special efforts were made to include contributors working with refugee organizations in camps, as government officials, or as program officers of international or local nongovernmental organizations. Daily life for these contributors is often fraught with difficulties such as environmental disasters, or conflict and violence. For this reason a number of our original authors were unable to submit their chapters; we thank them for their efforts regardless of the outcome.

Our sincere thanks go to all our contributors who have brought new thinking and original writing in the explication of the issues they are dealing with. It is through these analyses that we begin to understand the complexities of providing education to refugees across many contrasting situations—for example, from refugee camps in Africa or Asia to mainstream schools in Western countries. We particularly thank them for their willing responsiveness to the multiple requests for revisions and their patience dealing with the long timeline to publication.

We also thank the chapter reviewers whose careful reading and thoughtful comments enhanced the arguments put forward in various chapters. Our thanks also go to Elinor Brown and Rhonda Craven for supporting the publication of this book as part of the IAP series on Equity Issues in Education.

Refugee and Immigrant Students, pages vii–viii
Copyright © 2012 by Information Age Publishing

In preparing this volume, we came to have a deep appreciation and respect for the unstinting efforts of refugees as they seek to provide education for their children, and to the fortitude and resilience of the children as they strive to make the most of whatever opportunity they have. We hope this book will serve as a testament to their commitment and an inspiration to all who are concerned with these issues.

FOREWORD

FOR MY GRANDPARENTS

Carlos E. Cortés

When I received the editors' kind invitation to write the foreword to this important and revealing book, my brain told me to say no. I had too many other projects. Then my heart took over. I had to say yes. I owed it to my grandparents.

You see, three of my grandparents were immigrants to the United States, maybe refugees. You be the judge. The distinctions between refugees and immigrants can often be fuzzy, sometimes legalistic.

My grandfather, also named Carlos Cortés, fled from revolutionary Mexico in 1913. He had been a supporter of Francisco Madero, who became president of Mexico after the 1911 overthrow of longtime dictator Porfirio Díaz. But, in 1913, when Madero was assassinated by General Victoriano Huerta, Granddad Cortés learned that he, too, was on Huerta's hit list. It was get out or else.

We have no record of whether or not he had the proper documents to enter the United States. If he didn't, I'm glad he didn't bother to stop and wait for the processing of the requisite paperwork while Huerta's thugs were out to kill him. Paperwork is not always a refugee's luxury.

My mother's parents were immigrants, too, also maybe refugees. My grandmother, born Ada Weinsaft, came from Austria in the last years of the nineteenth century. My grandfather, Morris Hoffman, came from Ukraine in the first decade of the twentieth century.

Both were part of Jewish families fleeing from European anti-Semitism, which often exploded into bloody pogroms that devastated Jewish villages and communities. Their memories of their homelands were so painful that they refused to share much about their stories.

LUCK OF THE DRAW

Three of my grandparents may have been refugees, but, relatively speaking, they were also lucky refugees. Granddad Cortés was a well-educated member of the Mexican landowning aristocracy. Although he lost most of his wealth when he fled to the United States, he still had his engineering degree and class-bred self-confidence, as well as well as the cultural cushion of an American-born wife. He soon found a job with Shell Oil in California.

In contrast, the Hoffmans and Weinsafts were working class with little formal education. Yet they benefited from settling in Kansas City, Missouri, which had a strong, supportive Jewish community. There Grandma and Granddad Hoffman met and courted in Yiddish, the common language of Eastern European Jews. They opened a tiny grocery store and sold produce in the Kansas City market. Then Grandma managed apartments so that Granddad could go to night school and, subsequently, start his own small construction business.

My grandparents established a legacy for their children and grandchildren. Part of that legacy was intermarriage: my father the inheritor of a strong Mexican Catholic tradition, my mother a Reform Jew.

Their marriage launched my personal multicultural odyssey: experiencing clashes between dissonant cultures; pulled religiously in opposing directions; learning to speak—or at least defend myself in—Spanish and Yiddish as well as English; growing up without the comfort of a defined social niche; and being marginal to all social categories in racially segregated, religiously divided, class-conscious post-World War II Kansas City, Missouri.

That's the story I tell in my new autobiography, *Rose Hill: An Intermarriage before Its Time.* It's a story of the legacy of disruption, emigration, resettlement, and intermarriage.

AN EDUCATIONAL CHALLENGE

Every refugee and immigrant family has a story. Part of that story is their educational experience, too often the absence or inadequacy of educational opportunities. That's what makes this book so important.

Education for Refugees and Immigrants: Creating Equitable Pathways for the Future is an eye-opening book of scholarship, hope, and human compassion. It offers myriad compelling ideas for improving education in a world of continuous global movement, often driven by political, military, economic, and social chaos, as well as by natural disasters.

The book is global in scope, bringing together scholars and practitioners from seven countries, with original articles that concern people and educational systems from thirteen nations. By galvanizing these writers to illuminate the challenges and opportunities of educating those whose lives have been disrupted, editors Florence McCarthy and Margaret Vickers have provided a noteworthy service. Their book should jog our thinking and propel us to more effective action in meeting those educational challenges.

The book's introduction lays out the ongoing process of global migration, particularly the tragedy of international refugees: the oppression they encountered in their home countries, the agony of dislocation, the dissonance and deprivations of resettlement, and the traumas of readjustment. This is a story seen from time to time on television and covered occasionally in newspapers and magazines. But it is a story experienced on a daily basis by tens of millions around the globe.

The statistics the authors provide are stark. According to the United Nations High Commissioner for Refugees, in 2009 there were 43.3 million forcibly displaced people: 983,000 asylum-seekers, more than 15 million international refugees, and over 27 million internally displaced people. Forty-one percent of the refugees and asylum-seekers were children under the age of 18 representing 71 countries.

Yet in that same year, 2009, only 112,400 refugees were admitted for resettlement in 19 countries. This means that millions have remained for years, sometimes decades, in refugee camps. In those situations, educational services are limited.

As the book elucidates, this is a global phenomenon. Most refugees and asylum-seekers end up in other countries in their own region. Increasingly these refugees are becoming dispersed into urban areas, where it is difficult for support agencies to identify them and provide services, including education.

RETHINKING THE FUTURE

But what makes this book both visionary and pragmatic is that it goes well beyond chronicling woes. Its emphasis is on offering experience-grounded ideas for improving the lives of refugees and immigrants, particularly in the area of education. Moreover, although the book does not shy away from exploring the devastating aspects of the refugee experience, it avoids dwelling on victimology and rejects applying a deficit framework. Rather it offers hope, emphasizing the potential strengths of refugees, including their cultural capital and survival skills.

Throughout the book the emphasis is on the search for educational equity. Articles highlight educational approaches that build from experiential knowledge, draw upon multiple languages, consider group identity, grapple with the complexities of inclusion, address family concerns, promote parental involvement, involve liaison with community agencies, and view cultural differences as educational strengths. The authors also make cogent suggestions for structural, pedagogical, and conceptual reform, with targets ranging from individual teachers to educational systems to social, economic, political, and cultural contexts.

At the same time, the authors explore the complexities of acculturation and the pedagogical, situational, and systemic obstacles to educational equity. They also illuminate the all-too-frequent failure of educators and other societal leaders to address the unique situations of refugees as contrasted with immigrants in general. These obstacles include cultural biases and unexamined false assumptions, as well as outdated conceptualizations, political and fiscal constraints, and the inadequacy of teacher preparation programs.

This is a revealing and inspiring book. It should be read carefully, considered thoroughly, and applied thoughtfully. Let's hope it is also a book that impels us to more nuanced analysis and more effective action.

—**Carlos E. Cortés**
Professor Emeritus of History
University of California, Riverside

INTRODUCTION

EDUCATION FOR IMMIGRANTS AND REFUGEES

Creating Equitable Pathways for the Future

Florence E. McCarthy and Margaret H. Vickers
University of Western Sydney

Acquiring an education has been a traditional avenue for mobility, employment, and a better future for millions of people. It is a basic human right that has long been recognized as essential for realizing the potential of individuals and the economic well-being of states (World Bank, 2005). Participation in education is now also widely recognized as critically important in responding to emergencies and creating greater stability in fragile states (Inter-Agency Network for Education in Emergencies, 2010). Major initiatives such as Education for All and the Millennium Development Goals from the United Nations and its attendant organizations exemplify the importance given to education as a major element in the effort to improve the lives of people (United Nations High Commissioner for Refugees [UNHCR], 2002). The attempt to provide primary education to all children by

Refugee and Immigrant Students, pages xiii–xxv
Copyright © 2012 by Information Age Publishing
All rights of reproduction in any form reserved.

2015 mobilizes national governments, international donors and agencies, nongovernmental organizations, educators and participants, and numerous foundations to provide support for meeting this goal.

The focus of this book is on just one segment of the world's population that requires educational assistance: people fleeing conflict, violence, and/ or fear of persecution and seeking refuge in protected spaces—that is, refugees (UNHCR, 2002), and immigrants—people who voluntarily leave their places of origin to acquire employment, greater security, or better conditions abroad (International Organization for Migration, 2008). Given that the majority of the literature dealing with the global movement of people has focused on immigrants (McBrien, 2005), the major emphasis in this volume will be on refugees and the complex learning environments that are created when millions of people are forced to leave the security of their homelands and enter an anomalous situation of often prolonged dependency, insecurity, and limited opportunities in refugee camps or in urban situations in hosting countries.

REFUGEES ON A WORLD SCALE

In 2009, growing out of continued disruptions cause by prolonged armed conflict, natural disasters, and economic turbulence, there were 43.3 million forcibly displaced people in the world, the highest number since the mid-1990s (UNHCR, 2010). "Forcibly displaced" refers to people who fled their homes because of conflict, violence, or threat of persecution. Of these, over 15 million people were refugees, 983,000 were asylum-seekers, and over 27 million persons were internally displaced people (UNHCR, 2010). Refugees are people who have fled their countries of origin fearing persecution or threats of violence based on religion, race, nationality, political association, or membership of a particular social group (UNHCR, 2002). Asylum-seekers are people who are outside their country of nationality or their usual country of residence and apply to the government of the country they are in for recognition as a refugee as well as permission to stay should they be recognized (Refugee Council of Australia, 2011). Their application for refugee status is based on fear of persecution in their own country for reasons of race, religion, nationality, membership of a particular social group, or political opinion (RCOA, 2011).

A large proportion of asylum-seekers and refugees are children. Of the 15.2 million persons who were displaced as asylum-seekers and refugees, 41% are children below 18 years of age. Many of these children are unaccompanied or are orphans. In 2009, more than 18,700 applications were lodged by unaccompanied and separated children from 71 countries, the highest number in four years (UNHCR, 2010, p. i).

Currently, a total of 26 million people, including refugees and internally displaced persons, are defined as "persons of concern" who are entitled to receive protection or assistance from the UNHCR. Not included in the UNHCR mandate are Palestinians, economic migrants, stateless people, and people affected by natural disasters (UNHCR, 2010). These people come under the purview of other UN organizations. The 26 million people of concern to the UNHCR represent a million more persons than in 2008 (UNHCR, 2010). Repatriation, resettlement, and integration are the three traditional, durable solutions supported by the UNHCR for this population. While the numbers of displaced people increased worldwide, the numbers repatriating to their countries of origin in 2009 fell to 251,000 refugees, the lowest figure since 1990. This decline was caused by the resumption of conflict in areas such as Somalia, the Congo, and Afghanistan, which prevented refugees from returning home (UNHCR 2010). In contrast, more than two million locally displaced people were able to return to their home area, which is the highest number in more than a decade (UNHCR, 2010). These are people who had fled from their original homes, moving to more secure areas within their own countries. Moving beyond repatriation, resettlement, and integration, a fourth solution for refugee populations is increasingly being advocated. This is a rights-based approach to displacement that recognizes that mobility among refugees who are seeking rights they have lost as exiles is essential to international protection efforts (Long & Crisp, 2010).

Although many refugees seek resettlement in a country that accepts refugees, only very small proportions achieve it. Of the total numbers of refugees applying for resettlement to accepting countries such as Australia, the United States, Canada, and Germany, only one percent is accepted in any year. Even though the numbers are small, the program is important as it provides protection and support to people who fear reprisals or persecution if they were to return home. There are many more people who apply for resettlement than are ever accepted. In 2009, for example, 112,400 refugees were admitted for resettlement into 19 countries. This represented an increase of 25% over 2008 (UNHCR, 2010), but is only a small fraction of all those seeking this outcome.

One consequence of this imbalance between those seeking resettlement or repatriation and those actually securing it is that the length of time people stay in refugee camps has become quite prolonged. The effects of prolonged stays in severely under-resourced situations usually means that education facilities may be limited to primary instruction; services such as health or counselling are scarce; and teacher training, other job training, and formal employment opportunities are limited or nonexistent. Personal security is often problematic with robberies, rape, and assault occurring, which devastate people's lives. Movement outside the camps may be limited in some situations, and individuals may be born in and/or spend 10 to 30 years in these environments.

The vast majority of refugees and asylum-seekers find shelter in countries within their own regions. They are often hosted by countries that face their own significant issues of governance and political stability, social infrastructure, and economic growth. So it is that less developed countries in Africa and the Middle East in particular, and in South Asia are the sites where most refugees and asylum-seekers find shelter. Countries such as Pakistan, Syria, Jordan, Iran, South Africa, Chad, Tanzania, and India provide support to the great majority of the world's refugees (UNHCR, 2010). This places great strain on the budgets and infrastructure of hosting governments, and on the provision of social services to local populations. Financial support from UN organizations, more affluent nations, and international organizations is insufficient to make education a reality for all (Dolan, 2008).

ISSUES IN THE PROVISION OF EDUCATION TO CHILDREN AND YOUTH WITH REFUGEE EXPERIENCE

Since the end of the Cold War it is evident that the nature of conflict has changed in both its intensity and its form, and that this is true for conflicts around the world (Paulson & Rappleye, 2007). Where battles were once fought within demarcated battlefields, conflicts now occur primarily within national boundaries, and in the "towns, villages and homes of civilians" (Davies, 2004, p. 3). It is estimated that between 1989 and 1992 alone there were 82 such armed conflicts in the world (Gallagher, 2004). As a result of this type of conflict, an estimated one million children have lost their lives, and a further six million children have been seriously injured or disabled (World Bank, 2005, p. xi).

The sense of urgency has grown among international organizations, national governments, foundations, and nongovernmental organizations to address conflict and to develop clearer understandings of the way education systems can be complicit in the creation of conflict as well as contribute to building peace and the reconstruction of societies and fragile states (Paulson & Rappleye, 2007, p. 342). Education, with its systems and promise, has become a widely accepted and critical aspect of the reconstruction of societies in post-crisis situations, and its contributions range from contributing to peace and social cohesion to facilitating economic recovery (World Bank, 2005).

It is apparent that without the abatement of armed conflict, the drain on the monetary and material resources of states will continue to mount. The demand to provide education even at the primary level is a daunting task, and the likelihood of increasing numbers of children requiring assistance is only too likely.

Just as refugee populations are not static or placid, they also change in their configurations and locations. For example, while in the past most refugees were located in rural-based refugee camps, at present more than 40% of refugees are found in urban areas, and these numbers are constantly increasing (UNHCR, 2009). Refugees in urban settings are more likely to be dispersed among the local population, where it is more difficult to provide protection and services to them through the UNHCR, other donors, or NGOs. When urban refugees do not enjoy full legal rights—and this is often the case—then they have no legal recourse in the face of mistreatment or exploitation (Bailey, 2004). It is easy for them to be exploited at work or fall foul of sex traffickers, drug dealers, or other antisocial elements (UNHCR, 2009). Nevertheless, they are drawn to urban centers because of the belief that schools may be better in these places than in the camps. However, while this may be accurate to some extent, the fact of the limited provision of educational infrastructure in many urban centers, even to local students, means that refugee students may be denied access to local schools or forced to pay exorbitant fees.

EQUITY THEMES IN THE EDUCATION OF REFUGEES AND IMMIGRANTS

Each chapter in this volume deals with some aspect of educational equity for immigrant and refugee students. Three broad areas are canvassed: institutional practices that aim to improve learning environments, pedagogical approaches within classrooms and in teacher preparation programs that contribute to better curricula and more sensitive and aware teachers, and system-level policies that recognize the long-term learning requirements of students with immigrant or refugee backgrounds. Individual contributions are grouped under these three headings, and they combine an analysis of salient issues within different cultural and national contexts. The purposeful mixing of chapters with different national locations in different sections of the book has been done to reinforce the point that issues in educational equity cut across national boundaries and require global attention for their amelioration.

Among the refugee and immigrant populations discussed in the various chapters are people from Sri Lanka, Bhutan, Burma/Myanmar, Eritrea, Burundi, Rwanda, Somalia, Sudan, Vietnam, Sierra Leone, Liberia, Ethiopia, and Uganda. Contributors from six countries are represented: Australia, Canada, India, Uganda, Singapore, the United Kingdom, and the United States. All of the contributors work directly with refugee populations, whether as academics involved in research or in forms of community engagement, or as practitioners with Government Ministries or the United Nations agencies. Each article has been specifically written for this book.

Contributors to this volume were invited to participate based on an extensive review of the literature dealing with the education of students with refugee experience. Care was taken to cast as wide a net as possible to include analyses or descriptions of work going on around the world in the provision of education to refugee populations. The initial list of contributors also included academics and practitioners from South Africa and Pakistan, however, a combination of natural and national disasters and personal issues intervened to prevent their participation.

A shared perspective among the contributors to the book is the focus on the agency and resilience of people with refugee experience, illustrating, for example, the value of the cultural knowledges and survival skills they exhibit and the potential they represent to their hosting or settlement countries. The chapter authors are critical of approaches that assume a deficit framework, for example, by discussing refugee children as lacking social and cultural capital (Arzubiaga, Nogueron, & Sullivan, 2009), or by focusing on trauma and subsequently conceptualizing refugees as "victims." While trauma is certainly part of the refugee experience, refugees themselves are unlikely to dwell on this part of their experience. If they don't, neither should we as contributors or readers.

The articles in this book deal comprehensively with responses being made in more affluent countries, in refugee camps, and in hosting countries to provide education for students with refugee and immigrant backgrounds. Chapters deal with a range of issues and perspectives and are organized around the major components of educational systems: pedagogy, institutional practices, and policy initiatives. Each area will be considered in turn.

PEDAGOGICAL INITIATIVES IN ADDRESSING ISSUES OF EDUCATIONAL EQUITY

Educational systems, wherever their location, face enormous challenges in seeking to create learning activities for children who have limited, interrupted, or no prior formal education. Responses exemplified through chapters in this section implicitly suggest that schools themselves may be in need of transformation, not only to meet the needs of refugee and immigrant children, but by implication, to better fulfill the learning potential of all children. For example, in the innovative and progressive responses being made by teachers, schools, and students, we see in the chapter by Anna Kirov an approach being developed in some Canadian preschool centers. These centers feature intercultural, multilingual, and inclusive learning environments where newcomer parents play significant parts. Recognizing that children and their parents have a "wealth of knowledges," an approach has been created incorporating the knowledge-making processes of participating cultural and linguistic groups, simultaneously using four languages in the classroom, each taught by first-language facilitators, and working with parents in setting program goals and designing relevant curriculum. One of the outcomes of the program has been that refugee parents and children have come to value their own cultural and linguistic heritages as well as feeling less isolated in Canadian society.

In the chapter by Karen Dooley, the effort of some ESL teachers to create pathways by which newcomer students can participate as intellectual class members speaks to the "positioning competence" of teachers (Dooley) and the ways such teachers respect their students and constantly attempt to find ways to draw upon their experiential knowledge to engage them in the learning processes in the classroom. Using the concepts "smart links" and "smart paths," Dooley illustrates the skills some teachers employ in fashioning links between students' prior ways of knowing and the concepts in subject-matter curriculum (smart links). These teachers also map out for refugee students the ways to move between conceptual and procedural knowledge (smart paths). These kinds of creative teaching techniques enhance the refugee students' abilities to show "they know something," thereby enhancing their status in the classroom and reinforcing their place as fully participating class members. Creating this inclusive learning environment suggests what new forms of teachers' capital are required to meet the demands of student populations characterized by sharply differentiated learning histories and mobility patterns.

Susan Banki reverses the usual practice of considering what schools have to offer refugee students, and instead argues that refugees have the potential to offer valuable contributions to the educational systems they enter. Banki critically addresses the nature of diversity and difference in the classroom, maintaining that oversimplified versions of multicultural education fail to recognize the importance of acknowledging and celebrating differences in ethnicities, religions, cultures, and other sources of difference. Such differences contribute to what she terms a "pedagogy of estrangement" that can be a valuable source of teaching and learning as students grapple with understanding the nature of difference and conflict. Using the concept of "relational closeness," Banki suggests that the presence of refugee students in classrooms has the potential to introduce new skills and create the possibility of bringing to life situations and concepts about which local students may be quite uninformed. The importance of this chapter is its call for forms of education that use differences among children as important learning tools, and its suggestion to "reverse the lens" about the nature of contributions refugee children can make to learning situations.

Drawing on her research along the Thai border with Karen refugees from Burma/Myanmar, Su-Ann Oh writes of the relational tension between education and ethno-cultural nationalist identity. Education in camps, as in national settings, is politically charged as well as contextually specific. In the case of the Burmese Karen people who are the majority, but not the only ethnic group fleeing the repression of the Burmese regime, the relevance of formal education to identity formation in the Karen refugee camps is explored. Oh insightfully argues that inclusion in the formal educational system is what matters in the camps. However, inclusion includes learning the Skaw Karen language, Karen history, religion, and the formal rules of schooling. It thus becomes a center for the reproduction and transmission of Karen identity. For families who do not share this affiliation with the Karen people, it is difficult for their children to participate in the camp schools that are run by the Karen people. Children of other ethnicities and religions (the Karen are predominantly Christian) therefore tend to be excluded from educational opportunities. The importance of this chapter is in illustrating how political interests can shape educational equity, and how curriculum can convey more than subject matter material.

SCHOOL–COMMUNITY PARTNERSHIPS AND EDUCATIONAL EQUITY

Around the world, in wealthy countries as well as in developing ones, schools have found themselves overwhelmed by the complex task of meeting the needs of children with refugee backgrounds. As a result, community organizations, nongovernmental organizations, and local government agencies are increasingly taking on supportive roles. As Marian Rossiter and Tracey Derwing point out, however, the good intentions of these various stakeholders often are minimized through lack of consistent coordination and the failure of governments to reform their newcomer support policies in response to current needs. Basing their analysis on the learning environment of Edmonton, Alberta (Canada), the authors show how policies of the federal government, for example the age cap, work to disadvantage older students who are seeking to finish or re-enter secondary schooling. ESL delivery is decided by district school boards, but implementation depends on actual schools. Severe economic constraints limit what is available for newcomers and many of the language issues of English language learners (ELLs) go unaddressed. Each stakeholder, in other words, faces difficulties or structural weaknesses that work against the adequate provision of education to refugee students. Without systematic change, including adequate and sustained funding, stable programming, and consistent coordination and involvement of all stakeholders, "a disproportionate percentage of students will continue to fail to achieve their potential" (Rossiter & Derwing, Chapter 5, this volume).

Turning to the United States, Lynn McBrien and Jillian Ford make the point that the dominant concern of schools and communities across the U.S. is to cater to the overwhelming numbers of immigrants who have arrived in the country. This means that the often more complex concerns of refugee families and their children are rarely adequately addressed. In their chapter, McBrien and Ford explore the efforts of one community-based program that deals exclusively with refugee families. This private, nonprofit agency provides multilayered services, particularly the School Liaison Program that employs and trains refugee adults from specific cultural or national backgrounds to provide liaison services for refugee families from similar cultures or nations. By mediating the interests of the schools with the concerns and issues of refugee families and with the services provided by community agencies, liaison staff have created better forms of communication, cooperation, and understanding among all participants. For example, teachers and staff demonstrate alterations in their attitudes, beliefs, and behaviors towards refugee children as an outcome of working with the liaison staff. Parents also achieved a better understanding of the information they received from the schools, encouraging their children to attend after school and summer programs, and contacting the liaison people if they or their children had difficulties in school. For the children, this resulted in greater protection against bullying, teasing, and being hurt at school.

Similarly, Linda Silka explores the competing demands placed on schools in a midsized American city as they seek to provide academic instruction to newcomer students, whether of refugee or immigrant backgrounds, while at the same time promoting the acculturation of these students to the dominant culture. Silka reports on a number of programs that attempted to promote greater participation of newcomer students in standard academic reward programs. She deftly demonstrates how a lack of awareness among educators of their own cultural bias and unexamined assumptions about the nature of newcomer students' interests and issues led to the failure of numerous well-intentioned but flawed initiatives. Using the concept of "placed-based" partnerships, Silka illustrates how the linking of local contexts with the cultural knowledges of refugee or immigrant students and their parents can lead to innovative programs that stimulate the interest of refugee/immigrant students in their cultures of origin, interest parents in sharing and participating in local initiatives that meet their needs (for example, learning computer skills), and create pathways that promote intercultural understanding and interest.

SYSTEMIC ISSUES AND POLICIES
IN EDUCATIONAL EQUITY

While pre-settlement experiences deeply influence refugee identities and needs, it is widely accepted that the post-settlement context has a significant and long-term influence on their abilities to establish secure relationships, create personal well-being, and achieve social integration in their new countries (Matthews, 2008; Rutter, 1998). Academic success is only part of the picture, yet how schools respond to students with little, interrupted, or no educational experience becomes a telling marker shaping the likely academic success and social acculturation of these students.

The chapter by Florence McCarthy and Margaret Vickers analyzes the current policy environment structuring the provision of refugee education in Australia. While the commonwealth government provides centralized funding through the New Arrivals Program (NAP), educational systems in the states and territories across Australia are constrained in the responses they can make to their refugee populations because of shortages in funding and limited systematic support. Additionally, outdated conceptualizations of who a refugee is at the commonwealth level contribute to inadequate policy provisions for English language learning and cultural adjustment for most refugee students. While some universities are creating new intercultural opportunities for pre-service teachers to mentor and come to know refugee students, this is still far from recognized as a basic requirement of teacher capital for teachers in the future. It is apparent from this chapter that the larger social and political context with its often contradictory demands, significantly limits the abilities of schools to adequately meet the myriad social and educational needs of refugee students. The authors argue that in addition, schools themselves need transformation in ways that celebrate differences and creates learning spaces where all students can find a place and be secure.

The chapter by Jill Rutter reviews equity in education for migrant and refugee children in the United Kingdom. It argues that governmental and nongovernmental organizations involved in planning interventions to support greater equity in education need to reframe the way they see migrant and refugee children and pay greater attention to broader measures of equality, including income equality and maternal education.

Shifting to Africa, a different set of issues is presented in the chapter by Timothy Brown. His concern is the difficulties and trade-offs inherent in refugee environments as the traditional focus on emergency crisis gives way to the need to respond to prolonged and extended stays of people in refugee camps. Severely limited funding for long-term educational provision often means that education is only available for some students but that many miss out. Using Sudanese refugees in Uganda as a case study, Brown discusses the dilemmas that are faced by the donor community, including the UN agencies, international and local national governments, local schools, and refugee populations in situations where there is intense competition over educational funding priorities. Should the emphasis be on primary school provision only? But if so, then what to do with children as they finish primary school and seek further education? It is dilemmas such as these that are deftly presented in this chapter. While it is clear that organizations such as the Inter-Agency Network for Education in Emergencies (INEE) have been established to provide coordination, prevent overlap, and establish guidelines for curriculum and other inputs, issues such as the provision of post-primary education will remain critically important in countries hosting refugees or engaging in state reconstruction far into the future.

India represents a country that is not a signatory to the various UN conventions such as the Status of Refugees (1951) or the 1967 Protocol on the Status of Refugees. It also does not have a general domestic law governing refugees. However, the country is currently host to countless thousands of refugees from Tibet, Nepal, Bhutan, and Sri Lanka. In this chapter, K.C. Saha explores the experience of Sri Lankan Tamil refugees in India in the state of Tamil Nadu. The focus of this chapter is on the development of a local refugee organization, the Organization for Eelam Refugees Rehabilitation (OfERR), and the difference this type of organization has made in promoting the interests of Tamil refugees while providing services and supports to them. What is instructive in this article is the ability of a well-organized refugee organization to influence and be a proactive player in the creation of local policies and opportunities influencing refugee life. OfERR has been able to mediate refugee interests with those of the local population in gaining outcomes, for example, that benefit both local and refugee communities. The chapter includes lessons to be learned from this highly successful organization.

THE NEED FOR REFORM: PEDAGOGIES, PARTNERSHIPS, AND POLICIES

An overarching theme emerging from the chapters in this volume is that in order to achieve educational equity for students with refugee backgrounds, significant innovation and reform is required in all dimensions of education. While small and important changes are being made in refugee camps, schools, universities, communities, and nongovernmental agencies around the world, there is an enormous gulf between the present situation and the ultimate goal of delivering fair and equitable educational opportunities to refugee students. Of the over 15 million refugee and asylum-seekers in the world, 41% are children under 18 years of age. The lack of concerted and consistent educational provision for these children robs them of productive futures and constitutes a mammoth loss of human potential which, in the long run, affects us all.

The critical role of education has expanded in recent times, and is now perceived as being critical in contributing to stability in conflict-prone situations. Additionally, education provision is essential for the reconstruction of conflict-affected states and in the economic recovery of countries. Nowhere is the connection between the personal needs of people and the larger interests of governments more apparent. Whether the recognition of this critical connection will be sufficiently recognized and acted upon remains a critical question of our time. Given the mammoth global problems facing us, we can clearly argue that no human potential should go to waste, as solutions to what face us requires the best efforts of us all.

REFERENCES

Arzubiaga, A. E., Nogueron, S. C., & Sullivan, A. L. (2009). The education of children in im/migrant families. *Review of Research in Education, 33,* 246–271.

Bailey, S. (2004). *Is legal status enough? Legal status and livelihood obstacles for urban refugees.* Unpublished master's thesis, The Fletcher School, Tufts University, Boston, MA.

Davies, L. (2004). *Education and conflict: Complexity and chaos.* London, UK: Routledge Falmer.

Dolan, J. (2008). *Last in line, last in school 2008. How donors can support education for children affected by conflict and emergencies.* London, UK: International Save the Children Alliance.

Gallagher, T. (2004). *Education in divided societies.* New York, NY: Palgrave Macmillian.

Inter-Agency Network for Education in Emergencies. (2010). *Guiding documents and legal frameworks for the network.* Retrieved from http://www.ineesite.org/index.php/post/guiding_inee_documents_legal_frameworks/

International Organization for Migration. (2008). Global estimates and trends. In United Nations. *Trends in total migrant stock: The 2005 revision.* Retrieved from http://www.iom.int/jahia/Jahia/pid/254

Long, K., & Crisp, J. (2010). Migration, mobility and solutions: An evolving perspective. *Forced Migration Review, 35,* 56–57.

Matthews, J. (2008). Schooling and settlement: Refugee education in Australia. *International Studies in Sociology of Education, 18*(1), 31–45.

McBrien, J. L. (2005). Educational needs and barriers for refugee students in the United States: A review of the literature. *Review of Educational Research, 75*(3), 329–364.

Paulson, J., & Rappleye, J. (2007). Education and conflict: Essay review. *International Journal of Educational Development, 27,* 340–347

Refugee Council of Australia. (2011). Frequently asked questions. Retrieved from www.refugeecouncil.org.au.arp/faqs.html

Rutter, J. (1998). Refugees in today's world. In J. Rutter & C. Jones (Eds.), *Refugee education: Mapping the field* (pp. 12–30). London, UK: Trentham Books

United Nations High Commissioner for Refugees. (2002). *Definitions and obligations: Basic definitions.* Canberra, Australia: Regional Office. Retrieved from http://www.unhcr.org.au/basicdef.shtml

United Nations High Commissioner for Refugees. (2009). *Refugee education in urban settings.* Case studies from Nairobi, Kampala, Amman, Damascus. Geneva: Division for Programme Support and Management UNHCR

United Nations High Commissioner for Refugees. (2010*). 2009 Global trends: Refugees, asylum-seekers, returnees, internally displaced and stateless persons.* Geneva: UNHCR

World Bank. (2005). *Reshaping the future: Education and postconflict reconstruction.* Washington, DC: World Bank.

PART I

PEDAGOGICAL INITIATIVES ADDRESSING ISSUES
OF EDUCATIONAL EQUITY FOR IMMIGRANTS
AND REFUGEES

CHAPTER 1

POSITIONING REFUGEE STUDENTS AS INTELLECTUAL CLASS MEMBERS

Karen Dooley
Queensland University of Technology

ABSTRACT

With diversification of student populations around the world, new criteria of teacher competence emerge. One of these is skill in positioning all students for participation in the intellectual work of the classroom. This form of competence is particularly important when cleavages of educational opportunity are sharp. This chapter describes two techniques employed by teachers of students with little, no, or severely interrupted schooling: (1) smart links, and (2) smart paths. "Smart links" are connections between students' ways of knowing and other ways of knowing, while "smart paths" are clear routes between different ways of knowing. Data are drawn from interviews with English as a second language (ESL) teachers and African paraprofessionals that were conducted as part of a study of engagement of middle school-aged Sudanese, Eritrean, Burundian, and Rwandan refugees in Australian schools. They provide evidence of alternatives to deficit discourses about students for whom pre-existing programs have proven inadequate.

Refugee and Immigrant Students, pages 3–20
Copyright © 2012 by Information Age Publishing

> *[T]he profession of teacher... should no longer be defined simply according to traditional criteria of competence but rather by ability to transmit to all, with the use of* new pedagogical techniques, *what some students... have acquired from their family* milieu.
>
> —Bourdieu, 2008, p. 44, emphasis in the original

In recent years, African refugees have become a distinctive presence in some Australian secondary schools. The students are diverse in terms of their languages; ethnicity; social background; countries of origin and transit en route to Australia; and personal histories before, during, and after taking refuge. There are points of similarity too: most of the students are learning English as a second language (ESL), and many have little, no, or severely interrupted formal education. For these students, pre-existing ESL programs have typically been inadequate (Matthews, 2008; Sidhu & Taylor, 2007). As teachers have grappled with the students' needs, many have felt ill-equipped—initially at least (Miller, Mitchell, & Brown, 2005; Oliver, Haig, & Grote, 2009). In these conditions, talk of student "lack" has emerged, even on the part of some who have long challenged deficit discourses about ESL students. In the words of one of the principals who participated in the study reported on in this chapter, "a lot of teachers... [are] saying... the kids can't do this and they can't do this and they can't do this. And [they're] really struggling—competent ESL people." An ESL teacher from another school spoke similarly, "the deputy is going 'you know those kids come to my room and they can't express themselves... and they can't do this, this and this."

In the talk relayed by the principal and the ESL teacher, a form of "top-down" discourse is in play (English, 2009). This discourse ascribes an authoritative role to the curriculum; students who do not meet curriculum-based expectations are represented as "lacking." As a consequence, access to knowledge and intellectual power remains inequitably distributed, thereby reproducing divisions between the type of student for whom the curriculum was designed and all others. In Australia, ESL teachers have long challenged deficit representations of ESL students—most recently in relation to literacy curricula designed around native speakers of standard Australian English (e.g., Lo Bianco & Wickert, 2001). But as the principal's observations suggest, a form of top-down discourse has emerged in the ESL field in recent years, although not without challenge from within it. Asked to comment on some of the representations of refugee young people that were in circulation at the time of the study, one of the ESL teacher participants countered that it is schooling that is lacking, not the students: "They [the students] do have cognitive things, but it's not, whatever it is, it isn't something we are valuing in our education process and, again, what is it?" For this teacher, the problem was that local schooling had failed to engage the refugee students' intellectual capabilities, although the nature of these was unclear to her.

Teachers who participated in the study reported on here have developed strategies, which might be described as the "new pedagogic techniques" of this chapter's epigraph, that enable the students to participate fully in Australian schools. In this chapter I examine two of these strategies: "smart links" and "smart paths." Smart links are connections between students' ways of knowing and other ways of knowing, while smart paths are clear routes between different ways of knowing. The data I use in the chapter were produced as part of a study of engagement of middle school-aged Sudanese, Eritrean, Burundian, and Rwandan refugees in Australian schools.

The study is timely. Local research has reported that some refugees, including Liberian, Sudanese, Ethiopian, Rwandan, and Sierra Leonean young people, feel that they are less noticed, welcomed, and respected by teachers and peers than other students, and that their perspectives are devalued in some Australian classrooms (Hewson, 2006; Ramirez & Matthews, 2008; Refugee Health Research Centre, 2007a, 2007b). Similar findings have emerged from Canadian research conducted with refugee parents from Congo, Rwanda, Burundi, Djibouti, Eritrea, Somalia, and Sudan (Dachyshyn, 2008), and with students from Ethiopia, Senegal, Somalia, and Djibouti (Ibrahim, 1999, 2004). These findings are consistent with those of the broader literature in the UK (McDonald, 1998) and the U.S. (Yau, 1995) that reports on the experiences of Africans and other refugees in western school systems.

In a study of Somalis resettled in Norway (Fangen, 2006), the disrespect and sense of unimportance reported in the broader refugee literature has been named "everyday humiliation." Here "humiliation" means "the psychological feeling of being put down, of not being acknowledged as equally competent or of equal worth" (Fangen, 2006, p. 70). Everyday humiliation is distinct from genocide and other severe humiliation experienced by refugees. It takes many forms. In schools and other institutions everyday humiliation arises when refugees are teased, bullied, scorned, ridiculed, laughed at, harassed, embarrassed, or cruelly criticized; excluded from or denied access to an activity; made to feel invisible, discounted, small, or insignificant; and viewed by others as inadequate or incompetent. It is worth noting that intent is not necessary: humiliation can be inadvertent. A study in the Netherlands, for example, has shown how African students' knowledge of even their own everyday experience can be discounted when western teachers do not cede any epistemological authority in the classroom (Hanson, Boogaard, & Herrlitz, 2003).

Evidence of everyday humiliation in the classroom emerged from the study I report in this chapter (Dooley, 2009a). Being knowledgeable is a key to some forms of status, prestige, and esteem in school. As explained by a Congolese paraprofessional: "the child has spent time in the refugee camp; he has learnt up to Year 10...in the area of maths he is something, and that's how you feel the status." Yet, in the move to Australia some students have lost the intellectual status they enjoyed in Africa (Gifford, Correa-Valez, & Sampson, 2009; Refugee Health Education Research Centre, 2007a, 2007b). Sophia, an Eritrean who had topped her class in Sudan for six consecutive years, put it poignantly: "I was smart in Africa." By contrast, in Australia she felt "very embarrassed" by her academic performance. Like some of the other students in the study, Sophia was angry at being laughed at or criticized by peers for asking clarifying questions in class (Dooley, 2009a). The teacher and African paraprofessional data corroborated this student data. As one teacher put it, "sometimes the students...will feel humiliated that they don't understand." Another teacher alluded to the problem when she spoke of building student resilience in class. She said that she advised students to hold onto their dreams of high marks: "Concentrate on your speech and don't worry [when they laugh at you]...you want to get an A."

My aim here is not to reiterate or elaborate my findings about everyday humiliation, but to look instead at how ESL teachers interviewed for the study are enabling students with little, no, or severely interrupted schooling to participate intellectually in class in ways that do not render them vulnerable to humiliation—intentional or otherwise. All the student participants spoke of such teachers, as did school personnel. The Congolese paraprofessional said of the teachers at the intensive language school: "They are good teachers here; they amaze me, the teachers here." The ESL teachers at one of the high schools spoke similarly of the mainstream teachers: "They're very supportive and they are very interested in learning about every new group and meeting the needs of those students." An ESL teacher reflected similarly on her own efforts in this regard: "there are so many activities that I have done...to make them feel special, and of course they will open up and give you the 100%." A recent Australian study conducted in both intensive language and mainstream schools (Hammond, 2009) found that such teachers are distinguished by their respect for every student as an individual and person, and as a capable learner. It is the attribution of capability to learners that I am interested in here.

To date, the literature has primarily been concerned with documenting either educational challenges facing African students and their teachers in western countries of African migration and refugee resettlement (Brown, Miller, & Mitchell, 2006; Cassity & Gow, 2005; Oliver et al., 2009), or the inability of teachers to recognize and effectively bring the students' language, literacy, and academic capabilities into the classroom (Hanson et al., 2003; Perry, 2007; Smythe & Toohey, 2009). Provision for the students has received less attention, although there has been research on vocabulary instruction for Sudanese science students in an Australian secondary school (Miller, 2009), multicultural education for Somali and Moroccan students in a Dutch primary school (Hanson et al., 2003), and documentary film-making for Sudanese, Liberian, and other refugees in an Australian high school (Hewson, 2006). My aim is to add to this body of knowledge by looking at how some teachers work with the knowledge resources that refugees with little, no, or severely interrupted schooling in Africa bring to the middle-year classrooms of Australian secondary schools. Given increased student mobility in a world in which opportunities for schooling are distributed unevenly both within and between nations (Arzubiaga, Nogueron, & Sullivan, 2009), the study might be of wider interest.

This chapter has four sections. In the first I present a theoretical framework for looking at pedagogy and teacher judgement of student capability. Concepts of "capital" (Bourdieu, 1990) are used to describe student and teacher knowledge resources. Pedagogy is understood as processes for making knowledge. Capability is understood as accretions to our natures arising from knowledge processes in everyday life, or as residues from knowledge processes of formal schooling (Kalantzis & Cope, 2005). In the second section, I introduce the study reported here, describing the methods by which data were produced and analyzed. In the third section, I present data showing how ESL teachers in the participating schools are creating smart links and smart paths for refugees who have arrived from Africa with little, no, or severely interrupted schooling. In the final section I turn to implications for thinking about what should count as teacher competence in conditions of diversity.

RECOGNIZING AND BUILDING INTELLECTUAL CAPABILITY

In this chapter I understand everyday humiliation as a psychological effect of absence of symbolic capital. "Capital" here means an individual's power. This power can be economic (e.g., money), social (e.g., contacts), cultural (e.g., knowledge), or symbolic. In its symbolic form, capital inheres in honor, esteem, reputation, and prestige (Bourdieu, 1990). The disrespect and sense of unimportance described in the refugee literature is evidence of absence of esteem and prestige—absence of symbolic capital. This form of capital is accumulated when an individual's economic, social, or cultural capital is recognized by others; it is the "form which is assumed by different kinds of capital when they are perceived and recognized as legitimate" (Bourdieu, 1990, p. 128). Symbolic capital is destroyed easily by criticism and suspicion. It can be withheld, withdrawn or lost—as in the loss of "smartness" sustained by some refugee students in the move to Australia.

The point to note here is that, to some extent, accumulation of symbolic capital in the classroom rests in the first instance on teachers valuing students' resources as cultural capital relevant to classroom learning activities. In the words of one of the teachers quoted earlier, in the participating schools the challenge is one of "valuing in our education process" the African students' resources for knowing. ESL literature in general (Heller, 2008), and African refugee literature in particular (Smythe & Toohey, 2009), identify teacher inability in this regard as a source of student disadvantage.

To some extent, however, accumulation of symbolic capital also rests on students' acquisition of new resources for success in the contemporary Australian school system. The Congolese paraprofessional, who was studying for an advanced degree, emphasized the difficulties of this, even for someone as highly educated as he is: "how much I suffer myself to blend with these people." The suffering he spoke of was his struggle to enter into a learning community where it was taken for granted that "blackboard" denoted an online learning space rather than a chalkboard. This participant described how he had trailed his peers—"I was behind"—because he had spent three weeks waiting for material to appear on a chalkboard.

My interest here is in how teachers recognize and broaden students' knowledge resources for success in Australian schools. By "knowledge resources," I refer to both products and ways of knowing (Kalantzis & Cope, 2005). As product, knowledge inheres in facts, values, interests, and sensibilities learned by individuals in their particular worlds. As process, knowledge entails coming to know in different ways: *experiencing*—acquiring deep understanding through extended immersion in a situation; *conceptualizing*—acquiring the underlying concepts and theories of a discipline or system; *analyzing*—linking cause with effect, interest with behavior, and purpose with outcome; and *applying*—repeating something or doing it anew. Particular cultures, disciplines, and pedagogies entail peculiar preferences for and configurations of knowledge processes. Previous research with African students in the west has looked at pedagogies for teaching conceptual (Miller, 2009), experiential (Hanson et al., 2003), and critical analytic (Hewson, 2006; Ibrahim, 1999, 2004) knowledge processes—although not necessarily in these terms.

Capitalizing on knowledge resources is a key to students' accumulation of "participation competence" in the intellectual activity of the classroom—cultural capital for "being a student" (Curry, 2008). When recognized and legitimated by teachers, this type of cultural capital assumes the form of symbolic capital; students are, and may feel, esteemed rather than disrespected, dismissed, or invisible. One object of the study reported here was to examine the teacher competence that enables student participation competence. This is consistent with an extensive literature that shows that the capabilities teachers recognize in their students are brought forth in part by their own thinking and practices. Three decades of research on discourse in classrooms in general (Morine-Dershimer, 2006) and in ESL settings in particular (Yoon, 2008) shows that not only does student participation influence teacher belief about student ability, but also that this belief shapes differential opportunities for participation. Moreover, when teachers promote more inclusive participation in existing activities or provide opportunities for participation in new activities, hitherto un-imagined student abilities can be revealed, shifting teacher perceptions and attitudes. Given the humiliating effects of peer interactions evident in my data set, it is also worth noting that the ways teachers interact with ESL or refugee students seem to set the tone for peer interaction (Anderson, 2001; Yoon, 2008).

THE STUDY

The data presented in this chapter are drawn primarily from interviews conducted with administrators, teachers, and African paraprofessionals in an intensive English language school and three mainstream high schools. The interviewees worked at institutions attended by the eight African middle-school students who were the focus of the study. "Middle years" here refers to students enrolled in the junior secondary school grades, although the focal students were up to two years older than is typical for those grades in Australia. "African" refers to young people who have arrived in Australia as refugees in recent years. The students, their parents and guardians, and personnel from their schools were all interviewed for the study.

The students who took part in the study were from Eritrea, Sudan, Rwanda, and Burundi—the countries of origin of most, but not all, of the African students in the participating schools when the research was conducted. Like most of the other refugees arriving from Africa, all had spent lengthy periods in transit countries and had at least two, and in most cases more, years less schooling than their age peers on arrival in Australia. With one exception, the students all needed more than the usual six months to complete the intensive English program. Five of the students finished after seven to thirteen months and two after eighteen to twenty months. More-over, the students' English proficiency levels on exit were relatively low. His-torically, an exit level of four on the seven-point ESL Bandscales (McKay, 1995) was typical. At this level, students are likely to engage successfully with mainstream junior secondary schooling provided they have systematic English language support. Only three of the student participants left the intensive language school having achieved this level of proficiency for any of the macroskills of speaking, listening, reading, and writing.

The study was conducted over a period of five semesters in 2006–2008. All the participating schools are located in one Australian city and have been serving international students and/or migrants and refugees for two to three decades. Refugees, primarily from Africa, constituted 80% of the student population at the intensive English language school, and of these, 70% had little, no, or severely interrupted schooling. African students also constituted sizable minorities in the three mainstream high schools the students transitioned into during the course of the study—38, 18, and 14%, respectively, at high schools A, B, and C. Like the focal students, many of the students in these cohorts had spent a lengthy period at the intensive language school and exited with low levels of English proficiency.

The interviews from which the data presented in this chapter are drawn were conducted at the intensive language school in 2006, and in the mainstream high schools during 2008. Interview questions addressed opportunities for social, language and academic development. Interviews were digitally audio-recorded for later verbatim transcription.

Data were analyzed qualitatively using a deductive-inductive method (Bernstein, 1996). A code-and-retrieve procedure was used during the first stage of analysis. For the purposes of this chapter, every interview with an administrator, teacher, or African paraprofessional was subject to repeated readings to build a literal understanding of what the interviewees had said. Data about student knowledge were then extracted from the transcripts and organized into a single file. Fine-grained analyses were then conducted within the theoretical framework introduced earlier in this chapter. Analytic categories and decisions about what would count as evidence of each category were refined inductively. With each refinement the entire data file was reanalyzed, and the original transcripts were consulted to clarify meaning and to check for additional relevant data.

The findings showed how the study teachers were enabling refugee students from Africa to participate in the intellectual work of the classroom. I turn now to data illustrating two of these ways: smart links and smart paths.

"Smart Links" for Conceptual Development

As noted earlier, conceptual processes of knowing were of concern for the refugee students and their teachers. "Conceptual" here means acquisition of abstract ideas for naming things, and of theories that link these concepts into the explanations that constitute science, mathematics, and other disciplines of schooling (Kalantzis & Cope, 2005). All the adult school personnel involved in the study attributed the students' conceptual needs to prior histories of little, no, or severely interrupted schooling; all invoked the students' experiences of war and flight by way of explanation. A highly educated Sudanese teacher working as a paraprofessional at the time of the interviews elaborated, "the refugee schooling... means maybe he or she attended maybe three classes before they could move to another place because the area might be bombed up... so in a year... they have two classes or three classes." All participants recognized the considerable diversity of student histories in this regard and the experience of the student participants exemplified this. Of the eight students, one had enjoyed six years of regular town schooling in Sudan after fleeing Eritrea, some of the Rwandans and Burundians had at least four years of well-organized camp schooling in Tanzania, but the Sudanese students had spent several years in more *ad hoc* arrangements in Egypt. Diversity of prior schooling experience is also evident among the refugee students in other Australian states (Brown et al., 2006; Cassity & Gow, 2005; Oliver et al., 2009).

The Congolese paraprofessional was especially emphatic about the conceptual implications of social diversity amongst the refugee students. This participant, a secondary school teacher of many years' standing in Africa, emphasized the effects of social background on the conceptual capabilities with which the African students had arrived in Australia: "They come from different families; some are educated; some of them are not educated." Some of the differences this participant spoke of were of a kind described in this chapter's Bourdieusian epigraph as educationally salient differences of "family *milieu*." These were the differences that saw some of the refugees requiring a foundation class that had been created to develop basic orientations to schooling: "if... mother's not educated, the child also, and he is impacted on... this is also a problem." The participant explained that it was families from remote border areas wo had been able to flee his country most easily. With the exception of families of teachers, administrators, and nurses who had been posted to those areas, most of these refugees had primary schooling at best. For the children, there have been severe conceptual difficulties in Australian schools, but this is "not because they're refugees; it's because of being from remote areas." In contrast, there have been fewer conceptual difficulties for refugees from more advantaged social backgrounds: "These boys, they bring some of the things [mathematics concepts] in their own languages."

The teacher, paraprofessional, and principal participants noted that disrupted school histories have only been consequential because of Australia's age-based school placement policy—a point of contrast with African norms that is of contention between Africans and the Australian school system (e.g., Gifford et al., 2009). A Liberian paraprofessional explained the difficulties even for "smart kids": "You're not, only, just going to learn straight away what's, what they're teaching you in Year 10. You haven't been to Year 9, 8, 7, 6 and maybe 5.... Some of them are smart enough to catch up, but no matter how smart you are, it takes time for you to really fill in the gap."

Making smart links between students' experiential ways of knowing and the conceptualizing required for academic success was one strategy by which the study teachers had addressed this knowledge gap.

The following data illustrate smart links. The data have been excerpted from an interview with three teachers at the intensive language school. It is indicative of the data set in the sense that all but two of the nine teacher participants spoke explicitly of forging links between students' everyday experiential knowledge and conceptual knowledge processes required in the content areas of English, HPE (Health and Physical Education), and SOSE (Studies of Society and Environment). The examples given by the English language and subject English teachers concerned concepts and theories relating to the content of texts the students needed to write (Dooley, 2009b) and to the features of those texts. The latter included the functions of narrative and procedural genres, the logical relationships represented by conjunctions in a comparative report, and the concepts of "fiction," "nonfiction," "science fiction," and "plot."

The data presented here are drawn from an interview involving two of the researchers and three ESL teachers. The teachers requested that they be interviewed together. The data have been excerpted from the section of the interview where the teachers talked about the African students' opportunities for language development. Like all the other school-based adult participants, these teachers stated that the students generally require help not only with language, but also academic concepts that had been assumed in their work with previous cohorts of ESL students. One of the teachers began by saying that her treatment of literary concepts was less reliant on written language than it had been in the past.

> I find I'm doing a lot more talking because if there's the oracy there they can see, sort of, concepts that we're talking about, but we've started reading this book called *Tomorrow's Girl,* which is this little reader about a girl that comes from the future—2099—back to 1999 because she's interested in this island that's become an awful concrete jungle and she knows that something happened in 1999 and the fellow who owns the island is going to develop it and her job, she wants to go back and stop him from doing that. Now, conceptually, that's huge. "Fiction" and "nonfiction," they're not sure what's fiction and what's nonfiction, and then, science fiction, what's science fiction. And I've been trying to link it to telly they've been watching, which then goes onto Big Brother which is, "no, that's reality!" And then movies they might have seen. You're thinking all the time: What is it they might have seen or experienced that we could talk about?

This teacher, like the other school-based adult participants, identified oral language as the students' strength. Working with this strength, she was making more extensive use of talk to introduce literary concepts than she had in the past. The knowledge processes invoked in this talk are of interest here. The teacher elicited knowledge of text that the students had picked up from immersion in "telly" and movies to try to establish the concept of science fiction. In this way she linked the students' everyday experiential knowledge processes with the processes of conceptualization about the text required by subject English. Everyday knowledge was recognized as capital for participation in the classroom activity. The aim was to create valuable conceptual knowledge. The teacher claimed modest success: "Sometimes it works; sometimes it doesn't."

In the data set, the use of experiential knowledge processes on the part of the teacher was overtly associated with classroom participation on the part of the students. A teacher from high school C drew a distinction between the refugee students' capacity to participate in experiential and other knowledge processes. Her example concerned a spelling guessing game common in second-language classrooms. She said that although the students could participate in debates and other activities that required them to talk about their personal experiences, they struggled with the game:

> They [the students] are actually giving their personal experiences and they are participating in class. You know, it's not that they don't know, they may, ah, sort of be confused about the spelling and playing name games, "now name of a person, place, animal and thing, starts with B," so they are all thinking about what to say.

The guessing game described by this teacher requires conceptualization, specifically the processes of naming by classifying "people, places, animals, and things" and "words that start with B." The teacher stated that the students have at least some of the requisite information—"it's not that they [the students] don't know"—but are unable to bring it into these processes—"they may ah, sort of be confused about... playing name games." The point of interest here is that the teacher explicitly associated participation in activities requiring experiential knowledge processes with displays of intelligence on the part of the students. She preceded the example by rejecting deficit representations of the students' intellectual capabilities: "[in my class] they'll be answering intelligent questions, debate... they are actually giving their personal experiences and they are participating in class."

The conclusion that might be drawn here is that one form of teacher competence for intercultural classroom encounters lies in teachers' interest in seeking smart links and their skill in doing so. In this case they were links between experiential and conceptual knowledge processes. As the teacher quoted earlier put it: "you're thinking all the time: what is it they might have seen or experienced that we could talk about?" I suggest that this competence might be understood as cultural capital for being a teacher in conditions of student diversity. It is *positioning competence*: a capacity to position diverse students for participation in the intellectual work of the classroom.

"Smart Paths"

A "smart link" is a moment of connection between two different knowledge processes—in the examples described above, experiential and conceptual knowledge. In contrast, a "smart path" is a route teachers map out to enable students to move among knowledge processes. Study participants pointed to the necessity of this kind of provision for refugee students.

The African paraprofessionals in particular indicated that there was more to working with the refugee students than merely building the conceptual knowledge that many of them needed for content area success in Australia. It was also necessary to broaden the students' ways of knowing beyond conceptual levels. These participants described the pedagogy they knew as teachers and/or students in Africa as more "theoretical" than pedagogy in Australia. The Sudanese paraprofessional explained:

> Maybe they have learned theories in Africa. And sometimes just only, just by heart, learn it by heart and they know the formula. They can put it, write it down, correctly, but they've never been in the lab to experience that or to put that in an essay.

Like the other paraprofessionals, this participant suggested that prior schooling had equipped refugee students with some, but not all, of the knowledge processes required in Australian schools. He explicitly mentioned the likelihood of students having some conceptual knowledge of science, as distinct from experiential knowledge. Furthermore, his use of lab work and essay writing as examples implies the possibility of differences in relation to analytic, applicative, and other conceptual processes valued in African and Australian schools.

Participants were not asked to explain differences between pedagogies in Africa and Australia. The Congolese paraprofessional did so spontaneously, however, mentioning political repression in countries of origin—"you cannot think, you can think, then they tell you not to go beyond your thinking"—and limited resources in transit countries—"where the things are needed, they cannot get access to that." In the literature, explanations of African pedagogic settings invoke poverty, which makes transmissive pedagogies most feasible (Abd-Kadir & Hardmann, 2007); the persistence of colonial models of education as transmission (Kanu, 2003, 2007; Opoku-Amankwa, 2009); second and foreign language mediums of instruction that constrain the potential for teacher and student oral interaction (Cleghorn,

Merritt & Abagi, 1989; Abd-Kadir & Hardmann, 2007; Opoku-Amankwa, 2009); and cultural norms for respectful adult–child interaction (Cleghorn et al., 1989).

For the teachers who took part in the study, differences between students' knowledge processes and the repertoire of such processes required for success in Australian schools have raised pedagogic challenges. This challenge was described by the Congolese paraprofessional: "Science, you have the trees, and now here there's laboratories, there is computer, there is everything. It's too much for him to get knowledge in a normal way, like children born here." To clarify, "trees" are mentioned here as resources rather settings for learning: "there's equipment like trees, but where the things are needed, they cannot get access to that." This participant was speaking of a particular camp school setting that had more advantages than those experienced by some of the refugee students: "They've even built some shelters [for classrooms]."

One response to the challenge of broadening the students' knowledge processes in Australia has been to create 'smart paths' that are clear routes to ways of knowing. In what follows, I develop an example drawn from an interview with a content area teacher at the intensive English language school. The data show routes to both "conceptual" and "applying" knowledge processes.

To begin, it is worth looking at the broader context within which the teacher created smart paths for the students. Asked to describe his aims for the students, the teacher replied:

> My academic goal is to teach . . . investigative skills in science . . . so that when they go to high schools at least they have the basics. They know the names of the equipment. They know how to behave in a lab when they do experiments. They have the basic skills in animals, the conceptual skills in animals, plants, and body part . . . a basic grounding and then they can build on that once they go to high school because really by then they will have learned the essential key words and the skills in those areas.

This teacher aimed to equip the refugee students with a repertoire of new experiential knowledge—scientific "keywords" including "the names of equipment." He aimed to develop "conceptual skills in animals, plants and body parts," although the precise nature of these remained unspecified in the interview. He aimed also to equip the students to learn in the lab—a setting where the knowledge process of application, at the least, is likely to come into play. I turn now to the smart paths by which this teacher systematically broadened students' ways of knowing.

The teacher said that he took every opportunity for laboratory experiences because these are very motivating for the students: "They like to do hands-on activities. That's why every time they have a double science lesson we do a [practical experiment]." From his perspective, the aim of practical experiments was to build processes of conceptualization and application for high-school science: "We are hoping that we would cement the concept and the skill that is needed for the particular scientific aspect." To this end, he provided smart paths that enabled students to systematically develop these knowledge processes. In the lessons before the practicals he introduced the students to both concepts and procedures:

> **Teacher:** The instruction has to be very clear ..."next you put three drops of chemical in there, after that, and then, finally, you know, like you need to follow that" kind of, yeah
> **Interviewer:** Procedures?
> **Teacher:** And conceptual, it's heavily scaffolded, steps clearly demonstrated on the white board, and every step you stop, make sure they understood . . .

Immediately before the practical, the teacher explicitly elicited conceptual information from the previous lessons: "So what do you think will happen . . . in this activity we are doing today, how do you link up what we learnt the other day to this?" The practical itself was structured with a worksheet reinforcing the preparatory lesson. Follow-up discussions were scheduled too: "So, what happened? We discussed this yesterday." In short, the sequence of interactive routines used by the teacher provided clear routes to both conceptual and procedural knowledge. The teacher claimed success: "And that helps them with, you know, doing the prac, and whatever, actually, we are doing there."

Smart paths like those described here are clear routes to mastery of some aspect of one or another knowledge process—in this case, knowing through conceptualization and applying. This pedagogic strategy differs from smart links between knowledge processes, for example the links between experiential and conceptual knowledge described in the previous section of this chapter. Teachers' interest in seeking smart paths, and skill in doing so, can be viewed as teacher positioning competence for classroom encounters in conditions of student diversity, that is, as cultural capital for being a teacher.

TEACHER CULTURAL CAPITAL FOR ENABLING REFUGEE STUDENTS TO PARTICIPATE SMARTLY IN SCHOOL

The epigraph that opens this chapter highlights Bourdieu's (2008) suggestion that criteria of teacher competence need to account for capacity with "new pedagogic techniques" that redress disadvantages arising from prior pedagogic experience. The disadvantage relevant to the data arises not only from differences of "family *milieu*," as in Bourdieu's work, but also from quantitative and qualitative differences in prior formal education (e.g., Curry, 2008). My analyses identify two pedagogic techniques that some teachers have developed for working equitably in these conditions: smart links between familiar and unfamiliar ways of knowing, and smart paths to ways of knowing valued in the school system. The interest in creating these techniques, and skill in using them, can be understood as *positioning competence*—a form of cultural capital that enables teachers to promote all students' participation in the intellectual work of the classroom.

Participation in classroom activities matters: It is a dimension of effective teaching, and it is an essential, although not sufficient condition for student learning (Louden et al., 2005). Yet the efforts of engaged refugee students to participate in the intellectual work of the classroom can lead to everyday humiliation (e.g., Dooley, 2009a). In these conditions, positioning competence is crucial; it might be viewed as complementary to the cultural capital for being a student that has been described as *participation competence* (Curry, 2008). It is a form of capital that is likely to become more important in conditions of unprecedented heterogeneity in the classrooms of a world where cleavages of educational provision are sharp and mobility between contexts is increasing—and not only for refugee students.

ACKNOWLEDGEMENTS

This study was funded by Australian Research Council Linkage Grant LP0561597. I owe a debt of gratitude to the participants and the industry partners, Milpera State High School, Queensland Program of Assistance for Survivors of Torture and Trauma (QPASTT), Multicultural Affairs Queensland (MQA), and Queensland Studies Authority (QSA). I thank my co-investigators, Erica McWilliam and Felicity McArdle, and research assistant Jennifer Tan. I acknowledge the contribution of Penny McKay, who was instrumental in designing the study and securing funding, but became ill and passed away during the course of the work.

REFERENCES

Abd-Kadir, J., & Hardman, F. (2007). The discourse of whole class teaching: A comparative study of Kenyan and Nigerian primary English lessons. *Language and Education, 21*(1), 1–15.

Anderson, P. (2001). 'You don't belong here in Germany . . .' On the social situation of refugee children in Germany. *Journal of Refugee Studies, 14*(2), 187–199.

Arzubiaga, A. E., Nogueron, S. C., & Sullivan, A. L. (2009). The education of children in immigrant families. *Review of Research in Education, 33*, 246–271

Bernstein, B. (1996). *Pedagogy, symbolic control and identity: Theory, research, critique.* London: Taylor & Francis.

Bourdieu, P. (1990). *In other words: Essays towards a reflexive sociology.* Cambridge: Polity Press.

Bourdieu, P. (2008). Appeal for the organization of a general assembly of teaching and research. In P. Bordieu (Ed.), *Political interventions: Social science and political action* (pp. 41–45). London, UK: Verso.

Brown, J., Miller, J., & Mitchell, J. (2006). Interrupted schooling and the acquisition of literacy: Experiences of Sudanese refugees in Victorian secondary schools. *Australian Journal of Language and Literacy, 29*(2), 150–162.

Cassity, E., & Gow, G. (2005). Making up for lost time: The experiences of Southern Sudanese young refugees in high schools. *Youth Studies Australia, 24*(3), 51–55.

Cleghorn, A., Merritt, M., & Abagi, J.O. (1989). Language policy and science instruction in Kenyan primary schools. *Comparative Education Review, 33*(1), 21–39.

Curry, M. J. (2008). A "head start and a credit": Analyzing cultural capital in the basic writing/ESOL classroom. In J. Albright & A. Luke (Eds.), *Pierre Bourdieu and literacy education* (pp. 279–298). New York, NY: Routledge.

Dachyshyn, D.M. (2008). Refugee families with preschool children: Adjustment to life in Canada. In L. Adams & A. Kirova (Eds.), *Global migration and education: Schools, children and families* (pp. 251–262). Mahwah, NJ: Lawrence Erlbaum Associates.

Dooley, K. (2009a). Language and inclusion in mainstream classrooms. In J. Miller, A. Kosogriz, & M. Gearon (Eds.), *Culturally and linguistically diverse classrooms: New dilemmas for teachers* (pp. 75–91). Bristol, UK: Multilingual Matters.

Dooley, K. (2009b) Re-thinking pedagogy for middle school students with little, no or severely interrupted schooling. *English Teaching: Practice and Critique, 8*(1), 5–22.

English, B. (2009). Who is responsible for educating English language learners? Discursive construction of roles and responsibilities in an inquiry community. *Language and Education, 23*(6), 487–507.

Erickson, F., Bagrodia, R., Cook-Sather, A., Espinoza, M., Jurow, S., Shultz, J. J., & Spencer, J. (2008). Students' experience of school curriculum: the everyday circumstances of granting and withholding assent to learn. In F. M. Connelly, M. F. He, & J. Phillion (Eds.), *The SAGE handbook of curriculum and instruction* (pp. 198–218). Thousand Oaks, CA: SAGE Publications.

Fangen, K. (2006). Humiliation experienced by Somali refugees in Norway. *Journal of Refugee Studies, 19*(1), 69–93.

Gifford, S., Correa-Valez, I., & Sampson, R. (2009). *Good starts for recently arrived youth with refugee backgrounds: promoting wellbeing in the first three years of settlement in Melbourne, Australia.* Retrieved from http://www.latrobe.edu.au/larrc/documents-larrc/reports/report-good-starts.pdf

Hammond, J. (2009). High challenge, high support programmes with English as a second language learners: A teacher–researcher collaboration. In J. Miller, A. Kosogriz, & M. Gearon (Eds.), *Culturally and linguistically diverse classrooms: New dilemmas for teachers* (pp. 56–74). Bristol, UK: Multilingual Matters.

Hanson, M., Boogaard, M., & Herrlitz, W. (2003). "Sometimes Dutch and sometimes Somali": Children's participation in multicultural interactions in Dutch primary schools. *Linguistics and Education, 14*(1), 27–50.

Heller, M. (2008). Bourdieu and "literacy" education. In J. Albright & A. Luke (Eds.), *Pierre Bourdieu and literacy education* (pp. 50–67). New York, NY: Routledge.

Hewson, S. (2006). Inside out: Boys' voices: Identity and refugee students in a secondary school. In K. Cadman & K. O'Regan (Eds.), *TESOL in Context, Series 'S': Special Edition 2006, 34–48.*

Ibrahim, A. (1999). Becoming black: Rap and hip-hop, race, gender, identity, and the politics of ESL learning. *TESOL Quarterly, 33*(3), 349–369.

Ibrahim, A. (2004). Operating under erasure: Hip-Hop and the pedagogy of affective. *Journal of Curriculum Theorising, 20*(1), 113–133.

Kalantzis, M., & Cope, B. (2005). *Learning by design.* Altona, Victoria: Common Ground Publishing.

Kanu, Y. (2003). Curriculum as cultural practice: Postcolonial imagination. *Journal of the Canadian Association for Curriculum Studies, 1*(1), 67–81.

Kanu, Y. (2007). Tradition and educational reconstruction in Africa in postcolonial and global times: The case for Sierra Leone. *African Studies Quarterly, 9*(3), 65–81.

Lo Bianco, J., & Wickert, R. (Eds.). (2001). *Australian policy activism in language and literacy.* Melbourne: Language Australia.

Louden, W., Rohl, M., Pugh, C. B., Brown, C., Cairney, T., Elderfield, J., ... Rowe, K. (2005). *In teachers' hands: Effective literacy teaching practices in the early years of schooling.* Canberra, ACT: Commonwealth of Australia.

Matthews, J. (2008). Schooling and settlement: Refugee education in Australia. *International Studies in Sociology of Education, 18*(1), 31–45.

McDonald, J. (1998). Refugee students' experiences of the UK education system. In J. Rutter & C. Jones (Eds.), *Refugee education: Mapping the field* (pp. 149–170). London, UK: Trentham Books.

McKay, P. (1995). Developing ESL proficiency descriptions for the school context: The NLLIA ESL Bandscales. In G. Brindley (Ed.), *Language assessment in action* (pp. 31–63). Sydney, NSW: National Centre for English Language Teaching and Research.

Miller, J. (2009). Teaching refugee learners with interrupted education in science: vocabulary, literacy and pedagogy. *International Journal of Science Education. 31*(4), 571–592.

Miller, J., Mitchell, J., & Brown, J. (2005). African refugees with interrupted schooling in the high school mainstream: Dilemmas for teachers. *Prospect, 20*(2), 19–33.

Morine-Dershimer, G. (2006). Classroom management and classroom discourse. In C. M. Evertson & C. S. Weinstein (Eds.), *Handbook of classroom management: research, practice and contemporary issues* (pp. 127–156). Mahwah, NJ: Lawrence Erlbaum Associates.

Oliver, R., Haig, Y., & Grote, E. (2009). Addressing the educational challenges faced by African refugee background students: Perceptions of West Australian stakeholders. *TESOL in Context, 19*(1), 23–38.

Opoku-Amankwa, K. (2009). 'Teacher only calls her pets': Teacher's selective attention and the invisible life of a diverse classroom in Ghana. *Language and Education, 23*(3), 249–262.

Perry, K. H. (2009). Genres, contexts and literacy practices: literacy brokering among Sudanese refugee families. *Reading Research Quarterly, 44*(3), 256–276.

Ramirez, M., & Matthews, J. (2008). Living in the NOW: young people from refugee backgrounds pursuing respect, risk and fun. *Journal of Youth Studies, 11*(1), 83–92.

Refugee Health Research Centre. (2007a). What facilitates success of refugee girls at school? *Good starts for refugee youth, Broadsheet # 3*, October. Retrieved from *http://www.latrobe.edu.au/larrc/documents-larrc/broadsheets/goodstarts-broadsheet-3-refugee-girls-school.pdf*

Refugee Health Research Centre. (2007b). What keeps refugee boys in school? *Good starts for refugee youth, Broadsheet # 1*, August. Retrieved from http://www.latrobe.edu.au/larrc/documents-larrc/broadsheets/goodstarts-broadsheet-1-refugee-boys-and-school.pdf

Sidhu, R., & Taylor, S. (2007). Educational provision for refugee youth in Australia: Left to chance? *Journal of Sociology, 43*(3), 283–300.

Smythe, S., & Toohey, K. (2009). Bringing home and community to school: institutional constraints and pedagogic possibilities. In J. Miller, A. Kosogriz, & M. Gearon (Eds.), *Culturally and linguistically diverse classrooms: new dilemmas for teachers* (pp. 271–290). Bristol, UK: Multilingual Matters.

Yau, M. (1995). *Refugee students in Toronto schools: An exploratory study.* Toronto, ON: Board of Education, Research Services.

Yoon, B. (2008). Uninvited guests: The influence of teachers' roles and pedagogies on the positioning of English language learners in the regular classroom. *American Educational Research Journal, 45*(2), 495–522.

CHAPTER 2

CREATING SHARED LEARNING SPACES

An Intercultural, Multilingual Early Learning Program for Preschool Children from Refugee Families

Anna Kirova
University of Alberta

ABSTRACT

The chapter describes an intercultural, multilingual early learning program that is genuinely responsive to the early learning needs of preschool children and their parents from three ethnocultural refugee communities. By recognizing parents and children as having a wealth of knowledges, the program challenged the deficit frameworks that defined these refugees as lacking in social and cultural capital. Based on the sociocultural-historical theory of learning (Vygotsky, 1978; Wertsch, 1991, 1998), the knowledge-making processes of these cultural and linguistic groups were central to understanding the diverse forms of learning and teaching occurring in this community-initiated, government-funded program. Consistent with Participatory Learning and Action methodology, data were co-constructed and generated collectively

Refugee and Immigrant Students, pages 21–42
Copyright © 2012 by Information Age Publishing

during all phases of the process. Unique features of the program include the simultaneous use of four languages in the classroom, each taught by a first-language facilitator with English as the common language; the process of weekly negotiations in planning the emerging curriculum; and parent and community involvement in setting the program's goals in designing culturally relevant curriculum and in evaluating the children's learning. These features are discussed and interpreted using minority rights frameworks.

SOCIETAL CONTEXT OF THE EARLY LEARNING PROJECT

Every year Canada receives about 300,000 newcomers: immigrants and refugees. In 2008, approximately 20% of newcomers were children below the age of 14, and 12.5% were refugees (Citizenship and Immigration Canada, 2008). Newcomers face common stressors that include under- or unemployment, language problems, separation from former social networks, loneliness, discrimination, family conflict, and cultural incompatibilities (Dachyshyn, 2008). However, refugee families with young children face additional challenges related to deep traumas. These include (1) parental feelings of guilt, failure, or grief for not having been able to provide for the basic safety and well-being of their children; (2) separation of family members and fear for the lives of relatives left behind; (3) experiences associated with the terrors of war such as death and torture, often including post-traumatic stress disorder; and (4) lack of hope of returning to their country of origin due to war or other devastation (Suarez-Orozco & Suarez-Orozco, 2001).

Refugee families with young children are among the least likely to receive the preschool support they need (Rutter, 1998). "Families and children have to fit into narrow eligibility categories, segregated into class, income, racial and lifestyle 'silos' to qualify for different ECEC [Early Childhood Education and Care] programs" (Friendly & Lero, 2005, p. 72). Thus, although childcare centers have experienced an increasing number of children born in Canada to immigrant or refugee parents (Chumak-Horbatsch, 2008), many barriers still need to be overcome in order for such programs to advance social inclusion for newcomer children. These barriers include limited space; complex enrollment processes; limited access to language services; poor transportation; a shortage of bilingual, bicultural providers and culturally competent staff; and inappropriate parental and community involvement strategies (Kirova, 2010).

To address some of these barriers, the board of trustees in one public school system in Canada realigned its district funding in 2007 to support an innovative model that would better serve English language learners that included refugee and immigrant children. The intercultural early learning program that evolved was a result of a unique partnership among the public school board, a multicultural health brokers cooperative, a Mennonite center for newcomers, the University of Alberta, and a Head Start program, along with key community partners from the Somali, Sudanese, and Kurdish communities. In three years, this broad partnership has demonstrated how early childhood education can contribute to newcomers' inclusion in the dominant society.

INTERCULTURAL EDUCATION AND THE UN CONVENTION ON THE RIGHTS OF A CHILD

Arising from the 1971 federal multiculturalism policy, multicultural education mainly focused on encouraging majority students to learn about other cultures, locating immigrants as "the other" or as outsiders. This has been criticized for solidifying boundaries between majority and minority cultures (Kirova, 2008), fostering isolation, and replicating racialized forms of injustice (Wideen & Bernard, 1999). As a response to such critique, intercultural education seeks to include all students. It aims to create a common space, a *vivre ensemble* (McAndrew, 1996), based on mutual understanding and recognition of similarities through dialogue. However, the recent movement towards human rights has modified the contours of intercultural education to include differences (ability, regional, economic, sexual, etc.) within, as well as between, cultural groups. This movement also has created questions of education in historically marginalized languages. Thus, unlike multicultural education, intercultural education discourse in Canada is faced with examining its relation to the human rights discourse.

Particularly important for the pilot program described here is the 1989 United Nations Convention on the Rights of a Child. According to Article 29 (c) of the convention, education should be directed at development of respect for the child's parents, cultural identity, language, and values; for the national values of the country in which the child is living and for the country of origin; and for civilizations different from his or her own. In regard to children who belong to ethnic, religious, or linguistic minorities, Article 30 asserts:

> In those States in which ethnic, religious or linguistic minorities or persons of indigenous origin exist, a child belonging to such a minority or who is indigenous shall not be denied the right, in community with other members of his or her group, to enjoy his or her own culture, to profess and practise his or her own religion, or to use his or her own language.

In spite of ongoing debates about the interpretation of the articles of the convention (May, 2008), it is evident that if applied to the Canadian context, the inclusion of minority children should go beyond the preeminent position of the English and the French in society. Thus, the convention challenges the preservation of the national and linguistic duality that is assumed to create a foundation for a shared Canadian identity. Churchill's (2002) analysis of the origins of the federal programs for official languages education and its impact on identity, diversity, and citizenship revealed that the impact of the official languages model upon major population sub-groups—such as recent immigrants, whose home languages are neither English nor French, and the aboriginal peoples who were marginalized prior to the implementation of the official languages law—has been that "identity needs have not been addressed by the official languages-in-education model" (p. 43). As a result, even when heritage language instruction is available for recent immigrants on a short-term, voluntary basis in the schools, it is not sufficient to maintain immigrant languages and cultures beyond the second and third generation. Day's (2000) even more critical view was that "integration within multiculturalism in a bilingual framework is best seen as a creative reproduction of the colonial method of strategic simulation of assimilation of the Other, and not as an overcoming or break with this past" (p. 197).

The use of an official language as a tool of assimilation is defined by some authors as linguistic and cultural genocide. "Education through the medium of majority languages or colonial languages has been the most powerful assimilating force for both indigenous children and immigrant/refugee minority children, thus likewise having a homogenizing function" (Skutnabb-Kangas, 2000, pp. 201–202). In addition, the pursuit of educational goals pertaining to global competitiveness rather than human rights perpetuates linguistic colonialism or "lingoracism" (Gounari, 2006, p. 77) in many immigrant-receiving countries. As an outcome of globalization, the homogenization promoted by the emphasis on the English language has acted as a "killing agent" of diversity (Skutnabb-Kangas, 2000, p. xi). Thus, by not aligning with the UN convention, public education has not accommodated the needs of the children from minority communities, nor has it supported the development of their talents and capacities so they can become valued, respected, and contributing members of society. In the context of international economic restructuring that demands a common international language and a common set of knowledge and skills, the linguistic and cultural capital of minority children and their parents and communities has been systematically invalidated.

The education of young children of immigrant and refugee backgrounds is of particular relevance because of the implications for their educational trajectories (Arzubiaga, Noguerón, & Sullivan, 2009). However, outside bilingual/heritage language programs, there is a scarcity of research on balanced bilingualism in preschool curriculum and pedagogy.

AN INTERCULTURAL, MULTILINGUAL
EARLY CHILDHOOD PROGRAM

A commitment to the linguistic and cultural capital of minority children, parents, and communities has been fundamental to the development of an innovative intercultural, multilingual early learning program. The pilot program discussed here aimed to be genuinely responsive to the early learning needs and rights of preschool children from Somali, Sudanese, and Kurdish refugee communities. Based on the sociocultural-historical theory of learning of Vygotsky (1978) and Wertsch (1991, 1998), reflecting on the knowledge-making processes of groups involved in the program became central to understanding the diverse forms of learning and teaching that were occurring. Unlike the efforts made by the mainstream child development research to identify certain scientific values, through which it is asserted that universal, decontextualized features of childhood can be understood (Göncü, 1999), this theoretical perspective emphasizes the importance of culture and context in children's development.

The findings of the study have contributed to a growing body of scholarship that highlights the need for learning from nondominant groups (e.g., Green & Luke, 2006; Kelly, Luke, & Green, 2008): groups that are increasingly recognized as having a wealth of knowledges. The knowledge-making processes of cultural and linguistic groups were seen as central to understanding the diverse forms of learning and teaching occurring in this intercultural, multilingual early childhood setting.

Research Questions, Design, and Methods

Two main questions guided the study, which used the Participatory Learning and Action (PLA) methodology (Chambers, 1999; Pain & Francis, 2003):

1. What approaches to working with ethnocultural communities and parents contribute to the development of an intercultural early learning program that strengthens the home language and culture for children of refugee families who are English language learners?
2. What approaches to curriculum and pedagogy lead to a genuine inclusion of both the children's home languages and cultural traditions, and the English language and Canadian cultural traditions in early learning programs?

Consistent with PLA methodology, data were co-constructed and generated collectively during all phases of the process through the following methods: focus groups (Bloor, Frankland, Thomas, & Robson, 2001); individual interviews with representatives of ethnocultural communities, parents, NGOs, and government organizations; open-ended research conversations (Herda, 1999); field notes; focused and casual observations of classroom practices; and analysis of documentation. Due to the multinational, multiethnic, multilingual backgrounds of the participants, cultural brokers from the Sudanese, Kurdish, and Somali communities and first-language facilitators provided interpretations in the classroom. Interviews were audiotaped and transcribed verbatim so participants could verify their accuracy and intended meaning.

Setting and Participants

The pilot program was situated at a prekindergarten to Grade 9 Canadian public school in a low socioeconomic area having a diverse ethnic, racial, and linguistic population. More than 20 languages were spoken by the children in the school. The program was designed to include up to 22 children who were three and a half years old by September 1 of each year; 52 children participated in 2007 to 2010. The model is now an established program, becoming a regular feature in the school district in the 2010–2011 school year.

The age of the children and the parents' desire to enroll their children in the program were the only selection criteria. These families came from Kurdish, Sudanese, and Somali communities which had already established a close relationship based on their collaborative work in developing a support system for new mothers. Families in the school's neighborhood who were interested in enrolling their children in the program were also welcomed.

A first-language facilitator (FLF) for each linguistic group was selected by the respective communities based on their knowledge of the culture and love for children. An English-speaking teacher was employed by the public school board. Although FLFs were not certificated teachers, they had experience working with young children in preschool settings in their countries of origin or in Canada. The FLFs did not change over the course of the pilot program; three English-speaking teachers and several substitute teachers worked at various times.

The Pilot Program

The program was offered four mornings a week, with children bussed to the school. Mondays were reserved for classroom planning with the FLFs, classroom teacher, and researcher, and the first Monday of each month for a planning meeting with all stakeholders. Instruction time was divided equally between English and the children's native languages. This decision was based on research findings (e.g., Coltrane, 2003; Wong Fillmore, 1991) suggesting that in partnership, parents and educational practitioners can and should work simultaneously toward developing language learning milestones in both English and the native languages, through exploration of language and literacy patterns in the home and the integration of culture and language into classroom learning. Maintenance of the home language (L1) was found to be more likely when L1 was supported in the community outside the home. Therefore, it was expected that children would develop their native languages not only in the school but also at home and through community events, so that they could maintain relationships with their parents, extended families, and communities (Hepburn, 2004). At the same time, developing English language proficiency would put them in a more equitable position in school. It is important to note that although existing heritage language programs in Canada, Europe, and United States (Cummins, 1992; Tavares, 2000) and dual language immersion programs (Olson, 2007) mostly have a similar configuration of L1 and L2 language instruction time, the pilot program described here was unique in that it involved four languages: Somali, Arabic (Sudanese dialect), Kurdish, and English.

Learnings Regarding Approaches to Working with Ethnocultural Communities and Parents

> The program is a place where an intercultural community is built rather than a place where problems are fixed. The program is built on the premise that there is richness in diversity, both among and within communities that allows for similarities to emerge. The children attending the program are not "at risk"; they are in the program because they deserve and have the right to learn in their mother tongue. (Participant, professional development day, February 5, 2010)

As this comment shows, the program was closely aligned with the UN Convention on the Rights of a Child. In addition to providing learning experiences in the children's home languages, the program was based on the assumption that the knowledges and practices of newcomer parents and communities have a significant impact on their children's learning and development. Thus, early childhood classroom practices are greatly enhanced when these become part of the children's early school experiences. In contrast with common Anglo middle-class forms of engagement such as parents' involvement on the agency board or helping the teacher in the classroom, the pilot program sought other forms of participation that took account of the ways in which refugee parents are overburdened.

> [They are] overburdened with other responsibilities, mostly making a living...taking care of so many children, so the life circumstances might not necessarily give them the opportunity to participate in the way that the programs are expecting them.... The social and economic exclusion that families are experiencing is a major set of factors and it might be a set of factors that we need to work through and figure out because just being very poor or being very overburdened and being really trapped in other priority issues, really render parents having very little time to be involved. (Settlement worker, steering committee meeting, 2008)

The ethnocultural communities were involved through FLFs and cultural brokers, who initially helped to set goals and make sure cultural expectations and traditions were embodied in the children's daily lives in school. However, throughout the project, efforts were made to involve communities, parents, FLFs, and cultural brokers in regular meetings. In addition, community and parent volunteers from all three communities helped in the classroom.

The key learnings regarding the approaches to working with ethnocultural communities and newcomer parents over three years are summarized below. Developing trust based on respect and a shared vision of goals and learning was crucial in working with communities and parents.

Goal Setting and Ongoing Revisiting of Goals by All Stakeholders

For a program to be successful, all stakeholders must be involved in goal setting and an ongoing revision of goals. The stakeholders defined the following goals for the program (Kirova, 2010):

1. To be genuinely responsive to the unique early learning needs of newcomer children growing up in a particularly complex social/economic and multicultural context.
2. To provide cultural and linguistic continuity for young newcomer children through both first language and English instruction.
3. To be culturally sensitive and inclusive of the newcomer families' perspectives.
4. To be holistic, strength-based, and equity-based, building on the combined expertise of government organizations, community partners, communities, and researchers.
5. To be collaborative, interrelational, and interdependent so that mutual learning becomes fundamental to success of the project.

These goals were reviewed at the end of each year. At end of the second year of the program, two new goals were added: (6) To help children develop a sense of belonging to both their home culture and language and the Canadian culture, and (7) To build a support system and partnership within the broader school community. Fine-tuning of the goals demonstrated the active engagement of all participants in a truly collaborative process that was reflective of the changing circumstances of the communities. It also created a sense of shared ownership in the goals.

Affirming the Cultural Capital of Communities and Parents

The pilot program affirmed parents and community members as vital sources of knowledge about their world, culture, and children. They were seen as key players in the development of the intercultural program as a shared space. However, it is important to note that at the beginning of the program, when asked what they wanted for their children, most parents said that they wanted them to learn English and to fit into Canadian society. It was only when the Kurdish cultural broker explained that they "do not think they have anything worthwhile to contribute and are afraid to embarrass their children" (classroom staff meeting, May 5, 2008) that it became apparent that parents have adopted the dominant groups' beliefs that they were unable to provide their children with appropriate education because they lack social and cultural capital (Arzubiaga et al., 2009). As members of minority groups, their expressed views were a result of a process of negative internalization, termed by Bourdieu (1991) "misrecognition" as a sign of "symbolic violence." It took the classroom staff and the researcher almost a year to gain the trust of the parents and for the parents to share their knowledge.

In the second year, a series of focus groups collected the shared wisdom of the communities and parents, who discussed the following key questions: (1) In what aspects of life (both in the home and outside of the home) do you expect your children to participate and how? (2) What do you want your young child to know about the world? (3) What do you consider an appropriate way of teaching children what they need to know? Are there any specific songs, games, stories, play materials that you consider absolutely crucial for your children's learning? If so, how do you think they can be incorporated into classroom practice?

The analysis of the discussions with the parents and the elders from the three communities led to the identification of these commonalities:

- *Learning happens through observation and participation in life.* This applies to all children of this age, although boys and girls are expected to learn different roles; e.g., boys learn to play soccer, and girls pretend to cook and take care of babies.

- *Elders play an essential role in young children's education.* Children often sit around the elders to sing songs and listen to stories that have a moral lesson or that teach the child how to handle a difficult or unsafe situation.
- *Children are expected to know their roots.* Every child has a family name song, and family history is told in a song that includes the names of predecessors. Children learn differences and similarities between their own and other cultures (as for dress, religion, and language).
- *Teaching respect for family members and elders in the community is a priority.* Showing respect means never saying "no" to a teacher, parent, or elder; not looking older members of the family/community in the eye when being scolded (the child must not appear as an equal); and being obedient.
- *Skills and creativity are developed through children's engagement in making toys for themselves.* Boys and girls make different types of toys with natural materials (e.g., trucks and dolls), make instruments with fruits and seeds, and draw in the sand.
- *As members of the family and community, children have responsibilities.* Children should know and follow the rules of the house (e.g., at bedtime and meal time). They are expected to dress and feed themselves independently, as well as clean up after themselves. Children are never idle; they help adults with cooking, building, or making ropes, and they make their own toys.

The act of sharing cultural expectations, norms, and approaches to learning and the expectation of parents and community leaders that there was a "real place" for these to be implemented created the feeling, expressed in the focus group, that "for the first time there is chance for our voices to be heard for real" (focus group, April 24, 2009). Parents began to realize that instead of being labeled as "regressive and premodern" (May, 2008, p. 48), their cultural practices and languages were recognized as valuable in the dominant education system. For example, singing as the most salient cultural way of being with young children was utilized on a minute-to-minute basis by the FLFs and cultural brokers. All children were introduced to the classroom community with their special name and family song, and the children learned to sing or at least recognize each other's songs. Singing was described by both the parents and the classroom staff as a way of "naturally reinforcing steps followed in complex or monotonous tasks" (Sudanese FLF). They saw the use of songs as a way of gently and indirectly guiding children's behaviors in the classroom. Songs derived from the activities in which either the adults and/or the children were involved on a daily basis—sweeping the floor, getting the tables ready for a snack, greeting each other in the morning, "making pita bread" on the play dough table, and so on. Rather than being a separate activity, singing was related to what the children were doing at the moment, and thus it was a spontaneous activity that accompanied whatever the children were doing. However, songs involved instructions (i.e., how to complete a task at hand) or expressed particular emotions, most commonly affection. Since songs have traditional morals embedded in them, as pointed out by the community members and parents, they were used by the classroom staff to both praise children and scold them. Including such cultural practices in the classroom created a shared sense of momentum among the members of the communities and a desire to be involved in their children's education.

Learnings Regarding Approaches to Curriculum and Pedagogy

It was through the classroom team's conversations that life-stories became interconnected in a shared understanding about the children in the program and the diverse worlds they needed to know and navigate on a daily basis. In the absence of a set curriculum, Grumet (1995) described "conversation [as] the process of making sense with a group of people of the systems that shape and organize the world that we can think about together" (p. 19). Taking a constructivist viewpoint, Bruner (1987) defined "world-making" or "life-making" as a process in which the life-stories of those involved "must mesh, so to speak, within a community of life stories; tellers and listeners must share some 'deep structure' about the nature of 'life'" (p. 21).

Negotiating Cultural Meanings in Selecting Curriculum Topics

The program's first goal was to provide cultural and linguistic continuity for young newcomer children through both first-language and English instruction. Therefore, the first major task in developing the curriculum was to go beyond a simplistic view of culture commonly represented in multicultural classrooms: a static, homogeneous, frozen-in-time, and normative "entity" that "does things to people" (Hoffman, 1996, p. 549), or as Trueba (1992) put it, "some sort of amorphous, reified static entity that causes people to behave in certain ways, to express and exhibit certain values, beliefs, and practices" (p. 80). Instead of the traditional multicultural approach to early childhood practice based on special celebrations of holidays, foods, costumes, or arts/crafts, the classroom team engaged an ongoing discussion about children's everyday experiences that cut across all four cultures.

Common topics emerged as FLFs and cultural brokers shared stories of their lives as children as well as current events in their respective cultural communities. Through these ongoing conversations, common topics emerged: families, babies, friendship, harvest, market, serving tea, houses, and animals (see Figure 2.1). Almost half of the families had an infant at

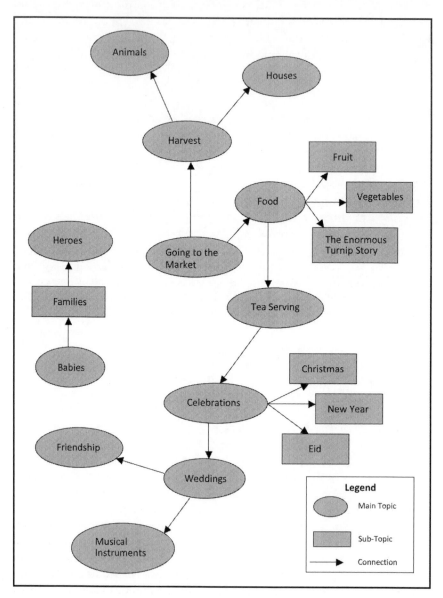

Figure 2.1 Topics map.

home, and in the classroom the ways in which all families care for a new-born were discussed. The FLFs also initiated discussions of family differences in both English and the children's respective home languages, having the children share a lullaby or a game used in their own homes. In this way the children learned what it means to care for a baby in general and how this care might differ from culture to culture. Thus, what was considered by the three communities important for their children to know about their own culture as well as about the other cultures was embedded in all aspects of children's learning in the classroom.

The view that language is best learned in a meaningful context was strongly supported by all stakeholders. Therefore, the topics developed in the program were illustrative of the view that content and materials are vehicles of language instruction. As a result, instead of acting as interpreters or translators from English to the children's home languages, FLFs engaged the children in culturally relevant activities that led to learning cultural traditions and the vocabularies pertinent to these traditions. This approach to language development allowed for meaningful introduction and use of cultural artefacts as part of the learning activities. Everyday objects brought to the classroom by the FLFs from their countries of origin were not used as decoration; rather, such cultural tools were seen as mediational means that were central in the cultural-developmental process (Wertsch, 1991, 1998). Therefore, artifacts and language as cultural tools were integral components of cultural settings and were used by both the FLFs and the children as they participated in the goal-oriented activities (see Kirova, 2010). From this point of view, the process of using cultural tools in learning, including learning a language, was not just a matter of reproducing a shared system, but, rather, is a creative processes, resulting in hybridity "as a social and cultural formation" (Luke & Luke, 2000, p. 283).

Finding a Balance Between Children's Needs and Strengths

Another major task in planning curriculum and pedagogy was making sure the discourse of deficit that constructed children of immigrants as needy, having fewer skills than their native peers (e.g., Magnuson, Lahaie, & Waldfogel, 2006) as well as having language deficiency or lacking alignment in social capital (e.g., Kao & Rutherford, 2007), was problematized on a day-to-day basis in the classroom. A central goal was to develop a shared understanding of the differences between classroom practices based on needs and those based on strengths. To achieve this, the classroom staff felt the need to contextualize the goals of the program. For example, while all stakeholders and classroom staff recognized that newcomer children have unique needs, there was a danger that the way in which these needs were articulated in discussion between the school authorities and the classroom teacher could perpetuate the discourse of deficit. Rich small- and large-group discussions with all stakeholders identified the following needs for children in the program:

- Be loved for who they are without being prejudged
- View their parents as capable caregivers despite a lack of English language proficiency
- Feel that they belong to both home and Canadian cultures
- Negotiate between home and school cultures
- Learn English as well as their home language
- Learn to navigate school rules
- Learn to be with children who don't speak their language
- Be confident in themselves in the face of being marginalized
- Maintain their cultural background
- See their family and community lives reflected in their classroom
- Have their unique strengths recognized

The classroom staff realized that needs such as belonging, affirmation, self-expression, and exploration were similar to mainstream children's needs, but there were also differences "in how we do this given the context of their lives. Concretely, this means much closer ties with families" (Kurdish language facilitator). Consistent with the cultural expectations of young children articulated at the communities' focus groups, another difference observed by the classroom staff was that newcomer children have a different interaction/learning style compared to their English-speaking, Canadian-born counterparts in that they relied more on nonverbal exchanges.

Being responsive to the children's unique needs meant that on a daily basis, the classroom staff needed to:

- Recognize that some unique needs are rooted in socioeconomic vulnerability
- Know the families' needs, situations, support for their children's learning, goals/hopes for their children
- Respect children's differences
- Develop an understanding of the families' experiences prior to emigrating
- Involve children in the learning process; find ways for them to express their curiosity and confusion; help them negotiate two different worlds

- Observe what the children are doing and what is catching their interest; use nonverbal expressions, such as a gentle touch and eye contact
- Recognize the cultural knowledge children bring to the classroom and how things are done in their home/culture; work with the child to extend their knowledge and skills. In this process, cultural brokers are invaluable resources.

The strengths of the children were seen in direct relationship to their already identified needs. As the Somali cultural broker put it,

> They have unique strengths that need to be recognized. We can get to know their strengths when we build their confidence and self-esteem in the classroom. Lots of times we see the children wandering around the classroom. We may think that they have some developmental issues because they are not paying attention to the teacher, when they are trying to make sense of the new setting and rules that need to be followed. (Monthly group meeting, 2009)

The children's ability to navigate across cultures and languages was seen as one of their main strengths. They were also resourceful (e.g., doing more with fewer materials and toys); able to learn by observing their environment; and astutely aware of gestures, tone, eye contact. Most of them had knowledge of at least two cultures and languages.

To be responsive to the children's unique strengths meant that on a day-to-day basis, staff needed to have the following mindset and approach:

- Begin every interaction with the belief that all children come with strengths; engage children as co-contributors of their learning through child-driven activities
- Foster a sense of competence and self-worth in children
- Identify and affirm what children bring to the classroom and who they are as unique individuals and as members of their cultural community
- Show the children the value of their cultural knowledge and experience

PARENTS' VIEWS OF THEIR CHILDREN'S LEARNING

Assessing children's learning in the program was not an easy task since stakeholders used a different cultural lens to define success. Research focused on creating an appropriate means to evaluate young children of immigrant and refugee families (Ogilvie et al., 2005) suggested that such assessment should not be done in a standardized fashion, isolated from the larger family context in which these children live. Consistent with the goals of the program, we put "addressing the needs of the families" first in the assessment process. The assessment activities were part of an iterative process, conducted at the pace and discretion deemed appropriate by the classroom team, parents, and cultural brokers. While this was a very complex process including a comparison between collected spontaneous speech samples and narrative samples from the children in both L1 and L2 at the beginning and end of the program, for the purposes of this chapter, only the views of the parents regarding their children's learning will be discussed.

Parents' views were solicited informally each year. At the end of year 3, the parents were formally invited to discuss observable changes regarding their children's feelings about themselves, ability to get along with others at home and at school, and use of the home language. The summary of these discussions showed that, like the parents of the first two years, they felt their children had become more responsible, had learned to share, had become more open to playing with other children even outside the school, and were now following rules at home for the first time. Some children had become a lot more confident, as expressed by these parents:

- "My daughter knows that she can do things by herself." (Sudanese father)
- "My son is very proud of what he can do. He is so excited about everything he does so he wants to show it to us." (Serbian mother)
- "My daughter too wants to show me everything she draws or makes." (Sudanese father)
- "I see a lot of change in him from the beginning of the school year. He can now sit still and do something while before he could not. He feels good about himself." (Sudanese mother)

Most parents noticed positive changes in terms of their children's use of their first language, including paying more attention to parents' talk in their home language and showing interest in the topics being discussed. For example, a Somali mother said, laughingly, "When we say something in our language we don't want him to hear, he now says, 'I heard you!'" Younger children were reported engaging older children in conversations in their mother tongue and teaching them words, or bringing new words from school and discussing them with their parents. Even Serbian children, whose home language was not supported in the classroom, became more attentive to their grandparents' requests and began to reply in Serbian. The parents acknowledged that they too have become a lot more conscious about using their home language with all their children, as well as encouraging other members of the community whose children were not part of the program to do the same.

Wherever I go I tell my people, "Talk to your children in our language because this will help them learn in school." They don't believe me first but then I tell them what my child is doing and they listen to me. (Sudanese mother)

The parents also identified changes that occurred in their relationships with their children. These were particularly noticeable in the area of engaging in playful interactions. As one Sudanese father put it,

Back home the relationship between the parent and the child are [sic] more limited. Kids would laugh at you if you wanted to play with them. Here, they demand it, they expect it; they see other parents play with their children and if I don't do the same, I feel bad. My children always ask me to go to the park and play. And I do even though I don't have time. . . . Back home we had the whole extended family so there were more people to play with the children. It is just us here.

Another noticeable change was in the way in which parents understood and were able to accommodate changes for their children's behavior required by the school, such as approaching adults directly with questions and looking them in the eyes when scolded. One Sudanese father said, "I don't have a problem with this. We are here in Canada and it is important for our children to learn to stand for themselves and be like the other children." A Somali father added, "I see her [my daughter] need to blend my culture and this culture in order to fit. So the program has helped a lot. If you live here, you have to be flexible."

IMPLICATIONS FOR EARLY CHILDHOOD THEORY AND PRACTICE

The main learnings regarding the research questions suggest that the goals of the program as implemented in everyday practice were in alignment with the articles on the rights of the minority children as outlined by the UN convention. Accessibility to such programs is a matter of social justice. With social inclusion conceptualized as "the goal and the process of developing the talents, skills and capacities of children to participate in the social and economic mainstream of community life by providing the opportunities and removing the barriers for children" (Freiler, as cited in Friendly & Lero, 2005, p. 59), the program exemplifies how early learning programs can contribute to social inclusion of marginalized populations. This was recognized by the local school authorities as well as the ethnocultural communities. The program has become a model for other schools that also have large populations of immigrant children. It was seen as an incubator for pedagogical innovations both in curriculum development and teaching approaches. These were shared regularly at the monthly PD day meetings involving the staff members of the other eight early learning programs within the public school board, many of which had a high number of English language learners (ELL) as well but provided instruction in English only. As a result of the example provided by the program, other communities have become energized and mobilized in articulating and gathering the knowledge about raising and educating young children they collectively hold. For example, two other ethnocultural communities, Vietnamese and Eritrean, started a daycare center where the two languages were used for regular instruction as well as English. The teaching team attended a few of the Monday morning planning sessions at the research site to learn about the planning process used in the program. Service providers (i.e., Multicultural Health Brokers' Co-op) report that conversations among different communities are filled with hope—there is a strong shared belief that something could actually happen in the system so that it can genuinely include their points of view.

However, in order for the program to make a contribution outside the specific context in which it took place, it is crucial to link the implications of the learnings to early childhood theory and practice. "Meaning is not lying around in nature waiting to be scooped up by the senses, rather it is constructed. It is produced in the acts of interpretation" (Dahlberg, Moss, & Pence, 2007, p. 147). Therefore, it is important to acknowledge the sociocultural-historical theory that provided the lens through which we made sense of the classroom practices. It provided grounding for examining the multidimensional relationship between culture, development, and power. In the societal context in which the project took place, the dominating universalist or decontextualized view of child development had created a discourse of deficits associated with the cultural and linguistic backgrounds of the children and families participating in the project. This had to be contested.

Through constant critical examination of the socio-political arrangements of power and access that the individuals in the project participated in, they came to better understand how conventional education arrangements have led to a privileging of particular forms of social and cultural capital (Bourdieu, 1990). Thus, the program not only addressed the fundamental epistemological question of what constitutes knowledge in general and child development and learning in particular, but also provided examples of how marginalized knowledge systems can and should be included in the ongoing process of knowledge reconstruction/co-construction.

Sociocultural-historical theory also allowed the study to focus on cultural practices as a unit of analysis of both the (minority) ethnic group's culture, and the (majority) school culture. The analysis of the activities and interactions of the "social others" such as teachers and peers (Vygotsky, 1978) within the respective cultures in the daily life of a classroom allowed for understanding how cultural practices are embodied by individuals participating in the project (Kirova, 2010). Because the concept of change is central to sociocultural-historical theory, it allowed all participants in the project to adopt a non-essentialist approach to cultural differences, which in turn allowed the creation of a hybrid or third space as one of negotiation of cultural space that offered opportunities for practices in and between varied modes of meaning. The fusion of cultures that occurred in this shared space was seen as an opportunity for multiple, even contradictory, cultural identities to coexist and develop. From this perspective, the presence of multiple languages was seen as an opportunity for an intentional and inter-subjective space between users to be created.

Of most importance, however, it must be acknowledged that while the theory provided the interpretive lens, it was the practices that emerged and were shaped by ongoing negotiations among all participants that held tremendous potential to generate new knowledge. In fact, the hope for the future of early childhood education is that new theories should be based on contextual, ever-evolving amalgamations of worldviews, knowledges, skills, values, and traditions present at each and every moment in the rich environment created by student and educator diversity. In this sense, the program provides an example of how the binary between theory and practice can be contested. It is an example of what Urban (2009) called creating "practice-based evidence" that the education field as a whole should engage in so the new understandings of the complex worlds in which both young children and early childhood educators navigate on a daily basis can emerge. For this to happen, the ongoing debates about who has the right to claim minority rights as they apply to education should not revolve around the question of whether we can afford the cost of programs that support children's linguistic and cultural rights. The question is: Can we afford not to have them?

REFERENCES

Arzubiaga, S. E., Noguerón, S. C., & Sullivan, A. L. (2009). The education of children in immigrant families. *Review of Research in Education, 33*, 246–271. doi:10.3102/0091732X08328243

Bloor, M., Frankland, J., Thomas, M., & Robson, K. (2001). *Focus groups in social research*. Thousand Oaks, CA: Sage.

Bourdieu, P. (1990). *The logic of practice*. Cambridge, UK: Polity Press.

Bourdieu, P. (1991). *Language and symbolic power*. Cambridge, UK: Polity Press.

Bruner, J. (1987). Life as narrative. *Social Research, 54*(1), 11–32.

Chambers, R. (1999). *Whose reality counts? Putting the first last*. Warwickshire, UK: Intermediate Technology.

Chumak-Horbatsch, R. (2008). Early bilingualism: Children of immigrants in an English-language childcare centre. *Psychology of Language and Communication, 12*(1), 3–27. doi:10.2478/v10057-008-0001-2

Churchill, S. (2002). *Language education, Canadian civic identity and the identities of Canadians.* Strasbourg, France: Council of Europe.

Citizenship and Immigration Canada. (2008). *Facts and figures Canada: Prairie provinces.* Ottawa, ON: Author.

Coltrane, B. (2003). *Working with young English language learners: Some considerations.* Center for Applied Linguistics (EDO-FL-03-01). Retrieved from www.cal.org/resources/digest/0301coltrane.html

Cummins, J. (1992). Heritage language teaching in Canadian schools. *Journal of Curriculum Studies, 24*(3), 281–286. doi:10.1080/0022027920240306

Dachyshyn, D. (2008). *Refugee families with preschool children: Transition to life in Canada.* Saarbrücken, Germany: VDM Verlag Dr. Müller Aktiengesellschaft.

Dahlberg, G., Moss, P., & Pence, A. (2007). *Beyond quality in early childhood education and care: Languages of evaluation* (2nd ed.). Abingdon, Oxon, UK: Routledge.

Day, R. (2000). *Multiculturalism and the history of Canadian diversity.* Toronto, ON: University of Toronto Press.

Friendly, M., & Lero, D. (2005). Social inclusion through early childhood education and care. In T. Richmond & A. Saloojee (Eds.), *Social inclusion: Canadian perspectives* (pp. 58–82). Halifax, NS: Fernwood.

Göncü, A. (1999). Children's and researchers' engagement in the world. In A. Göncü (Ed.), *Children's engagement in the world: Sociocultural perspectives* (pp. 3–25). Cambridge, UK: Cambridge University Press.

Gounari, P. (2006). How to tame a wild tongue: Language rights in the United States. *Human Architecture: Journal of the Sociology of Self-Knowledge* (Special Issue), *4,* 71–78.

Green, J., & Luke, A. (2006). Rethinking learning: What counts as learning and what learning counts. *Review of Research in Education, 30*(1), xi–xvi. doi:10.3102/0091732X030001011

Grumet, M. R. (1995). The curriculum: What are the basics and are we teaching them? In J. L. Kincheloe & S. R. Steinberg (Eds.), *Thirteen questions: Reframing education's conversation* (2nd ed., pp. 15–21). New York, NY: Lang.

Hepburn, K. S. (2004). *Building culturally and linguistically competent services to support young children and their families, and school readiness.* Baltimore, MD: The Annie E. Casey Foundation.

Herda, E. (1999). *Research conversations and narrative: A critical hermeneutic orientation in participatory inquiry.* Westport, CT: Praeger.

Hoffman, D. M. (1996). Culture and self in multicultural education: Reflections on discourse, text, and practice. *American Educational Research Journal, 33*(3), 545–569. doi:10.3102/00028312033003545

Kao, G., & Rutherford, L. T. (2007). Does social capital still matter? Immigrant minority disadvantages in school-specific social capital and its effects on academic achievement. *Sociological Perspectives, 50*(1), 27–52.

Kelly, G., Luke, A., & Green, J. (2008). What counts as knowledge in educational settings: Disciplinary knowledge, assessment and curriculum. *Review of Research in Education, 32,* vii–x. doi:10.3102/0091732X07311063

Kirova, A. (2008). Critical and emerging discourses in multicultural education literature: A review. *Canadian Ethnic Studies Special Issue: Multiculturalism Discourses, 40*(1), 102–124.

Kirova, A. (2010). Children's representations of cultural scripts in play: Facilitating transition from home to preschool in an intercultural early learning program for refugee children. *Diaspora, Indigenous, and Minority Education: An International Journal, 4*(2), 1–18. doi:10.1080/15595691003635765

Luke, A., & Luke, C. (2000). A situated perspective on cultural globalization. In N. Burbules & C. Torres (Eds.), *Globalization and education: Critical perspectives* (pp. 275–297). New York, NY: Routledge.

Magnuson, K., Lahaie, C., & Waldfogel, J. (2006). Preschool and school readiness of children of immigrants. *Social Science Quarterly, 87*(5), 1241–1262.

May, S. (2008). *Language and minority rights: Ethnicity, nationalism and the politics of language*. New York, NY: Routledge.

McAndrew, M. (1996). L'intégration des élèves des minorités ethniques dans les écoles de langue française au Québec: Éléments d'un bilan. In *L'éducation multiculturelle: École et société* (pp. 1–23). Winnipeg, MB: Canadian Association of Second Language Teachers. Retrieved from http://www.caslt.org/pdf/report3_integration.pdf

Ogilvie, L., Fleming, D., Burgess-Pino, E., Caufield, C., Chui, Y., Kirova, A., ... Ortiz, L. (2005). *Examining culturally appropriate assessment practices in early childhood (ECD) programs*. Unpublished manuscript, University of Alberta.

Olson, K. (2007). Lost opportunities to learn: The effects of education policy on primary language instruction for English learners. *Linguistics and Education, 18*(2), 121–141. doi:10.1016/j.linged.2007.07.001

Pain, R., & Francis, P. (2003). Reflections on participatory research. *Area, 35*(1), 46–54.

Rutter, J. (1998). Refugee children in the early years. *Multicultural Teaching, 17*(1), 23–26.

Skutnabb-Kangas, T. (2000). *Linguistic genocide in education, or worldwide diversity and human rights?* Mahwah, NJ: Erlbaum.

Suarez-Orozco, C., & Suarez-Orozco, M. (2001). *Children of immigrants*. Cambridge, MA: Harvard University Press.

Tavares, A. J. (2000). From *heritage* to international *languages*: Globalism and Western Canadian trends in *heritage language education*. *Canadian Ethnic Studies, 32*(1), 156–171.

Trueba, H. T. (1992). The Spindlers as ethnographers: The impact of their lives and work on American anthropology. In L. B. Boyer & R.M. Boyer (Eds.), *The psychoanalytic study of society* (Vol. 17, pp. 23–28). Hillsdale, NJ: Analytic.

United Nations Convention on the Rights of a Child. (1989). Retrieved from http://www2.ohchr.org/english/law/crc.htm

Urban, M. (2009, June). *Cloudy day navigation: Hermeneutic inquiry and practice-based evidence in early childhood education*. Presentation at the 17th Reconceptualization of Early Childhood Education Conference, Bethlehem, Palestine.

Vygotsky, L. S. (1978). *Mind and society: The development of higher mental processes*. Cambridge, MA: Harvard University Press.

Wertsch, J. V. (1991). *Voices of the mind: A sociocultural approach to mediated action.* Cambridge, MA: Harvard University Press.

Wertsch, J. V. (1998). *Mind as action.* New York, NY: Oxford University Press.

Wideen, M., & Barnard, K. A. (1999). *Impacts of immigration on education in British Columbia: An analysis of efforts to implement policies of multiculturalism in schools* (Working Paper Series, RIIM 99-02). Vancouver, BC, Canada: Vancouver Centre of Excellence.

Wong Fillmore, L. (1991). When learning a second language means losing the first. *Early Childhood Research Quarterly, 6*(3), 323–346. doi:10.1016/S0885-2006(05)80059-6

CHAPTER 3

REFUGEES AS EDUCATORS

The Potential for Positive Impact
on Educational Systems

Susan Banki
University of Sydney

ABSTRACT

Much of the literature on refugee education—indeed, on the acculturation
and integration of refugees in general—focuses on the obstacles refugees face
and on the ways in which the systems they enter are challenged by their presence. This chapter examines refugees and education from the opposite angle.
It argues that refugees have the potential to offer valuable contributions to the
educational systems they enter, particularly in resettlement countries. The first
part of the chapter draws on theoretical concepts in the sociological and psychological literatures to make the case for refugee contributions to an overall
educational system. The second part offers examples from refugee communities from Burma and Bhutan living in Australia, demonstrating the richness
and variety of skills that these communities possess. The third part briefly describes what these experiences and skills may bring to a learning environment.

The many challenges of educating refugee populations once they have
arrived in countries of resettlement are both intuitive and present in the

Refugee and Immigrant Students, pages 43–64
Copyright © 2012 by Information Age Publishing
All rights of reproduction in any form reserved.

academic and practitioner literature. The obstacles include linguistic and cultural challenges, trauma from refugee flight that makes concentration difficult, and adjustment to a new society that problematizes learning. There are also many empirical examples of refugees who have overcome such challenges and succeeded despite them. Both of these narratives, however, focus on the ways in which the educational system impacts refugees.

This chapter examines refugees and education from the opposite angle. It explores how refugees may impact an educational system. It argues that refugees have the potential to offer valuable contributions to education, particularly in resettlement countries. The first part of the chapter draws on theoretical concepts in the sociological and psychological literatures to make the case for refugee contributions to an overall educational system. The second part offers examples from refugee communities from Burma and Bhutan living in Australia, demonstrating the richness and variety of skills that these communities possess. The third part briefly describes what these experiences and skills may bring to a learning environment.

REFUGEES AND EDUCATION

While there is an extensive body of literature on the challenges of refugee integration and acculturation in general, the body of literature on refugee education is slim. Pinson and Arnot (2007) argue that the field requires far more empirical research, particularly studies with rigorous methodologies. Much of the current work, whether empirical (Bloch, 2002) or policy-based (Refugee Council of Australia [RCOA], 2010b; Remsbery, 2003), is centered around the job opportunities that refugees may locate post-education.

Where the literature is lacking, however, is in studying the impacts that refugees themselves have on educational systems. Some research does note that refugees offer wider contributions to the general community (Lalich, 2006; Madkhul, 2007; Miralles-Lombardo, Miralles, & Golding, 2008; RCOA, 2010a), but these do not have an educational focus.

Thus, the following sections seek to establish a theoretical and the beginnings of an empirical basis for arguing that refugees impact positively on broader educational systems. Drawing on the literatures of multicultural education and intergroup contact theory and applying field examples from refugee communities from Burma and Bhutan, the chapter demonstrates the potential for refugee contributions to education in Australia.

THE IMPORTANCE OF DIVERSITY IN EDUCATION

The broad notion of education for cultural diversity embraces a number of distinct constructions, some of which may be specific to particular countries or groups (i.e., multicultural education, social inclusion, pluralist education, anti-racist education, social justice education, and more recently, cosmopolitanism). The term "multicultural education" is used here to describe an overall approach that promotes the acknowledgement and acceptance of diversity and difference in the education system. Originally developed in the United States, the literature on multicultural education is ample in its breadth, depth, and longevity. Based on Kantian notions of universal human rights and intercultural understanding, the proponents of an education system that embraces diversity are many. It has been argued that a focus on pluralism in a country's educational system promotes social justice (Baptiste, 1979), tolerance (Parekh, 1986), and the values that maintain the pillars of the liberal state (Halstead, 2003). More theoretically, from the principle of critical pedagogy, the purpose of multicultural education in all its forms is to challenge dominant power structures, whether these are class-based (for example, McLaren, 1997), gender-based (hooks, 1981; Mohanty, 1991), or ethnicity-based (Bonilla-Silva & Embrick, 2006). Multicultural education also has its detractors. Maitzen (1997), for example, argues that multicultural and individualistic principles of teaching are incompatible and lead to an inconsistent pedagogical approach that is difficult to reconcile in the actual classroom.

The components of multicultural education encompass the spectrum of educational elements, from educational philosophy to school administration and resource allocation. Recognition of the importance of preparing instructors to teach multicultural themes and evaluate students accordingly, for example, has a longstanding emphasis (Frazier, 1977). Multicultural elements range from the specific—such as reforming curricula to reflect diverse racial, social, ethnic, and cultural perspectives (Banks, 1993a)—to a general overhaul of entire school systems (Nieto, 1992). Furthermore, analyses of the mechanisms and means of implementing multicultural education are not the realm of scholars alone. Policymakers, too, have joined the fray. Examples from policy documents in the United States (Tibbitts, 2002), Australia (Australian Government, 2010), and the UK (Remsbery, 2003) indicate that governments place importance on developing educational systems and tools that acknowledge diversity and call for inclusion.

What is less present, however, in both the academic and policy literature, is the question of how actual diversity in the classroom improves the implementation and execution of multicultural education. Some have recognized the importance of a diverse staff (for example, Grant & Sleeter, 1993), but the composition of students, and *the ways in which this diversity can contribute to improved educational outcomes for all students*, remains neglected. That is, how does having students from varied backgrounds influence all students' cognitive frameworks; the way that curricula are designed and taught; qualitative measures, such as student self-esteem and tolerance; and quantitative measures, such as student attendance and exam scores? Of course, literature as far back as the 1970s demonstrates a positive correlation between multicultural education and some of these qualitative measures in particular (Banks, 1991; Banks, 1993b), but linking these back to student diversity in the classroom specifically has proved problematic, as has obtaining sound data on quantitative measures.

In the field of migration studies, scholars have noted the hazards of an assimilation discourse, in which the migrant sheds her/his old cultural/ social traditions, as opposed to the adaptation discourse, in which migrants and indigenous populations adopt from one another (for example, Gold-lust & Richmond, 1974, pp. 194–196). Similarly, in education, one finds oversimplified versions of multicultural education that fail to recognize the importance of acknowledging and maintaining differences among cultures, ethnicities, and people with diverse backgrounds. An unquestioning insistence on the need to include "the other" regardless of the gaps that may exist in terms of a lack of shared understandings of the meanings of institutional practices can be problematic and may hinder attempts to understand and value cultural differences (Nesbitt, 2004).

Instead, Conroy (2009) suggests "a pedagogy of enstrangement" (p. 145), arguing that such an approach will sustain, rather than exclude, dynamic pluralism in education, because educators can utilize conflict and difference in the classroom to develop stronger shared understandings. Nesbitt and Conroy do not disagree about the need for diversity in the classroom, but only the approach that school systems and educators might take to most effectively enhance education in the face of such diversity.

Finally, the focus on diversity in the classroom is certainly not unique to refugee populations. Disability, race, gender, ethnicity, and nationality are all to be considered when one is seeking to develop respect for diversity through educational programs. Thus any conclusions that we can draw about the utility of diversity in the educational system, and in the classroom specifically, cannot be narrowed to refugee populations specifically. If this section demonstrates to some extent that difference and diversity enrich education for the larger population, what might other literatures say about the specific value of refugees? To answer this, we look to concepts that may offer insight into the unique experiences of refugees and how these may influence education.

THE ROLE OF RELATIONAL CLOSENESS TO REFUGEES

The presence of refugees within a classroom has the potential to add another positive dimension to an educational system that promotes multiculturalism. Over and above the diversity in ethnicity, race, and nationality that refugees provide, the nature of the refugee experience—fleeing persecution or generalized conflict—means this population is more likely to offer a window onto conflict and exile through first-hand experience. It is thus argued that non-refugee students who relate to refugee classmates may come to understand better key concepts such as equality, fear, sacrifice, survival, injustice, and persecution. Whether or not this provides a means of reducing the "otherness" of new populations, hence mirroring Conroy's pedagogy of enstrangement, is less important than the empathic responses that such relational closeness generates.

The term "relational closeness" has been used in the psychological literature to describe the extent of emotional investment (Mashek & Aron, 2004), while in communications studies it describes the thickness of the connections between individuals (King III, 1997). In this chapter, it describes the extent to which classmates can develop compassion and empathy for fellow students. The process by which this happens has been noted in several sub-literatures, among them psychology and sociology, in the study of the intergroup contact theory, as discussed below. While the empirical literature is silent on how relational closeness among refugees and the broader population may impact education, it can certainly be argued that the classroom setting offers an ideal space within which to develop refugee/non-refugee relationships that, in other contexts, might be considered unorganic.

INTERGROUP CONTACT THEORY AND ITS APPLICABILITY TO REFUGEES IN THE CLASSROOM

Intergroup contact theory argues that contact among individuals and groups of different backgrounds can alleviate conflict and tension. Allport's initial segregation housing study (1954) originally conceived of such contact as physical only, but the theory has been expanded to include parasocial parameters in which contact can come through mass media and other far-reaching communication instruments (Schiappa, 2008). Numerous empirical studies have sought to reinforce the theory's original assertion, focusing on racial divides (Pettigrew, 1971), homosexuality (Herek & Glunt, 1993), and the disabled (Harper & Wacker, 1985). Findings have been mixed in concluding whether contact among these groups increases the potential for cooperation or reduces it. Further, one in-depth critique differentiates between individual relations and group relations, positing that interpersonal contact has the possibility to improve individual cooperation, but not group cooperation (Forbes, 1997).

There has also been criticism that past studies have overlooked the potentially negative aspects of contact, such as increased intergroup anxiety (Stephan & Stephan, 1985). A call for more research on the negative impacts (Pettigrew & Tropp, 2006) has not, as of yet, yielded too many gains, but it has been noted that the methodological challenges of proving causality in either direction is a challenge (Green & Wong, 2009).

However strongly one espouses or eschews intergroup contact theory, it is recognized by most researchers that certain conditions are more likely to improve its chances of success. In the initial model, the four elements considered most important were equal status between the groups in the situation; common goals; intergroup cooperation; and the support of authorities, law, or custom (Allport, 1954). More recent research suggests that, rather than conditions, these four elements serve as *facilitators* for more cooperative outcomes (Pettigrew & Tropp, 2006, p. 766). Furthermore, institutional support, it was found, offers the strongest possibility of improving the relationship between contact and cooperation. It is not surprising, then, that the classroom setting with its institutional framework has been considered a good place for thinking about and applying the theory; both academic (Carithers, 1970; Harrington & Miller, 1992; McGlynn, Zembylas, Bekerman, & Gallagher, 2009) and policy examples (Banks & McGee-Banks, 2004) of intergroup contact studies demonstrate the possibility of creating such conditions in education settings.

The preceding paragraphs offer some evidence for the importance of relational closeness for enhancing cooperation between groups and even for improving education. While there is a small body of work on contact with migrants, however (for example, Voci & Hewstone, 2003), the literature is silent on how relational closeness with refugees may or may not impact education. In the policy arena, the need for "reciprocal education" has surfaced in Australia, with a particular focus on the mental health field (Procter, 2003). Procter's work is a first step toward recognizing the importance of reciprocity and reflexive learning, but more work needs to be done.

It is important to be mindful of the danger of viewing refugee students simply as victims of oppression. Scholars who have cautioned against an emphasis on "trauma discourses" have noted the homogeneity of policy responses to trauma, which threaten to undermine the specificity of refugee flight and may render students voiceless and limit the services and options available to them later (Boyden & de Berry, 2004; Rutter, 2006). This must be acknowledged and taken into account as classroom practices involving reciprocal learning are developed.

EMPIRICAL EXAMINATION: TWO REFUGEE POPULATIONS IN AUSTRALIA

The discussion in this chapter thus far has suggested that there are ways in which refugees might contribute to a more positive educational experience for the broader student population, but concedes that certain conditions are more likely to facilitate such an outcome. In the following section, two refugee communities in Australia are profiled, with a view to understanding their specific backgrounds and skills.

The purpose of these sections is to suggest possible educational enrichment for communities where refugee populations are located, rather than to demonstrate the effects of their presence on education thus far. As such, two relatively new populations to Australia have been selected for examination: Burmese refugees who have been living in Thailand and Bhutanese refugees who have been living in Nepal.

Compared to some other refugee populations, the Burmese and Bhutanese are relatively well-educated upon arrival to their resettlement countries. It could thus be argued that this chapter exaggerates the contributions of refugees to education, since these populations are already better educated. As the chapter argues, however, refugees bring far more than tangible education levels to the learning process.

Within refugee populations there are individuals whose tangible skills can be represented in terms of measurable outcomes, such as overall education levels, English proficiency, and vocational qualifications. In occupational terms, these may include teachers, medics, and midwives. What is less documented but no less evident, however, are the many intangible skills that refugees have developed through their experiences, backgrounds, and training.

The term "skills" is, as a result, interpreted broadly in this examination. This interpretation implicitly acknowledges the relevance of a vast literature on social capital, which argues that the relationships, networks, and sense of civic responsibility that can potentially be derived from social relationships offer an important resource for society. This resource is often presented in the context of the networks that produce social capital (for example, Castles, 2004; Massey, Arango, J., Hugo, G., Kouaouci, A., Pellegrino, A., & Taylor, 1993; Putnam, 1995). Just as strengthening social capital is important at all ages, the contributions of networks and individuals to education can occur at all educational levels, and in traditional as well as alternative educational settings. Each country section thus discusses the background, experiences, and training of refugees that have the potential to translate into a broad array of educational contributions.

Research on the refugee populations was conducted in three ways in the cases of both the Burmese and Bhutanese populations. First, a review of the secondary literature was completed to understand the contextual background that brought the populations to Australia. Second, field research was conducted in 2007 and 2008 in the locations from which the refugees have most recently come, in camps or settlements in Thailand and Nepal. Semi-structured interviews with refugees and key stakeholders were coded for confidentiality, as most respondents requested anonymity. Focus groups and direct observation supplemented the respondents' answers. Third, data about the specific population of refugees in Australia were collected. This last category includes data produced by Australia's Department of Immigration and Citizenship (DIAC). Unless otherwise noted, any information about resettled refugees in the following sections cited by DIAC is sourced from settlement reports that one can access online in order to obtain information about all manner of refugee populations in Australia, filtered by such criteria as age, education, country of birth, gender, etc. See the DIAC website on "Settlement Reporting" at http://www.immi.gov.au/settlement/ (accessed several times in June and July 2010 for various reports).

These three approaches have been used to weave together the aspects of each community that have the most potential to provide a rich ground for learning for the broader student population. The empirical section below will be followed by a discussion of how the skills detailed therein might offer potential valuable contributions to education in Australia.

REFUGEES FROM BURMA RESETTLED FROM THAILAND

The persecution of ethnic minorities and the destruction of their villages, forced labor, extrajudicial killings, devastating economic conditions, and the ongoing presence of an authoritarian regime securely in place since 1962 have all contributed to mass displacement out of Burma. The majority of Burma's displaced live in Thailand, which is estimated to host a population from Burma of 2,000,000 (Brees, 2008, p. 5). The vast majority are considered economic migrants by the Royal Thai Government (RTG); only a small fraction are recognized as refugees by the U.N. High Commissioner for Refugees (UNHCR).

Those eligible for resettlement include a small number of refugees who spent most of their exile living in urban areas (such as Bangkok) and those who have been living in nine refugee camps on the Thai–Burmese border. According to the Thailand Burma Border Consortium's website (www.tbbc.org), in June 2010, approximately 102,000 refugees were registered by UNHCR in the camps. Resettled refugees from urban areas hail from various ethnic groups from Burma and include Burmans (the ethnic majority in Burma) and ethnic minorities such as the Mon, Shan, Karen, and Chin. Until 2006, the refugees who resettled to Australia came primarily from urban areas and numbered in the hundreds. But since 2006, when a global resettlement program for refugees from Burma got underway, the numbers have increased and the composition of resettling refugees has changed.

According to DIAC, Australia has resettled more than 7,500 refugees from Burma in the past 10 years. Most of these (approximately 6,700), however, have arrived since 2006. In addition, today, the majority of those resettling to Australia come from the refugee camps, which are predominantly populated by the ethnic Karen. DIAC's public data on school-age refugees from Burma are incomplete, but if the proportions available in the settlement reporting database are an accurate reflection of the total, then about 12% of the resettling population between 2006 and 2010 are between the ages of 6 and 18.

DIAC acknowledges some of the skills and education that refugees have before arrival in Australia, including access to vocational training courses, agricultural training, and small business training (Commonwealth of Australia, 2006). While these are useful starting points for general information on how refugees' skills might translate into future jobs, the information provided is not linked to how refugees might use these skills to offer a positive contribution to Australia's educational system. Indeed, and supporting the original premise of this chapter, education is mentioned in the context of what needs refugees might have, such as ESL training (Commonwealth of Australia, 2006), rather than the broader experiences and psycho-social skills most refugees possess.

Background, Experiences, and Training That Have the Potential to Translate into Educational Contributions

Participating in Human Rights Education

Whether living in camps, settlements near camps, or urban areas, refugees from Burma living in Thailand have long had access to myriad human rights trainings of varied levels of intensity and sophistication. Some are sponsored by small, local community-based organizations (CBOs), some are nationally funded, and others are offered by international NGOs. Often these come under the ruse of "other kinds of training and education," since the RTG does not necessarily look kindly upon training that may be perceived as threatening to Thailand itself, or to Burma. Thailand's relationship with Burma is complex: On the one hand, it makes rather inconsistent attempts to appease Burma, but on the other, it provides a safe haven for refugees who flee from the regime.

Contrary to classic assumptions about the basic level of education provision for refugees in countries of first asylum, human rights education for refugees from Burma can be quite comprehensive. The Human Rights Education Institute of Burma (HREIB), for example, offers in-depth modules in the Burmese language on subjects such as women's rights, child rights, and the right to food, and covers specific topics such as international human rights instruments, group versus individual rights, transitional justice, and the history of human rights. These grassroots trainings not only provide the necessary human rights discourse and tools for refugee individuals seeking to effect change, but they are also offered in the mode of training of trainers to ensure a sustainable means by which to spread human rights information among refugee populations.

Documenting and Publishing Human Rights Reports

In a similar vein, many refugee organizations are eager to expose the human rights abuses that their members experienced in Burma. Such organizations produce and publish a plethora of human rights reports, often targeted toward international audiences. To ensure that the reports are not dismissed for their lack of credibility, refugees who belong to such organizations have undergone training, often quite rigorous, in research methods in order to properly document abuses. Examples of such training are widespread and include: training women to properly document instances of rape and other sexual violence perpetrated by the Burmese military; training medics to sample and collect accurate health data within rural areas of Burma (for example, on the prevalence of malaria); and training trainers to educate villagers inside Burma on how to document the effects of mining and dams on their social and cultural rights. There are many examples of the kinds of reports produced by individuals who have undergone such training, much of it grey literature (Backpack Health Worker Team, 2006; Human Rights Foundation of Monland, 2003; Shan Human Rights Foundation & Shan Women's Action Network, 2002).

Managing Scarce Resource Allocation

While the skills developed in managing scarce resources are not unique to refugee populations, certain elements of refugee camp life in particular mean that refugees are positioned to understand very well the challenges that come with trying to allocate limited quantities of food, clothing, and housing materials to a needy population. In camps on the Thai–Burmese border, refugees themselves are in charge of the camp committees that distribute UNHCR- and NGO-donated goods to the general population. While the process is overseen by staff from the Thailand Burma Border Consortium (TBBC), the refugees themselves manage the process and are accountable to the entire camp for their decisions. As one expatriate NGO employee working on the border noted: "Everyone knows where the food warehouses are, and when the food is distributed. People go to watch the food being given out, and their eyes are open wide. They get smart, even if they don't know formal maths.... It's an enormous responsibility to make sure that everyone feels treated fairly."

Developing Business Skills

According to RTG policy, refugees are neither permitted to work for other employees nor to own their own businesses (U.S. Committee for Refugees and Immigrants, 2008). Yet, given the aforementioned lack of resources, refugees do find ways to earn income to supplement their diets and to obtain other materials. While many refugees work on farms or in factories, others conduct small business transactions, such as selling goods inside or outside refugee camps.

The business acumen that refugees gain from such experience is not unique to refugees, but the sophistication that young refugee women bring to their work is indicative of their understanding of international markets. A Karen refugee woman working for a shop in Mae Sot, on the Thai–Burmese border, noted:

> Of course I like red and blue [the main colors of the Karen national flag and the primary traditional colors for married Karen women's and men's shirts] but when we make bags and clothing for our shops in Mae Sot I think about what the tourists want. Do Americans like red, white, and blue? This is their flag color also. But I think they want purple and black and green. The Japanese do not like white.... With bags, we Karen have one long strap over the shoulder. But now we make them with two shorter shoulder straps. This is how I see foreigners carrying their bags.

Such insights are likely due partially to the livelihood trainings that refugees have received. One CBO, Karen Women's Organization (KWO), is well known for its strong organizational capacity and provision of training for women and men in refugee camps all along the border. Its Income Generation Project supports the production and sales of Karen handicrafts made by women weavers in the camps. These products include bags, wallets, and purses; clothing and scarves; and pillow covers and placemats.

Managing Intranational Conflict

It might be assumed that refugees from Burma living in Thailand share similar goals having to do with reforming the current government in Burma. Any close reading of the various ethnic tensions among groups from Burma, however, reveals that there is much intranational conflict among the country's diverse ethnic groups. These tensions are also manifest among the refugee population in Thailand. Even within the same ethnic groups, competition for resources runs high. Refugees who interact with members of other ethnic groups (for example, when ethnic leaders meet, or when students come together for trainings), the process of sharing stories, arguing about lofty goals for reform in Burma, and making decisions about how to proceed on advocacy issues imbue refugees with valuable assets such as conflict resolution skills.

Of course, not all groups are able to resolve their differences; access to resources such as international media, international funding, and even asylum is so limited that bitter arguments are sure to occur. Still, the knowledge and understanding about intragroup conflict that refugees from Burma have developed due to their refugee experiences exemplify an intangible skill that refugees can bring to the resettlement context.

REFUGEES FROM BHUTAN RESETTLED IN NEPAL

Tens of thousands of refugees arrived in Nepal from Bhutan in the early 1990s and since then have primarily resided in seven refugee camps in eastern Nepal. Bhutan's little-known expulsion of part of its (primarily) ethnically Nepalese population is a contested subject that pits the official narrative of the Government of Bhutan (GoB) against the assertions of the refugee population. The GoB claims that flight from Bhutan was voluntary, that ethnic Nepali residents of Bhutan were never citizens, and that they left willingly for Nepal. Refugees insist that an exclusionary census in 1988 stripped many ethnic minorities of their citizenship, that their documents were taken away, and that they were forced out of the country. Perhaps due to the fact that Bhutan is considered a darling of the international aid community, abundant research on the refugee issue is not readily available. The most comprehensive treatment remains *Unbecoming Citizens* (Hutt, 2003). Banki (2008b) covers the recent contextual history that drove the expulsions. Attention to ethnic issues specifically can be found in Dhakal and Strawn (1994). For a legal analysis of the issue, see Saul (2000).

Until a mass resettlement program got under way in 2008, the camps in Nepal hosted more than 100,000 refugees (USCRI, 2008), most of whom shared the same language (Nepali) and religion (Hinduism) with the surrounding communities. In 2009, the number began to decrease for the first time in many years because 17,400 were resettled to countries such as the United States, Canada, and Australia, leaving about 86,000 in the camps (UN High Commissioner for Refugees, 2010). Like the refugees from Burma, refugees from Bhutan are a relatively well-educated population; about 13% of registered refugees have an education past 10th grade, and about 35% of camp residents can conduct their daily life in English (Banki, 2008a).

Prior to UNHCR's mass resettlement program, the number of resettled refugees in Australia from Bhutan was miniscule; according to DIAC, from 2000 to 2007, Australia resettled six refugees from Bhutan. In 2008, however, the number increased to 306 and in 2009 it stood at 468. Of these, according to DIAC, about 40 were school-age (ages 6 to 17) and another 200 were university-age (ages 18 to 24). While these numbers are extremely small, they will grow annually as Australia continues to resettle refugees from Bhutan.

As in the case of Burma, DIAC has prepared a community profile that highlights the skills of refugees from Bhutan and the offerings they received in the camps:

> All camps offer some skills development training for women including cotton weaving, tailoring, reading centre, women in micro business, micro credit, loan scheme, gender sensitization, and social awareness. Each camp has a children's forum and a disability centre that teaches sign language and lip reading skills. Many of the camps have a Bhutanese Community Development Centre for non-formal education, particularly for language classes in Nepali, English and Dzongkha. There is also some vocational training for vulnerable groups. (Commonwealth of Australia, 2007, pp. 6–7)

Background, Experiences, and Training That Have the Potential to Translate into Educational Contributions

Teaching in Challenging Environments

One of the noteworthy characteristics of Nepal's refugee population from Bhutan is the presence within its ranks of highly educated individuals who, prior to exile, worked as, for example, government officials, engineers, and teachers (Banki, 2008a). While not unique to this population, the fact that refugees share a common language with the majority population in Nepal has meant that educated individuals have the possibility of working outside of camp settings and of making significant contributions to Nepal.

The most powerful example of this contribution is the presence, all over Nepal, of teachers from the refugee camps. Refugees from Bhutan are often better educated, and speak better English, than local Nepalese schoolteachers because of both prior education and the schools in the camps. A Nepalese student who learned English from a refugee schoolteacher and subsequently became a translator in the camps said of her teacher that "he worked so hard every day. My English is so much better now and it will be very hard when he leaves for resettlement. More than English he showed me why I should work hard too, even when the system is unfair."

Refugees who become teachers at Nepalese schools obtain skills not only in teaching and discipline, but also learn to teach in challenging environments connected to their individual circumstances. Some of these teachers are the same age as the students they teach, requiring maturity and poise. They also have to navigate salaries and work schedules and the provision of grades from a position of little power. This skill is by no means unique to refugees from Bhutan; all refugee populations develop coping strategies in response to having very little formal power.

Developing Strategies for Contesting GoB Claims

A skill found among refugees from Bhutan that is not easily measured, but critical, is a comprehension of the forces that have shaped their exile and dictated their subsequent circumstances. This is evident in their sophisticated responses to and refutation of the documentation created by the GoB that contests their refugee claims and status. For example, many refugees who left Bhutan signed Voluntary Migration Forms (VMF), supposedly to indicate that the signers had left Bhutan voluntarily (Hutt, 1996). Subsequently the GoB used these to demonstrate to the international community that those who had been exiled had voluntarily relinquished their Bhutanese citizenship. As a countermeasure, refugees from Bhutan have developed strategies to ensure that this deception was made public. They produced their own supporting documentation—including passports, land records, and employment receipts—that showed the extent to which tens of thousands of individuals who had been deeply integrated into the fabric of Bhutan had been forcibly removed.

There are many other examples that show the ways in which refugees from Bhutan have empowered themselves through political engagement. Evans (2008) examined Bhutanese refugee youth from the camps, showing that they possess a strong understanding of the political and economic roots of their refugee status. Evans' focus has been on youth who joined Maoist groups. Many of these youth may have had trouble being accepted for resettlement. Evans' general argument—that refugee youth from Bhutan demonstrate a high capacity for independent decision-making based on analytic thinking—can also be applied to the general Bhutanese refugee population.

Understanding the Local Population

Much like refugees from Burma in Thailand, refugees from Bhutan in Nepal are not technically permitted to engage in any income-generating activities (Patrick, 2006). Refugees do, however, supplement meager food, housing, clothing, and fuel supplies with unofficial employment. First, NGOs such as Austcare (now Action Aid Australia) offer workshops in tailoring, traditional Bhutanese weaving, typing, embroidery, shoe making, mat making, and bamboo crafts (Austcare, 2004). Second, refugees leave the camp daily to work as laborers in construction and agriculture. The prospect of resettlement for refugees but not locals, however, has heightened tensions between them (Banki, 2008a). The tension associated with employment and resettlement both point to the need for social intelligence in sensitive situations. One international NGO officer who coordinated resettlement activities for Bhutanese refugees observed this refugee sensitivity:

I've hired so many construction workers at the last minute to get these buildings ready in time. I know there are refugees and non-refugees working together out there. And I know there's tension because of resettlement. But I see the way that the refugees interact with the locals, and I'm impressed. They get it—they know that prices are rising and that some local landowners will get rich! And they know that some will lose their main sources of labor. I don't tell them this—they know it far better than I do.

Organizational Learning

In Nepal, internal conflicts within the camp community and the way that leaders, youth, and non-leader camp refugees interact are reminders of the complex power structures that affect camp life. Anecdotal evidence from focus group discussions with the camp management committee in three camps indicate that the factors that most contribute to divisions among the camp population include socio-economic background prior to camp arrival, region from which refugees hail in Bhutan, ability to secure resources from NGOs within the camp, membership in camp and non-camp organizations, and camp sector residence. In recent years, these divisions have been aggravated by an even more significant catalyst: the desire to resettle to a third country or continue to promote repatriation (Banki, 2008a, 2008b).

Admittedly, complex power dynamics are certainly not unique to camp life. But one difference is that, because of the close quarters and the inability to leave, refugees are frequently forced to face their differences and deal with them directly. This certainly does not make the tensions go away, but it does mean that refugees addressing such issues may gain intangible social intelligence skills. Many of the psycho-social skills that refugees gain are not officially documented in the form of certificates and diplomas. Nevertheless, they represent important forms of social capital that enable people with refugee backgrounds to make important contributions to the countries in which they settle.

DISCUSSION

The previous section has offered some concrete examples of the types of skills that refugees from Burma and Bhutan bring from their countries of first asylum. The following section hopes to build on these examples to suggest possible means by which these skills may contribute to positive educational experiences for the general Australian student population. Broadly, these fall into three categories: contextual, practical, and social.

Contextual

First, knowing other students who have experienced *refugee flight from Burma and Bhutan* has the potential to allow non-refugee students to put a face to news stories that they may have heard or read about in the newspaper. In addition to piquing interest in current events and the wider international community, the phenomenon of *relational closeness* has the potential to convey to students precise and exemplified meanings for concepts such as exile, persecution, justice, and equity. In the context of modeling a Deweyan education system focused on creating well-rounded, cosmopolitan, and outward-looking citizens—something that geographically isolated Australia should strive for (Jakubowicz, 2009)—these are important components.

Practical

Second, skills from specific trainings, such as *human rights trainings, documentation research,* and *livelihood workshops* are useful tools that refugees may be able to share with their classmates. While it is true that non-refugee students, particularly in post-graduate programs, may receive similarly-named trainings, the content is likely to be different; refugees immediately apply the results of their trainings to the work they do. For example, they begin writing human rights reports during and after the time when they learn how to produce the documents, and they begin micro-businesses immediately after completing livelihood workshops. The practical conclusions and lessons learned that they come away with are ones that can be shared with co-students.

It is important to note that examples that discuss training opportunities in the previous sections are based on information collected prior to the resettlement of refugees to Australia or other countries. Thus it cannot be assumed that all refugees who have undergone such trainings are the ones who actually end up in resettlement countries like Australia. Empirical research, however, has shown that the most highly skilled refugees are likely to resettle first, in advance of the general refugee population (Banki, 2008a; Banki & Lang, 2007, 2008), which suggests that better trained refugees will be in the resettled refugee population. But neither DIAC's nor UNHCR's data are detailed enough to capture training modules as a proxy for education, so until further research is conducted in Australia, the presence of trained refugees among the resettled population remains merely a strong assumption.

Social

Third, refugees' navigation of *complex social relationships* while they resided in camp and urban settings in Thailand and Nepal points to a critically important skill that can be edifying for classmates in Australia. The urgency of collecting one's food quota from a camp leader with a different ethnic background, for example, compels refugees to consider such relationships with a keen eye. Such considerations, if shared appropriately with fellow students, can offer a fresh perspective on power dynamics and have the potential to improve students' social intelligence.

The three broad categories discussed above only briefly touch on the many ways in which refugee experiences and skills have the potential to contribute to education in Australia. But their focus on the contextual, practical, and social elements of educational contributions offers a framework to consider where refugee experiences and skills might be most useful in the future.

CONCLUSION

Unique differences exist both within and between different refugee groups from Burma and Bhutan. Furthermore, the goals, pedagogies, and administrative challenges of education on various levels vary widely. This chapter has provided a general overview in support of the argument that the experiences, backgrounds, and skills that refugees bring to countries of resettlement have the strong potential to improve education, not only for their own groups, but for the general student population at large.

Understanding the theoretical foundations for the ways refugees might enrich the classroom is simply the first step in developing curriculum and support mechanisms for ensuring that refugee experiences, backgrounds, and skills are effectively and sensitively shared with the general community of students. Stemming from this chapter, there are three important directions in which future research might go. Recent Australian reports focused on refugee issues call for similar measures (RCOA, 2010a).

First, empirical work that confirms the suggestions made here would go a long way to establishing respect for and an eagerness to engage refugee experiences in the classroom setting. The kinds of studies conducted by Khoo, McDonald, Giorgas, and Birrell (2002) that take a long-term approach and examine second-generation refugees indicate that refugee students often perform better than the general population. Similar studies could be conducted that compare classrooms with refugee students and classrooms without refugee students. Because some of the positive contributions discussed in these pages are not immediately apparent, similar long-term longitudinal studies are advised. Such studies would be better supplemented by qualitative research that plumbs the perceptions, opinions, and eventual job choices of refugees' classmates compared to those with no refugees in their classrooms. This kind of study would best be conducted in one school or region.

Second, the broadly defined skills discussed in this chapter are neither comprehensive for refugees from Burma and Bhutan, nor do they take into account the plethora of experiences and skills that refugees from other countries possess. Contributions to empathic understanding, social intelligence, and political analysis discussed in the previous section may also come from other refugee communities, and a project cataloging these broad skills would offer much to the education community.

Finally, the work of translating these skills into school-level curricula, teacher-preparation programs, allocations of staff to students, and development of extracurricular activities is an ongoing process that requires not only an awareness of the unique contributions of refugees, but a commitment to follow through with decisive action. On the practitioner level, this step will likely take the longest, but has the potential to effect the most change, for both refugees and the classrooms in which they study.

REFERENCES

Allport, G. W. (1954). *The nature of prejudice.* Reading, MA: Addison-Wesley.

Austcare. (2004). *AUSTCARE Exit Strategy for Micro-Skills Training Project / BRAVVE, Nepal.* Internal Document. Sydney, NSW: Author.

Australian Government. (2010). *Social inclusion principles for Australia.* Canberra, ACT: Author.

Banki, S. (2008a). *Anticipating the impact of resettlement: Bhutanese refugees in Nepal.* Sydney, NSW: Austcare, Griffith University.

Banki, S. (2008b). Resettlement of the Bhutanese from Nepal: The durable solution discourse. In H. Adelman (Ed.), *Protracted displacement in Asia: No place to call home.* (pp. 27–56). London, UK: Ashgate.

Banki, S., & Lang, H. (2007). *Planning for the future: The impact of resettlement on the remaining camp population.* Bangkok, Thailand: Committee for Coordination of Services to Displaced Persons in Thailand (CCSDPT).

Banki, S., & Lang,H. (2008). Protracted displacement on the Thai-Burmese border: The interrelated search for durable solutions. In H. Adelman (Ed.), *Protracted displacement in Asia: No place to call home.* (pp. 57–82). London, UK: Ashgate.

Banks, J. (1993a). Integrating the curriculum with ethnic content: Approaches and guidelines. In J. Banks & C. McGee-Banks (Eds.), *Multicultural education: Issues and perspectives* (pp. 189–207). Boston, MA: Allyn and Bacon.

Banks, J. (1993b). Multicultural education for young children: Racial and ethnic attitudes and their modification. In D. Spodek (Ed.), *Handbook of research on the education of young children* (pp. 236–250). New York, NY: Macmillan.

Banks, J. (1991). Multicultural education: Its effects on students' racial and gender role attitudes. In J. P. Shauer (Ed.), *Handbook of research on social studies teaching and learning* (pp. 459–469). New York, NY: Macmillan.

Banks, J., & McGee-Banks, C. (Eds.). (2004). *Handbook of research on multicultural education* (2nd ed.). San Francisco, CA: Jossey-Bass.

Baptiste, H. P. (1979). *Multicultural education: A synopsis.* Washington, DC: University Press America.

Backpack Health Worker Team (BHWT). (2006). *Chronic emergency: Health and human rights in eastern Burma.* Mae Sot, Thailand: Author.

Bloch, A. (2002). *Refugees' opportunities and barriers in employment and training.* London, UK: Department for Work and Pensions.

Bonilla-Silva, E., & Embrick, D. G. (2006). Racism without racists: "Killing me softly" with color blindness. In C. A. Rossatto, R. L. Allen, & M. Pruyn (Eds.), *Reinventing critical pedagogy* (pp. 21–34). Lanham, MD: Rowman & Littlefield.

Boyden, J., & de Berry, J. (Eds). (2004). *Children and youth on the front line: Ethnography, armed conflict and displacement.* Oxford, UK: Berghahn Books.

Brees, I. (2008). Forced displacement of Burmese people. *Forced Migration Review, 30,* 4–5.

Carithers, M. (1970). School desegregation and racial cleavage, 1954–1970: A review of the literature. *Journal of Social Issues, 26,* 25–47.

Castles, S. (2004). The factors that make and unmake migration policies. *International Migration Review, 38*(3), 852–885.

Commonwealth of Australia. (2006). *Burmese community profile.* Canberra, ACT: Department of Immigration and Citizenship (DIAC).

Commonwealth of Australia. (2007). *Bhutanese community profile.* Canberra, ACT: Department of Immigration and Citizenship (DIAC).

Conroy, J. C. (2009). The enstranged self: recovering some grounds for pluralism in education. *Journal of Moral Education, 38*(2), 145–164.

Dhakal, D. N. S., & Strawn, C. (1994). *Bhutan: A movement in exile.* Jaipur, India: Nirala Publications.

Evans, R. (2008). The two faces of empowerment in conflict. *Research in Comparative and International Education, 3*(1), 50–64.

Forbes, H. D. (1997). *Ethnic conflict: Commerce, culture, and the contact hypothesis.* New Haven, CT: Yale University Press.

Frazier, L. (1977). The multicultural facet of education. *Journal of Research and Development in Education, 11,* 10–16.

Goldlust, J., & Richmond, A. (1974). A multivariate model of immigrant adaptation. *International Migration Review, 8*(2), 193–225.

Grant, C. A., & Sleeter, C. E. (1993). Race, class, gender, exceptionality, and educational reform. In J. A. Banks & C. A. McGee-Banks (Eds), *Multicultural education: Issues and perspectives* (2nd ed., pp. 46–68). Boston, MA: Allyn and Bacon.

Green, D., & Wong, J. (2009). Tolerance and the contact hypothesis: A field experiment. In E. Borgida, C. M. Federico & J. L. Sullivan (Eds), *The political psychology of democratic citizenship* (pp. 228–244). New York, NY: Oxford University Press.

Halstead, J. M. (2003). Schooling and cultural maintenance for religious minorities in the liberal state. In K. McDonough & W. Feinberg (Eds.), *Citizenship and* education in liberal-democratic societies: Teaching for cosmopolitan values and collective identities (pp. 273–297). Oxford, UK: Oxford University Press.

Harper, D., & Wacker, D. (1985). Children's attitudes toward disabled peers and the effects of mainstreaming. *Academic Psychology Bulletin, 7,* 87–98.

Harrington, H., & Miller, N. (1992). Research and theory in intergroup relations: Issues of consensus and controversy. In J. Lynch, C. Modgil & S. Modgil (Eds.), *Cultural diversity and the schools* (pp. 159–178). London, UK: Falmer.

Herek, G., & Glunt, E. (1993). Interpersonal contact and heterosexuals' attitudes toward gay men: Results from a national survey. *Journal of Sex Research, 30*(3), 239–244.

hooks, b. (1981). *Ain't I a woman?* Boston, MA: South End Press.

Human Rights Foundation of Monland (Burma) (HURFOM). (2003). *No land to farm: A comprehensive report on land, real estates and properties confiscations in Mon's Area, Burma* (1998–2002). Bangkok, Thailand: Author.

Hutt, M. (1996). Ethnic nationalism, refugees and Bhutan. *Journal of Refugee Studies, 9*(4), 397–420.

Hutt, M. (2003). *Unbecoming citizens: Culture, nationhood, and the flight of refugees from Bhutan.* Delhi; Oxford, UK: Oxford University Press.

Jakubowicz, A. (2009). *Cultural diversity, cosmopolitan citizenship & education: Issues, options and implications for Australia.* A discussion paper for the Australian Education Union. Unpublished. Sydney, NSW: University of Technology Sydney.

Khoo, S., McDonald, P., Giorgas, D., & Birrell, B. (2002). *Second generation Australians.* Canberra, ACT: Department of Immigration and Multicultural and Indigenous Affairs (DIMIA).

King III, G. (1997). The effects of interpersonal closeness and issue seriousness on blowing the whistle. *Journal of Business Communication, 34*(4), 419–437.

Lalich, W. (2006). Collective action of 'Others' in Sydney. *Journal of Multidisciplinary International Studies, 3*(1), n.p.

Madkhul, D. (2007). *Supporting volunteering activities in Australian Muslim communities, particularly youth.* Canberra, ACT: Australian Multicultural Foundation and Volunteering Australia.

Maitzen, S. (1997). Diversity in the classroom. *Studies in Philosophy and Education, 16*(3), 293–302.

Mashek, D., & Aron, A. (Eds). (2004). *Handbook of closeness and intimacy.* New York, NY: Routledge.

Massey, D. S., Arango, J., Hugo, G., Kouaouci, A., Pellegrino, A., & Taylor, E. J. (1993). Theories of international migration: A review and appraisal. *Population and Development Review, 19*(3), 431–466.

McGlynn, C., Zembylas, M., Bekerman, Z., & Gallagher, T. (Eds). (2009). *Peace education in conflict and post-conflict societies.* New York, NY: Palgrave Macmillan.

McLaren, P. (1997). *Revolutionary multiculturalism: Pedagogies of dissent for the new millennium.* Boulder, CO: Westview.

Miralles-Lombardo, B., Miralles, J., & Golding, B. (2008). *Creating learning spaces for refugees: the role of multicultural organizations in Australia.* Adelaide, South Australia: National Centre for Vocational Education Research.

Mohanty, C. T. (1991). Under Western eyes: Feminist scholarship and colonial discourses. In C. T. Mohanty, A. Russo & L. Torres (Eds), *Third world women and the politics of feminism* (pp. 51–80). Bloomington, IN: Indiana University Press.

Nesbitt, E. (2004). *Intercultural education: Ethnographic and religious approaches.* Brighton, Sussex: Academic Press.

Nieto, S. (1992). *Affirming diversity: The sociopolitical context of multicultural education.* New York, NY: Longman.

Parekh, B. (1986). The concept of multicultural education. In S. Modgil, G. K. Verma, K. Mallick & C. Modgil (Eds), *Multicultural education: The interminable debate* (pp. 19–31). Philadelphia, PA: Falmer.

Patrick, E. (2006). *The perils of direct provision: UNHCR's response to the fuel needs of Bhutanese refugees in Nepal.* New York, NY: Women's Commission for Refugee Women and Children.

Pettigrew, T., & Tropp, L. (2006). A meta-analytic test of intergroup contact theory. *Journal of Personality and Social Psychology, 90*(5), 751–783.

Pettigrew, T. (1971). *Racially separate or together?* New York, NY: McGraw-Hill.

Pinson, H., & Arnot, M. (2007). Sociology of education and the wasteland of refugee education research. *British Journal of Sociology of Education, 28*(3), 399–407.

Procter, N. G. (2003). *Speaking of sadness and the heart of acceptance. Reciprocity in education: A model of interactive learning between migrant communities and mainstream health services.* Canberra, ACT: Multicultural Mental Health Australia, Australian Government, Department of Health and Ageing.

Putnam, R. (1995). Bowling alone: America's declining social capital. *Journal of Democracy, 6*(1), 65–78.

Refugee Council of Australia (RCOA). (2010a). *Economic, civic and social contributions of refugees and humanitarian entrants: A literature review.* Sydney, NSW: Author.

Refugee Council of Australia (RCOA). (2010b). *Finding the right time and place: Exploring post-compulsory education and training pathways for young people from refugee backgrounds in NSW.* Sydney, NSW: Author.

Remsbery, N. (2003). *The education of refugee children: policy and practice in the education of refugee and asylum-seeker children in England.* London, UK: Pupil Inclusion Unit, National Children's Bureau.

Rutter, J. (2006). *Refugee children in the UK.* Maidenhead, Berkshire: Open University Press.

Saul, B. (2000). Cultural nationalism, self-determination and human rights in Bhutan. *International Journal of Refugee Law, 12*(3), 321–353.

Schiappa, E. (2008). *Beyond representational correctness: Rethinking criticism of popular media.* Albany, NY: SUNY Press.

Shan Human Rights Foundation (SHRF) and Shan Women's Action Network (SWAN). (2002). *Licence to rape: The Burmese military regime's use of sexual violence in the ongoing war in Shan state.* Chiangmai, Thailand: Author.

Stephan, W., & Stephan, C. (1985). Intergroup anxiety. *Journal of Social Issues, 41*, 157–175.

Tibbitts, F. (2002). *Emerging models for human rights education: Human rights education—issues of democracy.* Washington, DC: U.S. Department of State.

UN High Commissioner for Refugees (UNHCR). (2010). UNHCR Global Report 2009. Geneva, Switzerland: Author.

U.S. Committee for Refugees and Immigrants (USCRI). (2008). *World refugee survey 2007*. Washington, DC: Author

Voci, A., & Hewstone, M. (2003). Intergroup contact and prejudice toward immigrants in Italy: The mediational role of anxiety and the moderational role of group salience. *Group Processes and Intergroup Relations, 6*, 37–54.

CHAPTER 4

IDENTITY AND INCLUSION

Education in Refugee Camps in Thailand

Su-Ann Oh
Institute of Southeast Asian Studies, Singapore

ABSTRACT

The role of schooling and formal education in refugee populations cannot be separated from the wider political environment—within refugee communities, the host state, the state of origin and the international refugee regime. This is because formal education is often used as a means of identity formation. In the refugee camps in Thailand, the reproduction and transmission of Karen identity in schools is bound up with Skaw Karen language, Karen history, religion, and formal forms of schooling. This chapter examines identity formation as the basis for inclusion and exclusion in education. It goes beyond an enumeration of the indicators of exclusion. Instead, it turns the question around and examines what being included means, and how those who do not subscribe to this are excluded. In addition, it examines how these conceptions of identity interact with structural inequalities. The discussion leads to the conclusion that identity and inclusion are indicators of the tension formed by the reproduction of an ethno-nationalist identity in schools in the setting of a multiethnic camp population. Attempts at addressing issues of access and equity, while valuable, have been piecemeal and limited be-

Refugee and Immigrant Students, pages 65–85
Copyright © 2012 by Information Age Publishing

65

cause they do not fully address this tension. Nevertheless, current attempts at a more integrated approach to inclusion may yield substantial gains in access and equity in the long run.

In refugee situations, the design and provision of education are surrounded by questions of purpose that are often difficult to answer. What should education prepare children and young people for? Repatriation, resettlement, and integration into the host country, or a protracted refugee situation? What should education prepare children for if they are prohibited from taking up employment in the host country? Attempting to answer these questions is like looking into an antique mirror—the reflections are ambiguous, indistinct, and obscure.

Furthermore, education is not just about the development of young people for employment purposes. The content and form of education are inextricably tied up in notions of identity and are thus mired in political sensitivities. In the effort to provide schooling to children and young people displaced by war and conflict, refugee communities, international nongovernmental organizations (NGOs), and host governments face challenging questions about what is to be taught and how it is to be taught (Preston, 1991; Sommers, 2002). What language should be used? What version of history is to be taught? What type of teaching and learning activities are most appropriate? What types of discipline methods can be used in the classroom?

> These are big questions, often going to the root of seemingly intractable political problems. Whose history, language, music or literature is taught in primary school—Israeli or Palestinian; Catholic or Protestant; Hindu, Sikh or Muslim; mujahedin or Royalist; Hutu or Tutsi—has much to do with expressions of power. (LeBlanc & Waters, 2005, p. 1)

The role of schools and formal education in refugee populations cannot be separated from the wider political environment—within refugee communities, the host state, and the state of origin. This is because formal education is used as a means of identity formation through socialization (including political socialization), cultural transmission, social control, and personal development. Schooling also plays the role of selection and allocation (of employment opportunities and other resources) and, sometimes, change and innovation.

It is not uncommon for refugee communities to use education and language as a way of asserting, legitimizing, and/or creating nationalist, ethnic, and cultural identities (Bush & Saltarelli, 2000). This, too, is true of the Karen from Burma. The use of Skaw Karen as the language of instruction in areas controlled by the Karen National Union (KNU) and in the refugee camps in schools is a way of establishing a particular version of Karen identity, as envisioned by the KNU. It is entirely natural that communities of people would want to promote certain forms of identity, but this does have implications for access and equity in education. While exclusion may not be intentional, it is systemic in that the Karen identity propagated in schools is not shared by all residents in the multiethnic refugee camps.

This chapter examines identity formation as the basis for inclusion and exclusion in education in the refugee camps. It goes beyond an enumeration of the indicators of exclusion. Instead, it turns the question around and examines what being included means, and how those who do not subscribe to this are excluded. In addition, it examines how these conceptions of identity interact with structural inequalities. It thus goes to the heart of issues of equity in education.

Before continuing, the scope of the paper has first to be clarified. Education encompasses a range of institutions, learners, content, and settings, and this paper considers all the different forms available in the camps. Next, the focus is on education in the seven predominantly Karen camps: There are considerably more data on education in the Karen camps as compared to that in the two Karenni camps in the north. The data were collected in 2005 and 2009 in education surveys conducted in the seven camps.

Finally, a brief note on the terms used is relevant here. In 1989, the Burmese government renamed the country *Myanmar Naing-ngan*. In this paper, the term *Burma* will be used to refer to the country, and Myanmar will be used where quoted by that name. *Burmese* is used to refer to the nationality of the people. *Karen* is used as an umbrella term for the myriad groups living in different parts of Burma and Thailand and who speak related languages. It includes the Skaw, Pwo, Kayah (also known as the Karenni) and White Karen (Smith, 1991). The word "Karen," as used by the Karen National Union (KNU), refers to Karen political and cultural identity. In this chapter, *Karen* is used to refer to the Skaw and Pwo subgroups, as is commonly defined by the residents in the camps.

REFUGEES FROM BURMA: THAILAND'S UNINVITED TEMPORARY GUESTS

Dotted along the Thai–Burmese border are nine official refugee camps housing almost 140,000 refugees from Burma. The porous border between Burma and Thailand runs for more than 2,000 kilometers along the edges of the Karen, the Karenni, and the Shan States on the Burmese side. Since the 1960s, these areas have been the sites of incursions by the Burmese military against communist and ethnic insurgency groups.

As a result, the refugee camps are inhabited by people of these ethnic groups who fled from armed conflict and structural violence. The seven refugee camps along the border between the Karen State and Thailand are predominantly made up of people from the Karen ethnic group. Besides these dominant groups, the camp population also consists of people from other ethnic groups (Pa-O, Burman, Chin, Kachin, for example) who previously lived in these and other states.

Semi-permanent refugee camps were set up along the Thai-Burmese border in 1984. Before that, temporary dwellings were erected by the small fluxes of people who were periodically displaced by seasonal fighting and who mostly returned to their villages when the fighting ceased. After 1984, it became apparent that the Karen refugees would not be able to return to their villages in Burma. Consequently, the Thai government allowed them to set up temporary camps with the understanding that once the situation permitted, they would return to Burma. Throughout, the overarching concern of the Thai government has been to ensure that the refugees do not engage in activities that would affect its political ties with Burma (Lang, 2002). This concern, along with fears of drawing more refugees to its border and of military incursions into its territory, is articulated under the rubric of security. Hence, its policies on education provision (as well as other services) in the camps are decided upon by the National Security Council (NSC) and implemented by the Ministry of Interior (MOI) and the Ministry of Education (MOE).

Accordingly, "official Thai policy has always stressed the *temporary* and *minimal* nature of its humanitarian commitment and has emphasized the imperative to prevent these minorities from engaging in any activities which may affect Thai–Burmese relations" (Lang, 2002, p. 86, emphasis added). Wider policies reflect this concern, which in turn influence policies on education.

The wider policies are translated into restrictions on the movement of refugees and their opportunities to earn a livelihood. These restrictions effectively exclude refugees from Thai public schooling. First, most of the refugee camps are located in remote areas with few transport links. Second, refugees are not allowed to leave camp without permission from the Thai authorities. Under Thai immigration laws, refugees or "displaced persons" occupy a particular administrative status, which only applies if they stay within the camps. The corollary of this is that shelter, rations, security, health services, education, and training are only available to them in the camps. Upon leaving, they fall into the administrative category of "illegal migrants." Illegal migrants are considered foreigners who do not have authorization to stay in Thailand and are not officially permitted access to public services such as education. Illegal migrants are also routinely rounded up and deported. In fact, it is estimated that about a million refugees from Burma end up as illegal migrants when they are denied entry into the camps or when they enter as migrants, legal or otherwise.

The free movement of refugees is very much viewed as a security risk by the National Security Council. In fact, it has vetoed proposals to allow refugees to attend Thai higher education institutions on those grounds.

Thus, the majority of refugee children and young people's schooling opportunities are confined to those in the camps. From the beginning, the refugees were allowed to set up and administer their own schools. A small number of NGOs provided education funding and support with the approval of the Thai government. However, it was only in 1996, 12 years after the camps had been set up, that a mandate for NGOs to provide support for education was granted (Bowles, 1998). At present, in the predominantly Karen camps in Thailand, the NGOs provide a series of essential services and financial and other support for education in the camps; they implement education and education-related programs (psychosocial, general education, English language, for example), capacity building (teacher training, education management) activities, curriculum design, coordination with the refugee community about distribution and implementation, and coordination and negotiation with the Thai government.

While the Thai government has maintained a laissez-faire approach to the refugees' educational endeavors, it has imposed specific restrictions that reflect its concerns with temporariness and minimalist intervention. As a rule, buildings in camp may only be constructed using temporary materials, and this also applies to buildings for educational purposes. Following from this, only semi-permanent buildings made up of bamboo and eucalyptus may be erected. The use of concrete is not permitted. Recent changes in the guidelines now permit the use of iron poles, small wooden poles, and steel roofs. The result is that school buildings, tables, and benches are made of bamboo, with the latter fixed to the ground. The "classrooms" are formed by dividing long rooms with bamboo partitions of about six feet; these are ineffective in keeping out the noise from other classes. In addition, the amount of space allocated for education purposes cannot be expanded. As a result, schools are crowded and hot, and the classrooms are filled with a loud cacophony of noise from the other classes. As in the rest of the camps, there is no electricity in the schools. The scarce resources for building schools and the limitations on materials and space pose challenges to providing good learning environments for the general student population, even more so for those with health and disability concerns (Oh & van der Stouwe, 2008).

Another restriction that the Thai authorities have imposed is that while expatriate staff members may work as advisors, they may not be employed as teachers in the camps. Following Thailand's high-profile experience of providing sanctuary to Indochinese refugees in the late 1970s, it has opted for "a relatively low-key, low-publicity affair, managed and negotiated by local refugee committees and their NGO counterparts" where it concerns the Burmese refugees (Lang, 2002, p. 91). The unanticipated benefit of this policy is that there is a high degree of community ownership over the education system. However, this has meant that teacher training is not as extensive and effective as it could be. The external teacher trainers provided by ZOA Refugee Care, the international NGO that currently supports education in all seven camps, travel to these camps throughout the year to train teachers and camp-based teacher trainers. However, this is not enough, given the high rates of teacher turnover and the low subject and skill base of the newer teachers. Further, there are not enough qualified people in camp to work as camp-based teacher trainers.

With regard to the content of schooling in the camps, the Thai government has maintained its distance. The only restriction that it stipulates is that the content of textbooks and publications distributed is not to contain political ideas, attitudes, or values. This hands-off approach changed slightly in 2005. For the first time, the Thai government, through the Ministry of Education, offered Thai language classes to camp residents. Its initial proposal was that it be taught in schools. The refugee community was enthusiastic about this, but the NGOs involved in education were wary of introducing Thai as another subject into the curriculum because students were already studying three languages—Skaw Karen, Burmese, and English—from kindergarten onwards. In the end, it was decided that Thai language classes would be provided to adults by the nonformal division of the Thai MOE and paid for by the UNHCR.

This was the most obvious and proactive campaign by the Thai government to exert some influence over the identity of the refugees through formal education. The principal reason for introducing Thai language classes, 20 years after the establishment of semi-permanent camps in Thailand, was motivated by the emergence of the idea (rightly or wrongly) that the Malay-Muslim separatist attacks in the South of Thailand were linked to certain teachers and students in Islamic schools in the South (Liow, 2009). In these schools, the language of instruction is Malay, and the Thai government was concerned that the dissonance in language and identity in the South would replicate itself in the camps in the Northwest. This precipitated the National Security Council to take preventive measures by introducing Thai culture and language into the refugee camps. In this instance, access to Thai language learning coincided with the NSC's security concerns about the identity of the refugees.

PATTERNS OF PARTICIPATION IN EDUCATION IN THE CAMPS

As the refugees do not have access to Thai education, the issues of education access and equity are situated solely in the schools in the refugee camps. One of the notable features of education in the camps in Thailand is that the system of schools and learning was set up and is staffed and managed by the refugees residing in the camps, with help from external organizations. Formal education begins at kindergarten, with children aged five years, followed by primary and secondary schooling consisting of grades 1 to 12. There are 70 schools in the seven predominantly Karen camps staffed by approximately 80 head teachers and 1,600 teachers. They support and foster the learning of more than 34,000 students.

Post-secondary learning programs are available in camp, but they are highly competitive—there are only 700 places per year. The other types of learning programs available fall outside the "formal" education system; these provide skills training, religious education, and other learning opportunities.

In 2009, there were 37,847 children between the ages of 0 and 12 out of a total population of 110,000 in the seven camps (KRC, 2009). There are no accurate figures for the number of young people between 12 and 18, as resident numbers are collected for the purpose of calculating food rations. Physical and bureaucratic access to primary schools appears to be good: The gross enrollment rate (GER) for the primary cycle was 104% for all camps in 2008–2009 (103.5% for male students and 106.2% for female students).

Some caveats about GER need to be enumerated. First, it is more than 100% because there are discrepancies in reported figures of the total number of students of primary-school age. The only up-to-date figures for the number of children in the camps come from the feeding figures used by the Thailand Burma Border Consortium (TBBC). Some children could have been left out of these figures because they had not been registered. Second, it is not possible to base the calculation on the school-age of the population because students are not always able to attend the grade that corresponds to their age. Thus the figure cited aggregates primary numbers rather than numbers for each grade level. Third, the TBBC feeding figures are divided into three broad age categories: 0–5 and 6–12. Thus, we do not have an accurate GER for secondary schools.

According to official camp education policy, the schools in the camps are accessible to all children and young people. In fact, the slogan adopted by the Karen Education Department —the body formerly in charge of education administration in the camps—was "Education for All." School administrators and education committee members work to ensure that this is the case, given the constraints imposed on them and the limited resources available to them. However, bureaucratic obstacles hinder the achievement of full access. There have been reports that students were not able to register at school. Inquiries into this by NGOs and the camp education committees have not completely resolved the discrepancy between schools' stated policy of accepting all students regardless of registration status and reports from students about not being able to register for school.

TABLE 4.1   Number of Primary and Secondary Students in the Seven Predominantly Karen Camps, 2005–2010

Academic year	Primary	Secondary	Total
2005–2006	26,156	11,446	37,602
2006–2007	25,394	12,754	38,148
2007–2008	23,482	12,861	36,343
2008–2009	20,129	16,346	36,475
2009–2010	20,235	13,813	34,048

The GER for the secondary cycle is not available as there are no figures for the number of students aged 13–18. However, there are participation figures for 2005 to 2009 (see Table 4.1).

In 2005, the UNHCR had a figure of 38,305 registered children and young people between the ages of 5 and 17 for these seven camps. Taking into account 1,426 "inside students," this provides an enrollment rate of 94% for 2005. This is a relatively high rate of enrollment. It is difficult to comment on whether more people are completing secondary schooling over the years, given the lack of data that tracks the progress of individuals throughout their schooling trajectory. This is complicated by the fact that there are constant flows of people in and out of the refugee camps as a result of seasonal employment, resettlement, and new arrivals.

For the academic years 2007–2010 the percentage of male students in the primary cycle is higher than that of female students, at slightly more than 51%. However, the proportion is reversed in the secondary cycle with female students ranging between 50 and 51% in the three years.

Patterns of participation show that access and retention are more pronounced along religious rather than gender lines. In the 2008–2009 academic year, 57.7% of the primary students were Christian, 34.9% were Buddhist, and 6.8% were Muslim. The rest were categorized under "other religions." For secondary students, the proportion of Christian students was higher than in the primary cycle, with Christian students representing 64% of the secondary student population. The Buddhist students made up roughly the same numbers as in the primary cycle, at about a third. The percentage of Muslim students was much lower than in the primary cohort, at 1.2%. This does not correspond with the percentage of people by religion in the camps, as will be discussed in more detail below.

Out of 2,130 parents interviewed in 2009, 27.4% responded that their children had dropped out of school. The figure reported by these parents was 583. The top five reasons that parents gave for their children leaving school were: marriage (30% of 583), lack of money (17.2%), family problems (9.3%), that the children did not want to continue studying (9.1%), and that the children had to help their family by working (8%). For each child who dropped out of school, parents were given a list of reasons and asked to choose one. The percentages for the responses given are an aggregate of the reasons given for all children, the total number being 583.

Following the work undertaken by Oh and van der Stouwe (2008), inclusion is conceptualized as consisting of three dimensions: access, quality and relevance, and management structures. Access means having the opportunity to enroll in learning programs and institutions and having physical access to buildings and other educational facilities. The quality and relevance dimension concerns all learners being able to engage fully in the learning process and to achieve the same outcomes as their peers. The third dimension is community management structures and how they influence inclusion in education.

Embedded in this conceptualization, but not explicitly articulated, is the concept of equity. Equity is about being able to gain fair and impartial access. Thus, while it may be said that there is free access to all, certain circumstances such as income distribution or power structures may make it more difficult for certain populations to gain access to education despite the fact that access is universal.

Several studies on inclusion in education have been conducted in the refugee camps to determine the factors that act as barriers to access and to retention in schools to explain the patterns of participation detailed above. The characteristics of exclusion have been presented under the categories of language, age, religion, financial, legal, cultural, and health impairments (Haikin, 2009; Oh, Thawda, van der Stouwe, & Say Naw, 2007). They are particularly useful in identifying the areas of exclusion and inequity that need to be addressed.

However, this approach is limited because it presents these factors as atomized, unrelated issues rather than as indicators of a larger phenomenon. This can present contradictory and puzzling scenarios of exclusion. Thus, it is argued here that in examining access and equity in education in the camps, there needs to be a framework to structure and weave the factors of exclusion *and* inclusion as a coherent whole. It is posited that identity and its formation in schools provides this framework. This allows us to arrive at a more nuanced and integrated picture of access and equity, and to examine whether practices of exclusion are systematic or random, intentional or unintentional.

IDENTITY: THE BASIS OF INCLUSION AND EXCLUSION

Formal education has characteristically been employed to promulgate, reify, and legitimize certain constructions of collective social identity, be they religious (Liow, 2009), ethnic (Bush & Saltarelli, 2000), political (Alzaroo & Hunt, 2003), ideological (Freire, 2000), cultural (Willis, 1977) or social class (Bernstein, 1971, 1973; Bourdieu, 1991). Identity formation in schools is particularly important to consider in refugee situations. Different community groups have an interest in shaping identity to establish and reproduce certain political and cultural values.

In Thailand, as we have seen, the host government, except for the introduction of Thai language lessons, has left the formation of identity in schools to the Karen refugees and the NGOs as it perceives no benefit in doing so, except for the introduction of Thai language lessons. The form and content of schooling has thus been shaped by the accepted wisdom of the international refugee regime—through NGOs—and the dominant Christian Karen leadership in the camps.

The international refugee regime promotes its own version of refugee identity. The past two decades have seen a focus on providing psychosocial intervention to large-scale refugee displacements as part of the humanitarian agenda (Eyber, 2002). In addition, the discourse on and conceptualization of refugee children have been framed around their vulnerability and role as victims (Boyden, 2003; Hart & Tyrer, 2006). The predominant approach that the UNHCR uses in reference to children is that of protection (UNICEF, 2005).

In the refugee camps in Thailand, the curricula for subjects such as English, mathematics, and science were designed by international NGO staff in consultation with the Karen education leadership; "living values" were instigated and then incorporated into the curriculum (interview, July 2010); psychosocial assistance in the form of Creating Opportunities for Psychosocial Enhancement (COPE) has been integrated into teacher training. As LeBlanc and Waters (2005) observed, "in their decision-making in seemingly technical areas to do with curriculum, pedagogy and school administration, they [educational administrators in refugee camps] plant the seeds of a future. This future may see repatriation, resettlement, the end of an old identity, or the beginning of a new one" (LeBlanc & Waters, 2005, p. 1).

It is also the case that NGOs, on occasion, unwittingly accept the power dynamics that already exist in the community. "In administering schools, humanitarian organisations make decisions which have consequences for how power is distributed. Teachers are identified and promoted, a language of instruction is chosen and specific norms of deference and respect are enforced" (LeBlanc & Waters, 2005, p. 1).

Commentators have observed that when the NGOs began working in the camps in Thailand, they accepted the existing power structures without questioning them (Bowles, 1997; South, 2007). These structures were set up with the help of the Committee for Coordination of Services to Displaced Persons in Thailand (CCSDPT) using the village structure that had existed in Karen State (Lang, 2002). The Karen Education Department (KED), the education arm of the KNU, was recognized as the administrative body for education in the seven camps: "[A]long the border, foreign aid insulated the KNU and its supporters from the realities of life in Burma, while empowering one among several competing concepts of Karen nationalism, which became the dominant form of discourse among border and exile/opposition communities" (South, 2007, p. 4).

In the past few years, some NGOs have worked to change the nature of their involvement in these structures and to encourage power sharing amongst those who have fewer political resources in the interest of expanding access and promoting equity in education. For example, the education NGOs have implemented programs and initiatives that promote inclusion in education, such as special education (World Education) and inclusion awareness and practices, in an attempt to embed inclusion at all levels and in all aspects of education provision and management (ZOA Refugee Care Thailand). On occasion, this matched the Karen leaders' conception of identity and its transmission in schools. On many other occasions, this did not.

Turning to the refugee community, there is no doubt that the role of schooling is considered vital in identity formation. In the case of the Karen, Rajah points out that education and language have been used by the Karen National Union (KNU) to cultivate a certain form of national consciousness in the areas it controls in Burma and in the refugee camps in Thailand.

> [I]n order to identify with that nationalism [separatist movement or the community envisioned by the KNU], there must first be a national consciousness. The key issue is the monopoly of control over identification with the state. In the territories controlled by the KNLA, however, it is possible to generate that kind of consciousness because the KNU and KNLA control one of the means of social reproduction, namely, schools. But education (or indoctrination) is not the only consideration. The use—or perhaps one should say the *possession*—of a Karen 'national language' (Sgaw Karen) and a script (even if originally based on the Burmese writing system) in these schools, as well as in administration and other forms of communication, is also symbolic and serves to establish, simultaneously, Karen identity and differences between Burmese and Karen. (Rajah, 1990, p. 121)

The control over schooling and the possession of a "national language" as efforts to create and propagate a nationalist identity are important in understanding the significance of education and schooling in the camps. This is revealed in the insistence on using Skaw Karen as the language of instruction and the teaching of Karen history and social sciences.

This control is manifested in the administrative structures in education. Education management is dominated by Christian Skaw Karen-speaking elites. In 2007, a study conducted in six of the seven camps found that all the nominated and elected members of the camp education committees were Christian. These committees make important decisions about the management of camp education resources and coordination. The camp education coordinator, who is invariably Christian Skaw Karen and a member of the Karen Refugee Committee Education Entity (KRCEE), is a member of this committee and has the most power and influence over educational matters (Oh et al., 2007).

The KRCEE is the education department of the Karen Refugee Committee (KRC). The KRC was formed by the Karen in 1984 to administer the refugee population (Lang, 2002). It is the administrative body through which assistance is provided. The KRCEE, on the other hand, was only established in April 2009. It took over from the Karen Education Department (KED) which is the department of education of the KNU, the "government-in-exile." When it was operating in the camps, the KED had overall responsibility for the administration of kindergarten, primary, secondary, vocational, and adult education in the refugee camps as well as education in the Karen State in Burma.

At present, the KRCEE operates freely in camps and has taken over KED policies on education. The KED is now only responsible for education in Karen State. At present, the KRCEE focuses on post-secondary education and does not have a specific focus on vocational and adult learning. It also coordinates the education activities in camp with the NGOs and community-based organizations (CBOs) working along the border.

Thus, the education in the camps is managed and controlled by the (mostly Christian) Karen leadership in accordance with their beliefs and values about what constitutes identity formation in schools. This is done in collaboration with education NGOs.

THE NATIONALIST KAREN: LANGUAGE, HISTORY AND RELIGION

There are two sets of students who are disadvantaged by the use of Skaw Karen as the language of instruction: those whose mother tongue is Skaw Karen but who are not literate in it, and those whose mother tongue is not Skaw Karen.

"Inside students" are students who lived in areas controlled by the State Peace and Development Council (SPDC) and crossed the border into the camps solely for the purpose of gaining access to the educational opportunities there. Many are Karen but are not well versed in written Skaw Karen; they studied in Burmese when they were in Burma. The UNHCR figures for the number of inside students in 2006 in Mae La, Umphiem-Mai, and Tham Hin camps was 1,559. However, this figure underreports actual numbers because many of them are unregistered. In addition, the numbers have since changed, but this is not recorded by the UNHCR as it has not been permitted to register newcomers since 2005.

On arriving at camp, these students often have difficulty adjusting to Skaw Karen as the language of instruction in the first few months or so (Oh & van der Stouwe, 2008). When asked about this during interviews in 2005, almost all of the 40 students in the sample reported needing time to adjust to the different language of instruction and having varying levels of difficulty doing so. However, one set of students played down the difficulties encountered and expressed pride in learning the language and Karen history, subjects which had not been part of their schooling experience in Burma. Further, these students conveyed a sense of privilege in their new and growing political awareness of the struggle of their people.

In this case, the use of Skaw Karen—as opposed to Pwo Karen or Burmese—as the language of instruction and the study of Karen history are seen as expressions of Karen nationalism and struggle. Thus, the difficulty encountered in studying in Skaw Karen is downplayed and seen to be something to be overcome, and not an exclusionary practice.

Despite the enthusiasm that the inside students professed for Skaw Karen as a language of instruction, there are still reports from teachers that inside students drop out due to language difficulties. The numbers are uncertain as there are no accurate figures for dropout at present. Moreover, the reasons for dropout are often a combination of factors, and these are not recorded by schools.

The other group of students who do not speak Skaw Karen as their mother tongue are residents who are not ethnically Karen. The biggest group of non-Karen define themselves ethnically as Muslim. They form the largest subset of people practicing Islam as their religion. In an education survey of 2,408 people conducted in 2009, 153 adults identified Islam as their religion. Of these, 127 (83%) considered themselves ethnic Muslims. The rest were Skaw Karen, Pwo Karen, Burman, Chin, Pa-O, Arakan, Na Gha, and of mixed heritage. The majority (94%) of the ethnic Muslims reported Burmese as their home language.

According to the UNHCR figures for 2005, the camps with the highest percentage of Muslims are Mae La, Umphiem-Mai, and Nu Po, ranging between 12% and 24% of the population (see Table 4.2).

Compared to the percentage of Muslims in the wider population, Muslim students were underrepresented in school in Mae La camp, but in the other two camps, their numbers roughly corresponded to those in the wider population. However, the figures become particularly stark in secondary school in all three camps: the percentage of Muslim students in the secondary student population ranged between 1.7% and 4%, out of a wider Muslim population ranging between 12% and 24%. In addition, the percentage of students who were Christian was overrepresented in secondary schools (see Table 4.3).

TABLE 4.2   Student and Camp Population by Religion

	Students (%) 2006–2007			Population (%) 2005		
	Buddhist	Christian	Muslim	Buddhist	Christian	Muslim
Mae La	44.3	47.5	7.8	41	44	15
Umphiem-Mai	38.8	43.7	17.4	36	40	24
Nu Po	35.0	53.7	11.2	32	56	12

Note: The population figures are from 2005 UNHCR reports; they are the most accurate as the UNHCR is the only organization that collects the religious affiliations of the camp population. However, it is not up-to-date as the UNHCR has not been allowed to register refugees after 2005.

For purposes of comparison, the ideal figures for the student population would have been those for 2005–2006. However, the figures of students by religion for 2005–2006 are not available. The student figures do not add up to 100% because students in the "other religion" category (which is negligible) are not included.

TABLE 4.3   Student Population by Religion by Cycle

	Primary students (%) 2006–2007			Secondary students (%) 2006–2007		
	Buddhist	Christian	Muslim	Buddhist	Christian	Muslim
Mae La	46.9	42.4	10.4	38.5	59.7	1.7
Umphiem-Mai	38.6	38.1	23.2	39.4	56.3	4.0
Nu Po	31.7	52.2	16.1	41.0	56.4	2.3

Note: For purposes of comparison, the ideal figures for the student population would have been those for 2005–2006. However, the figures of students by religion for 2005–2006 are not available.

The student figures do not add up to 100% because students in the "other religion" category (which is negligible) are not included.

High levels of Muslim participation in the primary level are widely attributed to the existence of schools where Burmese is used as the language of instruction. These schools are known colloquially as Muslim schools; they are not religious schools but are attended by the ethnic Muslims. As yet, camp-wide data showing that ethnic Muslim students drop out at the secondary level due to the language of instruction are not available. However, interviews that were conducted with some Muslim parents pointed to language as a barrier to access to secondary schools in Nu Po camp (Oh and van der Stouwe, 2008). Unlike for the "inside students," the use of Skaw Karen as a language of instruction was not perceived as a barrier to overcome, but as an exclusionary practice.

Different measures have been instituted to address the issue of language. The Muslim schools were set up by the Muslim community and the language of instruction is Burmese; their curriculum differs from the Skaw

Karen schools and the pass rate has been lowered (Oh & van der Stouwe, 2008). However, there are no secondary schools with Burmese as the language of instruction. In terms of religious identity, Koranic schools have been set up to fill this need. Similarly, there are Buddhist and Christian Mission schools in the camps.

There have been recommendations to use Burmese as the language of instruction, but, understandably, there is resistance on the part of the education leadership. However, this may not be the best solution either, since the use of Burmese as the language of instruction in the Karenni camps is also proving to be a challenge to students (Haikin, 2009).

The figures reveal that the appeal of secondary schooling is greater for Christians than it is for non-Christians. Besides the language of instruction, there are also issues of relevance relating to national identity: Karen nationalist identity is tied up with Christianity and formal education as the tool to self-determination.

> [T]he very notion of contemporary Karen nationalism was birthed in early mission schools even as formal schooling became one of the primary sites of the colonial process, including the imposition of western thought. This relationship between Eurocentric thought, western schooling and the attainment of Karen nationalist aspirations has become inextricably intertwined in nationalist rhetoric. (O'Brien, 2004, p. 7)

It would seem that in this nationalist framework the incentives for pursuing education are greater for the (Christian) Karen than the non-Karen, because therein lie status and respect for those who work towards advancing the Karen nation through the attainment of high levels of education. The sentiment among the (Christian) Skaw Karen is that education is of utmost importance, whereas the ethnic Muslims are more interested in pursuing business and trade (interview, July 2010). It is posited here that the non-Karen and ethnic Muslims have little or no stake in this nationalist agenda, nor do they gain status or prestige from it. Thus, while they do value education, it is easier for economic and other circumstances to override their motivations for schooling. It may also be said that the attribution of different domains of activity (education and trade) to distinct ethnic groups is an affirmation of power-sharing in camp politics.

Having said that, identity in the camps is not always clearly delineated. While the language and the history of the Karen may not speak to the ethnic identity of the non-Karen, these groups have also shown solidarity with the repression and struggle that the Karen have experienced. An NGO worker came across a Muslim school celebrating Karen Martyr's Day and was puzzled as to why they were commemorating a Karen event, particularly since the other (Karen) schools were not doing so. In answer to her bafflement, they explained that their (Muslim) community experiences the same hardships as the Karen and that they identified with the struggle against the Burman (interview, July 2010). Identity is multilayered and multifaceted. It would seem that some aspects of Karen schooling and identity appeal more to non-Karen identity than others, and these are areas that require further investigation for a more nuanced and precise understanding of exclusion *and* inclusion.

THE MODERN KAREN:
NORMAL AND NONFORMAL EDUCATION

The colonial project of transmitting western forms of knowledge through formal schooling has been embraced by the Christian Karen leadership as one of the main tools for self-determination (O'Brien, 2004). There is a belief among the leadership and shared by the Karen community that their education must be on par with international standards in order to build a modern, developed nation. When the head of the Karen Education Department (KED) was asked what he thought education was for, he replied that it was to build a modern Karen society and that this would be achieved when more people had attained university-level qualifications so that they would have the skills and knowledge to build a developed society (interview, April 2005). These same sentiments are echoed by teachers and education administrators.

The orientation towards the future is rational given present circumstances: there are no jobs available to the refugees in the Thai economy beyond those which are menial and illegal and the number of jobs in the camps is limited. What is noteworthy is that the Karen leadership have aspirations of an advanced society and they believe that this will come about through the provision and attainment of high levels of formal education. In fact, O'Brien (2004) argues that

> an inherent conflict exists between the concepts of formal schooling bound up in western assumptions about the larger project of nation building, and Karen knowledge, identity and culture. The conflict lies in the implausibility of coexistence between worlds, given one of which has historically devalued and/or displaced the other. (p. 61)

Without a doubt, formal forms of education are valued over nonformal ones. The priority has always been to establish schools based on general education models of kindergarten, primary, secondary, and further leading to tertiary education. The majority of the coordination, administration, funding, and attention are given to this sector by both the Karen education leadership and the international NGOs. When it was operating in the camps, the KED had overall responsibility for the administration of kindergarten, primary, secondary, vocational, and adult education in the refugee camps. When the KRCEE was created to take over, it narrowed this portfolio to basic, further, and higher education. In addition, ZOA Refugee Care, the main provider of education resources and services in the seven camps, spends half of its education budget on primary and secondary education (Oh, 2010a). The rest is divided among vocational training, English language learning, and a livelihoods project.

Students also internalize this value system. In 2005, 638 children aged 9, 12, and 15 were asked what they planned to do after completing secondary education. The majority (87%) wanted to further their studies. When asked what they planned to study, the children and young people indicated they wanted to pursue their education either through a further education program (highly competitive and limited places) or by studying subjects (languages, math, science, and so on). Medic training was the most popular, with 27% choosing that option. The learning/training programs that followed in popularity were those offered by the two most prestigious post-secondary education programs, university and teacher training (Oh, 2010b). It is significant that the top two choices were the highest available formal education opportunities in the camps and that university education, virtually impossible to attain, was third in popularity.

In itself, the emphasis on formal education is not uncommon. Formal education is prioritized in many countries and by the international education development community (including the Education for All campaign). However, in this setting, the belief in the supremacy of the formal system in delivering development means that those who do not manage to fit into this system are left with few suitable and valid choices to continue with their learning.

Students who lost years of schooling while internally displaced feel uncomfortable studying in classes where their peers are younger than they are; many drop out as a result. In addition, some students who were internally displaced have difficulty habituating to the classrooms. Others drop out because they cannot keep up, have health impairments, or have limited financial means (Haikin, 2009; Oh et al, 2007). Those who marry before completing secondary education, shamed by social and cultural norms, leave school voluntarily.

The opportunities available to them are inadequate because they do not provide learning pathways that lead to the attainment of the valued form of education—the completion of secondary schooling under the formal education system. When students who had dropped out of school were asked if they would like to continue with their education, they invariably said yes, and the learning they wanted to pursue was almost always the subjects that are available in the formal education system.

Programs with further learning opportunities are provided by the Karen Women's Organization (KWO) and night school in Tham Hin camp. The KWO further learning program aims to improve the basic knowledge of adults, but it does not necessarily use the formal education curriculum. Students who dropped out of the formal system do enroll in this program, but this is only a small proportion of the total number. The night school in Tham Hin camp, on the other hand, is an alternative secondary school program that provides students with the opportunity to complete their secondary education. However, the curious fact about this program is that almost all of those who enroll are teachers who want to complete their schooling, students who had been asked to leave school to become teachers, and students who had not been able to enroll in mainstream schools because they had arrived too late (Oh & Pakdeekhunthum, 2007). In 2007, only one student enrolled in this program had dropped out of school because she had gotten married. Furthermore, this program only provides learning at the higher grades, making it inaccessible to students who dropped out at the lower ones. It would seem that this learning program caters to the learning needs of people who did not complete their secondary education because of external circumstances, and not because of an inability to cope in mainstream education.

Besides the paucity of nonformal learning avenues and the relegation of such provision to non-KRCEE bodies, the priority given to formal education is manifested in the creation of the Karen Refugee Committee Institute of Higher Education (KRCIHE). This body is attempting to standardize higher education programs in the camps and is working with NGOs to develop curricula and to set up programs in community development, teacher training, and public health. On completing their studies, students will be awarded a bachelor's degree from KRCIHE (interview, July 2010).

The pursuit of higher education is a worthwhile endeavor. However, it has to be examined in the context of the camp and the positioning of the Karen education leadership. Higher education, as mentioned above, is seen as the means to the development of a modern, advanced Karen society. However, there needs to be some consideration for those who drop out of the formal system and do not progress to further and higher education (there are only 700 places for post-secondary schooling per year in all seven camps) and adults who are not literate given the limited resources available to the education sector.

At present, the nonformal and adult learning sectors receive less funding and attention from the Karen leadership. NGOs do provide programs and funding for skills development in these sectors, but they are limited. In addition, the NGOs have focused more on inclusion in formal education rather than in education as a whole.

CONCLUSION

The reproduction and transmission of Karen identity in schools is bound up with Skaw Karen language, Karen history, religion, and formal forms of schooling. This chapter has explored a small part of this identity, as expressed in the form and content of schooling, in order to flesh out and relate indicators of inclusion, access, and equity. While this identity is not inherently bad, its transmission in schools may alienate other groups that do not subscribe to this collective identity.

Since 2007, a more integrated approach has been employed by the main education NGO, ZOA Refugee Care, in its inclusion initiative. This has had an impact on awareness and attitudes in the camps and within its own ranks. It has questioned its own assumptions about the power dynamics among the different groups in the refugee community and tentatively posed this issue to the education leadership in the refugee community. Different refugee communities and organizations, NGOs, and the Karen education leadership have devised ways of addressing exclusion. However, these measures do not plug the gaps completely, nor do they fully address the issue of identity and inclusion at a systemic level. In addition, they are concentrated only in the formal education sector. Consequently, they are not completely effective and are limited in their efficacy.

The inherent tension of identity and inclusion is located in the reproduction of an entho-nationalist identity in schools in the setting of a multiethnic camp population. In the Karen imagining and construction of their nation, they have used ethnic and cultural origin as the basis for citizenship and belonging. Ethno-cultural nationalism requires individuals to possess the necessary ethnic attributes before full status and membership of the national community may be conferred (Brown, 2002). This runs up against a competing form of nationalism—civic nationalism, which asserts that "those who have transferred their political loyalties from ethnic minority and majority communities, and given them to the state, deserve the full rights and status of citizens" (Brown, 2002, p. 560). These two forms of nationalism are at odds with each other, and in the predominantly Karen refugee camps, the former dominates at present. It is this variance that needs to be scrutinized so that attempts to address issues of access and equity are coherent and integrated rather than piecemeal and *ad hoc.*

ACKNOWLEDGEMENTS

The author wishes to thank the Institute of Southeast Asian Studies, Singapore for its support; ZOA Refugee Care Thailand for the use of their statistical database; and Supee Rattanasamakkee (Say Naw), Implementation Manager, Duangporn Saussay, Country Director, and Simon Purnell, Strategic Operations Manager, ZOA Refugee Care Thailand, for sharing their knowledge and expertise.

REFERENCES

Alzaroo, S., & Hunt, G. L. (2003). Education in the context of conflict and instability: The Palestinian case. *Social Policy and Administration, 37*(2), 165–180.

Bernstein, B. (1971). *Class, codes and control.* London, UK: Routledge and Kegan Paul.

Bernstein, B. (Ed.). (1973). *Class, codes and control: Vol: 2.* London, UK: Routledge and Kegan Paul.

Bourdieu, P. (1991). *Language and symbolic power.* Cambridge, UK: Polity Press.

Bowles, E. (1997). *Assistance, protection, and policy in refugee camps on the Thailand–Burma border: An overview.* Refugee Studies Programme, Queen Elizabeth House, Oxford University.

Bowles, E. (1998). From village to camp: Refugee camp life in transition on the Thailand–Burma border. *Forced Migration Review, 2,* 11–14.

Boyden, J. (2003). Children under fire: Challenging assumptions about children's resilience. *Children, Youth and Environments, 13*(1). Retrieved from http://www.colorado.edu/journals/cye/13_1/Vol13_1Articles/CYE_CurrentIssue_Article_ChildrenUnderFire_Boyden.htm

Brown, D. (2002). Why might constructed nationalist and ethnic ideologies come into confrontation with each other? *The Pacific Review, 15*(4), 555–570.

Bush, K. D., & Saltarelli, D. (2000). *The two faces of education in ethnic conflict: Towards a peacebuilding education for children.* Florence, Italy: UNICEF.

Eyber, C. (2002). Psychosocial Issues. *FMO Research Guide.* Retrieved from http://www.forcedmigration.org/guides/fmo004/

Freire, P. (2000). *Pedagogy of the oppressed.* New York, NY: Continuum.

Haikin, M. (2009). *Survey of inclusion.* London, UK: Voluntary Services Overseas (VSO).

Hart, J., & Tyrer, B. (2006). *Research with children living in situations of armed conflict: concepts, ethics and methods.* RSC Working Paper No. 30.

KRC (Karen Refugee Committee) (2009). Newsletter and Monthly Report, May 2009. Thailand, KRC.

Lang, H. J. (2002). *Fear and sanctuary: Burmese refugees in Thailand.* Ithaca, NY: Southeast Asia Program Publications, Southeast Asia Program, Cornell University.

LeBlanc, K., & Waters, T. (2005). Schooling in refugee camps. *Humanitarian Exchange Magazine, 29*(March). Retrieved from http://www.odihpn.org/report.asp?id=2654

Liow, J. C. (2009). *Islam, education and reform in Southern Thailand: Tradition and transformation.* Singapore: Institute of Southeast Asian Studies.

O'Brien, S. (2004). *Karen perspectives on schooling in their communities: Indigenous knowledge and western models of education.* Unpublished MA thesis. University of Toronto.

Oh, S-A. (2010a). *Education in refugee camps in Thailand: policy, practice and paucity.* Background paper for EFA Global Monitoring Report 2011.

Oh, S-A. (2010b). Future dreaming. *Around the Globe, 7*(1), 27–29.

Oh, S-A., & Pakdeekhunthum, T.T. (2007). *The learning landscape: Adult learning in seven refugee camps along the Thai–Burmese border.* Maesot, Thailand: ZOA Refugee Care Thailand.

Oh, S-A., & van der Stouwe, M. (2008). Education, diversity, and inclusion in Burmese refugee camps in Thailand. *Comparative Education Review, 52*(4), 589–618.

Oh, S-A., Thawda, L., van der Stouwe, M., & Say Naw. (2007). *Having their say: Refugee camp residents and inclusive education. ZOA's commitment to educational inclusion.* Maesot, Thailand: ZOA Refugee Care Thailand.

Preston, R. (1991). The provision of education to refugees in places of temporary asylum. *Comparative Education, 27*(1), 61–81.

Rajah, A. (1990). Ethnicity, nationalism, and the nation-state: The Karen in Burma and Thailand. In G.Wijeyewardene (Ed.), *Ethnic groups across national boundaries in mainland Southeast Asia* (pp. 102–133). Singapore: ISEAS.

Smith, M. (1991). *Burma: insurgency and the politics of ethnicity.* London, UK: Zed Books.

Sommers, M. (2002). Children, education and war: reaching education for all (EFA) objectives in countries affected by conflict. *Conflict Prevention and Reconstruction Unit Working Papers* (paper no.1.). Washington, DC: The World Bank.

South, A. (2007). Karen nationalist communities: The "problem" of diversity. *Contemporary Southeast Asia, 29*(1), 55–76.

United Nations Children's Fund [UNICEF]. (2005). *The state of the world's children 2005: Childhood under threat.* New York, NY: UNICEF.

Willis, P. (1977). *Learning to labour.* Farnborough, UK: Saxon House.

PART II

REFUGEE AND IMMIGRANT SCHOOL–COMMUNITY
PARTNERSHIPS

CHAPTER 5

STILL FAR TO GO

Systematic Programming for Immigrant and Refugee Children and Youth

Marian J. Rossiter and Tracey M. Derwing
University of Alberta

ABSTRACT

Many stakeholders are involved in the provision of educational services for immigrant children and youth in Edmonton, Canada. Unfortunately, there has been limited coordination across stakeholders, leaving many students falling between the cracks. Federal government contributions are restricted by the Canadian Constitution; thus, federal input is limited to non-instructional support. The provincial government makes policy and funding decisions about English as a second language (ESL) programming. Universities educate kindergarten to grade 12 (K–12) teachers, but opportunities for pre-service teachers to learn about ESL issues are ad hoc. School boards determine how ESL is delivered across districts, but they face severe funding constraints in the current economic climate. If students are coded as ESL, their schools receive supplementary funding to provide language instruction; however, many needs are not met, and this contributes to high dropout rates. Several nongovernmental organizations have established out-of-school homework

Refugee and Immigrant Students, pages 89–106
Copyright © 2012 by Information Age Publishing

89

clubs to provide additional support. These well-intentioned efforts rely heavily on volunteers, only some of whom have the necessary skills. ESL parents are sometimes distraught because they perceive that their children are not receiving a good education. Although most stakeholders are sincere in their commitment to support immigrant children and youth, the lack of systematicity and coordination has resulted in terrible human costs. We make recommendations (including, for example, assessment, professional development for school staff, and elimination of the age cap) for providing these students with an equitable education.

Many stakeholders are involved in the provision of education for immigrant and refugee children and youth in Canada, including different levels of government, universities, school boards, schools, teachers, settlement agencies, and other volunteer organizations. Parents and the children and youth themselves are also key stakeholders, although often their input either is not sought or is limited by language barriers, cultural differences, and difficult living circumstances. In this chapter, we will describe the nature of these stakeholders' roles in Edmonton, a medium-sized city in western Canada. As will become apparent, each of the stakeholder groups listed above participates in the education of immigrant and refugee students, but there has been a lack of coordination and communication between them, such that many children and youth end up falling between the cracks. Although, as will be shown below, there is a great deal of concern about the welfare of immigrant and refugee children and youth, as well as many interventions, there is very little evidence that, overall, these initiatives have increased linguistic, academic, and integration success. This is not to say that all English language learners (ELLs) struggle academically; some of the top-achieving students in the school system are immigrant youth (Toohey & Derwing, 2008). Nonetheless, the numbers of immigrant and refugee students who drop out of school are unacceptable, and far higher than those of their Canadian-born counterparts (Watt & Roessingh, 2001).

DEMOGRAPHIC FACTORS

Over the last several years, Alberta, including Edmonton, the capital city, has received significant numbers of immigrants and refugees. Canada has three primary streams of immigration: economic class (61%), family class (26%) and refugee class (9%); another 4% of immigrants come in under special circumstances (Citizenship and Immigration Canada, 2010). In 2008, the source regions for the largest groups of newcomers to Alberta were Asia/Pacific (12,256), Europe (4,328), Africa/Middle East (4,175), and Central and South America (2,198) (Citizenship and Immigration Canada, 2008). Each year, for the last five years, Edmonton has received an average of slightly over 7,000 immigrants (adults and children). In 2009, Edmonton received 8,506 newcomer permanent residents, in addition to the temporary foreign workers in the city (15,768), some of whom also have children (Citizenship and Immigration Canada, 2010).

In 2001, Canada introduced the Immigrant and Refugee Protection Act, which specifies that refugees be chosen on the basis of greatest need. Prior to 2001, Canada chose refugees on the basis of adaptability, thus selecting individuals who were highly educated, healthy, and of working age. The change in policy has resulted in a different population of refugees with complex needs. Often refugees have significant education gaps and may not be literate in their first language. These issues place further demands on some refugee youth, who have a limited period of time to learn English and catch up with their peers on curriculum subject content.

ROLES OF KEY STAKEHOLDERS

Federal Government Role

Although the federal government makes the majority of the decisions about how many newcomers Alberta receives, it does not play a significant role in the education of immigrant children and youth because the Canadian Constitution dictates that education is a provincial responsibility. Therefore, federal input is limited to non-instructional support, such as social workers in schools. The federal government funds multicultural liaison workers (cultural brokers) in some school districts, but school boards report that there are insufficient funds to address all of the immigrant communities' needs. Ironically, the federal government has a generous language program for adult immigrants (Language Instruction for Newcomers to Canada, or LINC), but this program is not considered to be "education." It is deliberately called "training" because of the constitutional restriction; LINC is viewed as a prerequisite to employment. Because Canada is officially bilingual, the federal government promotes the learning of French in English-majority locales. Federal funding supports grade school French immersion in Edmonton, but there is no comparable funding for speakers of other languages who require English, the other official language.

Provincial Government Role

The provincial government is responsible for funding public education from kindergarten to grade 12 (K–12), developing curriculum and assessment, and making policy decisions about English as a second language

(ESL) programming, for example, deciding who is eligible for ESL support and for how long. Alberta Education is understaffed in this area and has been slow to respond to the increasing needs brought about by changing demographics in the schools. For the last four years, the focus of the department has been on the development of provincial ESL benchmarks (Alberta Education, 2009), adapted from the Calgary Board of Education.

Four years ago, Alberta Education undertook a review of ESL programming in Alberta schools (Howard Research and Management Consulting, 2006). The study was designed to inform the province of the factors that affect the academic success of ESL children and youth. Results indicated that few ESL specialists in the K–12 system had TESL qualifications and that most mainstream teachers were lacking the knowledge and strategies to enable ELLs to acquire English language skills and subject matter simultaneously. According to the report, at least 17% of the K–12 population in Alberta in 2006 were identified as ESL (5% of the ESL students were refugees). Most urban schools and an increasing number of schools in smaller centres had some ESL students. Howard (2006), however, found that:

> 63% of schools reported that staff designated to instruct ESL students have some ESL training (possibly as little as one professional development session). Twenty-seven [percent] (27%) of ESL designated teachers have no ESL training. Only 14% of schools reported that ESL designated teachers had an ESL diploma, certificate or degree in ESL. (Howard, 2006, p. 5)

In fact, neither Alberta Education nor the Alberta Teachers' Association requires K–12 teachers to have any specific preparation dealing with the accommodation of ELLs, despite the advantages that this would entail for schools.

Another responsibility of the province is the determination of the age cap. In Alberta, no student of 20 years of age or over can register in regular high schools. For refugee students who come as adolescents and who may have significant gaps in their education, the age cap presents a serious barrier to high school completion. Completion in alternative schools is often not an option because of financial constraints. Watt and Roessingh (1994) and Derwing, DeCorby, Ichikawa, and Jamieson (1999) reported push-out rates of over 30% and 10% respectively; that is, students who were forced to leave school because of the age cap. As a result of this policy, many immigrant and refugee youth do not complete high school, and this results in huge costs to society (Hankivsky, 2008).

A further difficulty for this particular group of students is a policy that requires that students be out of school for at least one year before they are eligible for provincial funding for occupational training (including additional time to complete high school as an occupational prerequisite) (Alberta Employment and Immigration, 2010). This "gap year" represents wasted time for students who are already facing challenges in making up for lost time in schooling.

School Boards

Edmonton has three school boards: Edmonton Public School Board (EPSB), which is open to all students; Edmonton Catholic School District (ECSD), which is intended for Catholic students but is open to students of all faiths; and the North Central Francophone School Board, which is intended for students whose first language (L1) or primary language is French. All three boards have significant populations of immigrant and refugee children and youth, but the ethnic mix differs somewhat from one board to the next. The Francophone board has large numbers of African students from countries where French is the language of instruction. Both the larger public and the Catholic boards have student bodies of greater ethnic diversity. Practices with ELLs differ somewhat across boards, and students' perceptions of the quality of ESL instruction also differ by board (Coalition for Equal Access to Education, 2009b). The Coalition for Equal Access to Education surveyed a non-random stratified subset of ELLs in the four largest school boards in Alberta (two in Calgary and two in Edmonton) to gain their perceptions of the quality of ESL instruction. Table 5.1 is adapted from the Coalition's study (note that the Francophone board was not included in this research). The results should be considered with caution, but it is the case that the Edmonton Catholic School District has long had a coherent strategy and has devoted considerable resources to its ESL programming, whereas schools in the Edmonton public system received reduced funding and support for ESL throughout the 1990s and early 2000s and have started only recently to rebuild their programming.

The boards of education are in an awkward position because their funding from the province is limited and yet they are required to meet contractual agreements for teachers and other staff amidst competing demands

TABLE 5.1 Students' Perceptions of the Quality of English as a Second Language Instruction

Agree/Strongly Agree I receive . . .	Alberta	Edmonton Public School Board	Edmonton Catholic School District
enough ESL support for daily communication.	69.0%	64.3%	79.4%
enough ESL support for good grades in subjects.	66.2%	57.1%	74.3%
enough ESL support for vocational school.	60.0%	50.0%	84.4%
enough ESL support for university or college.	63.0%	51.9%	80.0%

for a myriad of programming needs, of which ESL is only one. As a result, specialized support for ELLs is often very limited.

Schools

Immigrant students who are thought to need ESL are formally assessed by teachers, administrators, and/or ESL consultants, but inconsistencies in coding practices exist. In some cases, children are not assessed because their conversational English is quite good, although they may still have difficulty with academic English (Cummins, 1986). If students are coded as ESL, their schools are provided with a special allocation ($1,155 in 2010–2011) in addition to the individual base instruction grant. Funding is provided for a maximum of seven years for eligible ESL students (Alberta Education, 2010). School principals decide how the ESL funds will be spent; they must indicate that the students will receive instruction that will allow them to learn English, but there is no requirement that they use the funding directly for ESL instructional purposes. In other words, a child can be put in a mainstream classroom with no additional support if the principal feels that the teacher can accommodate the linguistic needs of the student. There must be a sufficient number of ELLs in a school to justify the hiring of a classroom aide; even more students are necessary to hire a teacher designated to work with ESL pupils. The Coalition for Equal Access to Education (2005) estimated that it took 69 funded ELLs to cover the costs of one full-time equivalent ESL teacher at that time.

The Role of the University of Alberta

It is the responsibility of the universities to educate K–12 teachers, but at the University of Alberta, the opportunities for pre-service teachers to learn how to meet the needs of ELLs are ad hoc at best. To date there is no requirement that elementary or secondary education pre-service teachers complete a course in how to teach literacy skills or adapt content for ELLs in mainstream classes. Despite the fact that a concentration in teaching ESL exists in secondary teacher education, few pre-service teachers are enrolled in this program, possibly because ESL is not classified as a "teachable subject area." Students are encouraged to focus on "teachable subjects"—that is, subjects that are tested in province-wide examinations. Another course has been developed for in-service teachers, but it is available to a very limited number of pre-service teachers. Until recently, K–12 immigrant issues were not a priority for the faculty, and with the exception of a few faculty members, these issues received little acknowledgement. Like many education faculties in Canada (Toohey & Beynon, 2005), the University of Alberta Faculty of Education does not attract a diverse student population at the undergraduate level. Most prospective teachers are white and Alberta-born. Immigrants from diverse ethnic backgrounds tend to aspire to university educations (Krahn & Taylor, 2005), but few are attracted to the teaching profession (Schmidt, 2009). Although the Faculty of Education does have an extensive TESL program to prepare instructors who wish to teach adult immigrants, there is no comprehensive TESL program to prepare teachers for the primary and secondary school levels. Paradoxically, while the primary providers for adult ESL programming have many well-qualified instructors on staff, there is a severe shortage of similarly trained teachers for primary and secondary schools.

Role of Volunteer Agencies

In recognition of the lack of support and lack of academic success of immigrant and refugee students, several volunteer agencies and settlement organizations have established out-of-school-time (OST) clubs. Until recently, these well-intentioned efforts tended to be somewhat uncoordinated and relied heavily on volunteers who may or may not have had the skills to assist students. In a survey conducted in 2009 (City of Edmonton, 2010), 149 OST programs were identified in Edmonton, 14 of which explicitly targeted immigrant children and youth. These programs operated on different schedules: some were before or after school, others were in the evenings or on weekends. The offerings ranged from once a week to seven times a week. Homework or academic achievement was the focus of some clubs, while others were designed to provide recreation, life skills support, and ethnocultural activities. In many instances, these clubs operated in school facilities, but with little or no direct collaboration with school staff. This lack of communication resulted in little continuity between classroom instruction and club activities. It was thus more difficult for teachers or volunteers to attend to the specific needs of individual students. Furthermore, the fact that the clubs existed allowed some school staff to assume that the learners' ESL needs were being met elsewhere. Although the clubs generally had at least one staff member, they were largely facilitated by volunteers from the community. Because of budgetary restrictions, organizational challenges, and limited staff, the clubs provided few training opportunities for volunteers. The clubs provided a vital service, in that the children and youth who attended were in a safe place during "critical hours"; however, the potential academic and linguistic benefits were not fully realized in many cases.

Parents

The parents in several immigrant communities are distressed because they believe that their children are not receiving a good education. One aspect of the Canadian school system that is particularly troublesome for them is the age-appropriate placement of ELLs in K–12 grades. The school boards and the province are in general agreement that all students should be placed with their age peers, but many immigrant parents would prefer that their children be placed in a grade commensurate with their prior formal education experience. Some parents feel that their children are being destined for failure because of the age policy. Another issue that concerns parents, according to the Coalition for Equal Access to Education (2009a), is the way in which schools deal with cultural diversity: fewer than a third of parents surveyed expressed overall satisfaction with this and more specific issues, such as the promotion of cultures, ongoing communication with families, and the availability of culturally focused services. Finally, many teachers expect that parents will be able to assist their children with homework, but in the case of many immigrant families, the parents may be working extra jobs and thus unable even to supervise, or they may have language and education barriers themselves. Even older siblings may not be available to assist with homework because they are often employed in the evenings to supplement the family income (Rossiter & Rossiter, 2009).

LACK OF SYSTEMATICITY

What we have seen is that there are multiple stakeholders involved in the education of immigrant children and youth, most of them well-intentioned, but that there is a lack of systematicity and coordination that results in extreme social costs, both to the individuals and to society at large. Furthermore, many of these programs reach only a minority of eligible students. A lack of employability skills (including literacy) and limited educational opportunities, in part because of the age cap, force youth to seek alternative ways to support themselves and their families. As Rossiter and Rossiter (2009) have shown, the involvement of immigrant and refugee youth in criminal and or gang activity is of growing concern in Edmonton and other Canadian cities.

PROMISING INITIATIVES

These concerns have led to the instigation of some promising initiatives in the last few years by governments, school boards, university faculty members, and volunteer agencies to expand and improve supports and services for immigrant and refugee children.

Provincial Government

The provincial government has devoted more resources within Alberta education to address growing ESL needs. The work with the K–12 ESL proficiency benchmarks is progressing. A possible benefit of using standardized benchmarks to report language proficiency is that all K–12 teachers will require some professional development to gain an understanding of ELLs and aspects of second language acquisition. In addition, the provincial government recently updated and extended a curriculum guide for teachers and administrators, to support the teaching and learning of ELLs in Kindergarten to Grade 9 classes. Furthermore, a pre-kindergarten early learning program has been implemented to encourage the maintenance of immigrant children's first language and their development of English (Kirova, 2010).

School Boards

There have been a number of developments at the school board level that will potentially enhance ELLs' academic achievement. ECSD for the last few years has had a peripatetic consultant working in mainstream classrooms with teachers to help them learn to adapt their teaching and materials to the needs of their ELLs. Each ESCD school has ESL support for its immigrant and refugee students, with the hope of eventually providing more extensive support to families as well. The consultant visits schools with high concentrations of ELLs and spends enough time in each school to ensure that the teachers receive sufficient professional development for working with ELLs. This work is in addition to the work of the ESL consultant for the board.

A pilot project in a curriculum subject, CALM (career and life management) was designed for refugee students at one Catholic high school. These were students who had been in Canada for no more than two years and were designated as being at risk (living independently and/or socially vulnerable). They ranged in age from 17–20 and were enrolled in grades 11 and 12. All had little or no formal school experience in their countries of origin. The pilot, entitled Project Youth: Integration and Education, focused on four main areas: basic life management skills, education planning, employment skills development, and career goal setting (Khalema & Ishiekwene, 2009). The curriculum was adapted to suit the needs of the learners and was individualized with follow-up. The program has now become permanent in the initial school site and has been replicated in other ECSD high schools. The ECSD has plans to establish an alternative learning high school completion center, which will be geared to students who have either been pushed out of high school by the age cap or have dropped out and who need a program to enable them to complete high school. The ECSD envisions a community school that will provide library and recreational facilities, in addition to space for social service agencies. Finally, the district has hired a facilitator to coordinate out-of-school-time programming and to encourage students to remain in school.

The Edmonton Public School Board has recently expanded its ESL consultant service and has created programs at magnet schools to maximize the use of resources. In 2004, the Northern Alberta Alliance for Race Relations (NAARR, now the Centre for Race and Culture) conducted a survey in Edmonton high schools and found an unacceptable degree of racial discrimination and bullying. They contacted both Edmonton public and Edmonton Catholic school boards and hosted two action committees to review and recommend relevant policies to both boards. In 2008, EPSB created a multicultural task force in response to the Edmonton public action committee's recommendations. The task force recommended the development of K–12 transition centers for at-risk refugee and immigrant children with limited English proficiency, little or no formal education experience, and a need for both social and emotional support (Edmonton Public School Board, 2009).

Both the EPSB and the ECSD have implemented early childhood programs in more than a dozen locations to enhance English language development, while at the same time maintaining proficiency in the children's first language.

University of Alberta

In an investigation focused on the infusion of diversity issues into their classroom teaching, three researchers at the University of Alberta (Dunn, Kirova, Cooley, & Ogilvie, 2007) examined their own teaching practices and the intercultural awareness of their students. One instructor taught a course on second language education, in which he explicitly taught the relationship between culture and language. A second taught an early childhood education course, in which students were required to work directly with young children whose first language was not English. Finally, an art instructor used intercultural themes in the creation of art. The researchers summarized their results by stating that "although all of the approaches held some benefits in promoting intercultural competence, each of the instructors acknowledged that their efforts in isolation would not fully equip students to deal with the realities of contemporary classrooms" (Dunn et al., 2007, p. 14). Although the University of Alberta is currently planning to develop a mandatory course in language and literacy for all undergraduate education students, it has yet to be implemented.

Several other innovative university research studies have been conducted in collaboration with schools. For instance, Kirova and Emme (2008) created a noon-hour photography club for newcomer students. They gave the elementary–junior high school students disposable cameras and asked them to create photo novellas of their experiences in school. The children's photo stories from playground and cafeteria settings, for example, illustrated friendship, rejection, exclusion, inclusion, and agency, and these were used by the researchers to help ELLs better understand their rights and the academic and social contexts within the school.

Abbott and Dunn (2009) undertook an innovative project in which they conducted focus groups with in-service K–12 mainstream classroom teachers regarding their ESL professional development needs. The participants indicated the need for: (1) cultural competency, (2) practical teaching strategies, (3) ESL teaching techniques, (4) communication skills for dealing with ESL parents and students, (5) techniques for teaching multilevel classes, and (6) knowledge of appropriate resources for ELLs (Abbott & Dunn, 2009, 3). Students in an introductory TESL course for mainstream teachers then created 16 presentations that responded to professional development requirements identified by the focus group. These presentations were shared with ESL consultants from the Edmonton public and Edmonton Catholic school boards and were posted to the following website for public access: http://www.ualberta.ca/~abbotted/. This project continues to meet the needs of local teachers in that each time the course is offered at the university, new student presentations that address some of the aforementioned research themes are developed and added to the TESL learning community web site.

Yohani (2010) has explored the role of cultural brokers who provide "day-to-day bridging, support and educational activities that assist children's adaptation through direct contact with families, school personnel, and community" (p. 9). She concluded that although cultural brokers play a vital role, they face particular challenges in determining to what extent they can advocate for ELLs in both school and ethnic community settings.

Rossiter and Rossiter (2009) consulted with stakeholders from a wide range of social service agencies, ethno-cultural groups, forensic mental health services, and the criminal justice system regarding immigrant and refugee youth involvement in criminal or gang activities. One of the risk factors identified was related to schools, where these youth may be subject to bullying, discrimination, and gang recruitment. Participants lamented the lack of understanding by school staff of students' educational, cultural, and family backgrounds, and identified other factors that exacerbated dropout rates. The findings have been presented to several stakeholders with recommendations for enhancing supports. A follow-up study is currently being conducted with immigrant youth who have come into conflict with the legal system and those who have become youth leaders and positive role models in their communities. Interviews with youth themselves will identify factors that they perceive to have had a significant impact on their settlement paths. A better understanding of their experiences will help to determine the particular supports, or gaps in supports, that they considered to be critical to their successful integration into Canadian society or to their pathways to crime.

At the University of Alberta but outside the Faculty of Education, there are other useful research initiatives taking place. A notable program of research is that of Paradis (e.g., Golberg, Paradis, & Crago, 2008), in the Department of Linguistics, who is developing a test that would help educational psychologists distinguish between normally developing ELLs and individuals with special needs. In order to make linguistic comparisons of the two groups, Paradis has had to collect a significant amount of baseline data. Given that some ELLs are incorrectly coded as special education students and some ELLs with special education needs are not identified as such, this test promises to make an important contribution to the ELL assessment field.

City of Edmonton

For many years, the City of Edmonton had no policies regarding immigrant and refugee residents. In 2005, however, the city initiated a campaign to attract and retain more newcomers (Derwing & Krahn, 2008). In the process, the city recognized that it had an important role to play in integrating immigrants into the larger community. The Office for Inclusion and Diversity hired several new staff members, and a wide range of integration initiatives were implemented. In 2008, a city taskforce on community safety was created to develop an action plan, REACH (City of Edmonton, 2009). One of the recommendations of the taskforce was to initiate a "turn away from gangs" program. Another was to develop programs to support ethnocultural communities. REACH Edmonton Council for Safe Communities, a nonprofit society, was founded in 2010 as a result of the REACH report recommendations. With a grant from Safe Community Innovation Fund, this council is providing "Schools as Community Hubs" funding for one ECSD and two EPSB schools. In addition to academic programs, these schools will provide wrap-around services for children, youth, and families in the community.

Volunteer Agencies

One particular initiative that has been sponsored by several community organizations, as well as the City of Edmonton, is the Africa Centre. This community center can be used by all African immigrants to Edmonton, and many different programs are available. There are numerous sports activities (soccer, basketball), an arts academy, a summer camp for African children and youth, African community youth leadership training, and a variety of after-school programs. The mission statement of the Centre is as follows: "to create opportunities for access and full participation of members of the African community in all aspects of society including economic, social, cultural and educational endeavors and contribute to the holistic development and wellness of the African individual, family and community" (Council for Advancement of African Canadians in Alberta, n.d.). This center is used extensively throughout the year by members of the African community from a wide range of countries.

The lack of coordination of out-of-school-time (OST) programs was addressed in a 2009 environmental scan coordinated by the Edmonton Public School Board and the United Way of Alberta's capital region (City of Edmonton, 2010). The scan identified some of the issues mentioned above and made recommendations for strategies to improve OST offerings. The first strategy is to obtain reliable information about children, youth, and parents and their needs, interests, and barriers to participation. The second strategy, promoting program quality, includes developing standards and monitoring programs to ensure that they are upheld. This strategy also entails ensuring that OST programs have access to good resources and culturally sensitive models. Expanding participation is the third strategy, to be achieved by removing barriers, setting objectives, monitoring progress, and establishing strong communications with families. Strategy number four, strengthening the ecology of OST programs, involves identifying the policies and practices of mainstream institutions (e.g., schools, governments, funders) that facilitate or hinder the delivery of seamless quality programming. In the summer of 2010, the strategies were introduced in programming offered in five different areas of the city. Big Brothers/Big Sisters Society of Edmonton coordinates the more than 20 organizations involved in the initiative. Based on evaluation of the summer program, changes in other OST offerings will be instituted during the next three years.

RECOMMENDATIONS

Despite the number of positive initiatives cited above, many immigrant and refugee children and youth will be left out. If they do not happen to attend a school that has a program suitable to their needs, or if they live in a neighborhood where they cannot easily access transportation to OST activities, or if they have to work to supplement the family income, they may still end up leaving school without a diploma, and some will end up in the justice system. Furthermore, many families are unaware of the programs designed for children and youth; communication across and within ethno-cultural communities should be developed extensively. Moreover, many of the new programs are not equipped to handle larger numbers, either in terms of staff and volunteers or in terms of physical capacity.

The provincial government should eliminate the age cap, which arbitrarily ends many promising students' education. Furthermore, if an individual drops out of school and requires funding to return, he or she must stay out for a period of 12 months and must be 18 years of age to go back to an adult high school or college. This waiting period should be waived.

The fact that there is no expectation on the part of the provincial government that teachers should have expertise or training in teaching ELLs has a negative impact on immigrant and refugee students. We recommend that Alberta Education require that all pre-service teachers be provided with courses that enhance intercultural sensitivity and give strategies for (1) improving language learning, (2) promoting literacy skills, and (3) adapting content to accommodate ELLs in mainstream classes. In-service teachers should also be required to provide evidence of professional development in these areas.

School boards must find a way to coordinate and fund their offerings for immigrant and refugee youth such that the dropout and pushout rates do not differ from those for Canadian-born students. Hankivsky (2008) has estimated that the annual cost to Canadians of high school non-completion (excluding public health care) is over 37 billion dollars. Although this number includes Canadian-born drop-outs, the percentage of immigrant and refugee youth who drop out or are pushed out is generally higher than that of their Canadian-born counterparts (Howard, 2006).

Assessment and coding of ELLs should be examined carefully. The long-term consequences of miscoding or not coding an individual who needs support are severe. Alberta Provincial Achievement Examinations, administered to all students in grades 6, 9, and 12, should be evaluated for their fairness to ELLs, and accommodations (e.g., auditory support, scribe, extra time) should be considered.

School principals and staff must recognize that whether or not an ELL has come through a transition center, he or she will still need both language and academic accommodations in the mainstream classroom. In addition, intercultural communication within student bodies must be fostered to avoid bullying and racism within schools.

Multicultural liaison workers or cultural brokers currently work in both ECSD and EPSB but under somewhat different conditions. Their mandates and funding mechanisms are distinct. It would be very useful to clarify the role of these workers and to provide them with standardized training so that they have a good understanding of school board policies, appropriate advocacy, and the resources that are available in the community to further address the needs of ELLs and their families.

Currently, foreign-trained teachers have their credentials assessed by the Teacher Development and Certification Branch of Alberta Education. The process of requalifying as a K–12 teacher is convoluted and discouraging to many potential applicants. Prospective teachers are often told that they must take additional course work at a university, but they are given very little guidance. The Calgary Board of Education, in conjunction with the University of Calgary, offers an Immigrant Bridging Program for Foreign Trained Teachers that includes practicum experiences in schools. A similar program should be offered in Edmonton to increase the number of immigrant teachers within the system who can serve as role models for immigrant and refugee youth, and who can contribute linguistic diversity and resources to schools.

Universities, particularly the University of Alberta, should follow up with other stakeholders on the development and implementation of the required course in language and literacy to determine whether it is sufficient or whether changes are required to meet the needs of school teachers. Ongoing changes should be made in response to community and school needs, and with direct input from school representatives. Furthermore, the faculty of education should actively recruit ethnically diverse pre-service teachers.

At present, OST programs tend to be staffed by volunteers, some of whom have little or no teaching experience or qualifications. OST programming that deals with academic development should be provided in close collaboration with schools and subject teachers. Furthermore, these programs should employ paid, bilingual, trained teachers; at the very least, there should be bilingual assistants to interpret in cases of low-proficiency students. The three-year OST strategy coordinated by REACH Edmonton Council for Safe Communities represents a good start in pulling different programs together, but more focus on evidence-based evaluation of linguistic, cultural, and academic outcomes is necessary.

Finally, for immigrant and refugee children and youth to achieve their goals and meet the expectations of society, a systematic, comprehensive approach to support is required. All stakeholders must be involved, from the funders and policymakers to schools and teachers, to settlement agencies, to ethno-cultural groups and to the families themselves. Despite the promising initiatives described above, there has been no systemic change to date. Without systemic change, sustained and adequate funding, and stable programming, we will continue to see a disproportionate percentage of students who fail to achieve their potential. This outcome is clearly not good for the ELLs themselves, but it comes at a high cost to society, as well.

NOTE

The provincial government is trying to address the age cap problem with a two-year extension, and a course in literacy is now required for Elementary and Secondary pre-service teachers at the University of Alberta.

ACKNOWLEDGEMENTS

We are grateful to our colleagues in settlement agencies, refugee sponsors, governments, and school boards for sharing their work with us and for their long-term commitment to immigrants and refugees. Many of these individuals have made significant differences in the lives of immigrant and refugee youth.

REFERENCES

Abbott, M., & Dunn, W. (2009). *Meeting low proficiency English as a second language learners' English language needs field experience project report summary.* Unpublished report submitted to Edmonton Catholic School District and Edmonton Public School Board.

Alberta Education. (2009). *Alberta K–12 ESL proficiency benchmarks.* Retrieved from http://www.learnalberta.ca/content/eslapb/index.html

Alberta Education. (2010). Funding manual for school authorities: 2010/2011 school year. Retrieved from http://education.alberta.ca/media/1213348/2 0102011fundingmanual.pdf

Alberta Employment and Immigration. (2010). *Learner policy and procedures.* Retrieved from http://employment.alberta.ca/AWonline/IS/5014.html

Citizenship and Immigration Canada. (2008). *Facts and figures, 2008— Immigration overview: Permanent and temporary residents.* Retrieved from http://www.cic. gc.ca/english/resources/statistics/facts2008/permanent/14.asp

Citizenship and Immigration Canada. (2010). *Facts and figures, 2009— Immigration overview: Permanent and temporary residents.* Retrieved from http://www.cic. gc.ca/english/resources/statistics/facts2009/index.asp

City of Edmonton. (2009). *Building a culture of community safety in Edmonton in one generation.* Edmonton, AB: Author.

City of Edmonton. (2010). *Faster alone, farther together: An out of school time strategy for immigrant and refugee children and youth in Edmonton.* Edmonton, AB: Author.

Coalition for Equal Access to Education. (2005). *Towards quality, equitable English as a second language education: A practical framework.* Calgary, AB: Author.

Coalition for Equal Access to Education. (2009a). *Cultural competence in Alberta schools: Perceptions of ESL families in four major school boards.* Calgary, AB: Author.

Coalition for Equal Access to Education. (2009b). *Evaluation of ESL Education in Alberta: Perceptions of ESL students in four major school boards.* Calgary, AB: Author.

Council for Advancement of African Canadians in Alberta. (n.d.). Africa Centre. Retrieved from http://www.africacentre.ca/about.php

Cummins J. (1986). Language proficiency and academic achievement. In J. Cummings (Ed.), *Bilingualism in education: Aspects of theory, research and practice,* (pp. 138–161). New York: Longman.

Derwing, T. M., Decorby, E., Ichikawa, J., & Jamieson, K. (1999). Some factors that affect the success of ESL high school students. *Canadian Modern Language Review, 55,* 532–547.

Derwing, T. M., & Krahn, H. (2008). Attracting and retaining immigrants outside the metropolis: Is the pie too small for everyone to have a piece? The case of Edmonton, Alberta. *Journal of International Migration and Integration, 9,* 359–380.

Dunn, W., Kirova, A., Cooley, M., & Ogilvie, G. (2007). Fostering intercultural competence in preservice teachers: Using infusion strategies in subject-area curriculum courses. *Prairie Metropolis Centre Working Paper Series,* WP05–06.

Edmonton Public School Board. (2009). *Annual education results report (2008–2009).* Edmonton, AB: Author.

Golberg, H., Paradis, J., & Crago, M. (2008). Lexical acquisition over time in minority L1 children learning English as a L2. *Applied Psycholinguistics, 29,* 1–25.

Hankivsky, O. (2008). *Cost estimates of dropping out of high school in Canada.* Ottawa, ON: Canadian Council on Learning.

Howard Research and Management Consulting. (2006). *Review of ESL K–12 program implementation in Alberta final report.* Calgary, AB: Howard Research and Management Consulting.

Khalema, N. E., & Ishiekwene, G. C. (2009, April). *Meeting the integration support needs of refugee youth: The role of community-based participatory partnerships.* Paper presented at the Prairie Metropolis Brown Bag Seminars, Edmonton, AB. Retrieved from http://pcerii.metropolis.net/frameset_e.html

Kirova, A. (2010, January). *Challenges and successes in the development of an intercultural early learning program for refugee children.* Paper presented at the Prairie Metropolis Centre Research Symposium, Edmonton, AB. Retrieved from http://pcerii.metropolis.net/frameset_e.html

Kirova, A., & Emme, M. (2008). Fotonovela as a research tool in image-based participatory research with immigrant children. *International Journal of Qualitative Methods, 7*(2), 35–56.

Krahn, H., & Taylor, A. (2005). Resilient teenagers: Explaining the high educational aspirations of visible-minority youth in Canada. *Journal of International Migration and Integration, 6,* 405–434.

Northern Alberta Alliance on Race Relations. (2004). *Equity in Edmonton schools: Research report.* Edmonton, AB: Author.

Rossiter, M. J., & Rossiter, K. R. (2009). Diamonds in the rough: Bridging gaps in supports for at-risk immigrant and refugee youth. *Journal of International Migration and Integration, 10,* 409–429.

Schmidt, C. (2009, October). *Supporting EAL immigrant youth and immigrant teachers in Manitoba.* Paper presented at the Prairie Metropolis Brown Bag Lunch Seminars, Edmonton, AB.

Toohey, K., & Beynon, J. (2005). Fighting structural and power: Two perspectives. *Curriculum Inquiry, 35*(4), 483–492.

Toohey, K., & Derwing, T. M. (2008). Hidden losses: How demographics can encourage incorrect assumptions about ESL high school students' success. *Alberta Journal of Educational Research, 54,* 178–193.

Watt, D., & Roessingh, H. (1994). ESL dropout: The myth of educational equity. *Alberta Journal of Educational Research, 40,* 283–296.

Watt, D., & Roessingh, H. (2001). The dynamics of ESL drop-out: Plus ça change . . . . *The Canadian Modern Language Review, 58,* 203–222.

Yohani, S. (2010). *Challenges and opportunities for educational cultural brokers in facilitating the school adaptation of refugee children.* Edmonton, AB: Prairie Metropolis Centre Working Paper Series. Retrieved from http://pcerii.metropolis.net/frameset_e.html

CHAPTER 6

SERVING THE NEEDS OF REFUGEE CHILDREN AND FAMILIES THROUGH A CULTURALLY APPROPRIATE LIAISON SERVICE

J. Lynn McBrien
University of South Florida

Jillian Ford
Kennesaw State University

ABSTRACT

Because refugee children account for a so small a percentage of the U.S. school-age population, there is a dearth of research that specifically addresses their needs, sometimes resulting in poor communications between refugee families and schools. Our mixed methods study focused on one urban refugee agency's liaison services designed to facilitate such communication. The program hired and trained refugee adults to serve as liaisons between school personnel and refugee families of their particular nationality and/or cultural background. Findings indicated both statistical significance and qualitative

Refugee and Immigrant Students, pages 107–126
Copyright © 2012 by Information Age Publishing

107

evidence that this community model makes a positive difference in the lives of refugee children and families, creating increased opportunities for school communications and partnerships.

Educational researchers in the United States have been slow to distinguish between students of voluntary immigrant families and refugee children. One reason may be that refugees account for a small percentage of the U.S. international population. The Office of Immigration Statistics (OIS, 2010) of the U.S. Department of Homeland Security, reported that in 2009, nearly 1,130,818 legal immigrants were admitted into the United States, but just 74,602 (6.6%) were refugees. Just under 527,000 refugees entered the United States between 2000 and 2010 (OIS, 2010). In 2009, 23,651 (38%) were defined as children.

Given that so small a percentage of foreign-born students are refugees and that refugees do share some characteristics with students of voluntary immigrant families, important studies on foreign-born students in the United States, such as the Children of Immigration Longitudinal Study (CILS; see Portes & Rumbaut, 2001), have subsumed refugees into the broader category of immigrant. As a result, many educators and educational policymakers have an incomplete understanding of the significant differences between the groups. We have spoken with numerous teachers who could not define a refugee, did not know the difference between refugees and other immigrants, and did not know which students in their classrooms were children of voluntary immigrants and which were refugees.

SIGNIFICANCE OF THE PROBLEM

Unfortunately for refugee students, this lack of information can cause misunderstanding and a reduction or lack of needed services through the school system. Other social services are also inadequate for refugee children when providers are unaware of their cultures or the circumstances that brought them to a new country. Even most agencies designed specifically for refugees concentrate their services on the adults, as they are the ones who must obtain jobs to provide food and housing for their families. Often the services for children are limited to insuring that they have the proper vaccines to register for school.

The current study examined multilayered services offered to refugee children and their parents at Refugee Family Services (RFS), a private refugee agency focusing on services needed after initial resettlement occurred. A highlight of the agency's services is the school liaison program. RFS hires and trains culturally appropriate liaison staff who create bridges of understanding between refugee families, school staff, and other community services. The research reported here took place between January 2006 and May 2007. Surveys and focus group protocols focused around the following research questions:

- How are parents involved with the RFS liaison program increasing involvement with their children and their schools?
- How has involvement with RFS affected teachers' and school administrators' attitudes towards refugee youth?
- What are outcomes of the RFS school liaison program?

Educators and policymakers do not currently have sufficient information regarding programs that can make a positive difference in the lives of refugee youth and their families. There are over 300 agencies scattered throughout the United States to help refugees with immediate resettlement needs, but few of them offer programs for refugee children. A search of the primary U.S. national clearinghouse for refugee youth and children's services, Bridging Refugee Youth and Children's Services (BRYCS, 2007), retrieved only 13 agency entries for "refugee children NOT immigrant." Of these services, three concentrated on mental health services, two were for preschool refugee children only, one was a two- to six-week transitional program only, one was only for refugee minors who were not accompanied by family, and one was targeted for African refugee children only. Thus, of the 13 listings for refugee children's programs, only five offered a combination of after-school tutoring, field trips, summer programs, and/or mentoring for refugee children from any country. The listing in the BRYCS clearinghouse may not be complete, but it does suggest the lack of comprehensive services available for refugee children and youth resettled in the United States.

REVIEW OF THE LITERATURE

As mentioned, refugee children and children of voluntary immigrants share numerous challenges. Usually they are faced with learning the language of their new country (though in the case of refugees, this may be the third or fourth language they have had to learn). They face the challenge of "code-switching"—taking on the culture of their new peers in school, and submitting to the culture of their parents or guardians at home. Again, for refugees, this may occur three or four times as they go from their native country to transition countries to a home of permanent resettlement. Because children tend to acculturate more readily than their parents, the disparate levels of acculturation between children and adults can be the cause of considerable friction (Portes & Rumbaut, 2001; Zhou, 2001).

Children's comparative ease with language acquisition over their parents' ability can also result in a problematic inversion of power in the home, especially when children must translate for their parents. Both immigrant and refugee children also tend to be victims of stereotypes, prejudice, and discrimination. Portes and Rumbaut (2001) found that discrimination was the greatest barrier to immigrant and refugee students' adaptation to a new country. McBrien (2009) found that refugee students frequently feel victimized by discrimination, with Muslim students indicating higher levels than non-Muslims.

The greatest difference between children of voluntary immigrants and refugees is the circumstances that bring them to a new country. In general, voluntary immigrants intentionally leave their country and choose a new home, often in hopes of bettering themselves economically. They tend to have time to plan for their move, and they may have time to prepare their children and to learn about the new culture and language, at least somewhat, prior to their departure. They often have relatives, friends, or an enclave awaiting their arrival.

Refugees, by definition, do not willingly choose to leave their countries. Rather, they depart reluctantly due to a "well-founded fear of being persecuted for reasons of race, religion, nationality, membership in a particular social group or political opinion" (UN High Commissioner for Refugees, 1951/1996, n.p.). Refugee children are likely to suffer trauma at one or more of their transitions (UNICEF, 2007). The three phases of refugee migration (pre-flight, flight, and post-flight) may cover the span of many years before a refugee is finally resettled. During pre-flight, they usually experience fear due to threats by an oppositional force, and they may experience violence to their homes, their family members, or to themselves (Boyden, de Berry, Feeny, & Hart,2002). In flight, children may be separated from family members. They may be forcefully taken to become child soldiers or sex slaves to insurgents. And in post-flight, refugees face issues of prejudice, discrimination, and acculturation, often multiple times before they find themselves in a place of permanent resettlement. Refugees may request a particular country for resettlement, but it is not guaranteed, and extended families are broken apart frequently by designated host countries. Facing multiple bureaucratic procedures as they try to procure a permanent home can cause refugees to become wary of authorities, as can discrimination faced in new surroundings. For example, if the UNHCR refers a refugee to apply for resettlement in the United States, applicants will undergo numerous interviews with Overseas Processing Entity staff working for the U.S. Department of State, followed by staff of the U.S. Department of Homeland Security (USRAP, 2010).

Refugee students are often lost in the turmoil of transition. Birman, Trickett, and Bacchus (2001) conducted a case study in Maryland with Somali refugees that found that these refugee students suffered alienation due to teasing, fighting with U.S. students, and misunderstandings that caused many of them to drop out. Mosselson (2006) found that refugee students would work to obtain high grades in order to reduce the attention being paid to them, even though they were in need of psychological counseling due to depression. A review of literature on refugee students in the United States (McBrien, 2005) found that these students are frequently challenged by issues of past trauma, current marginalization and rejection, discrimination, and lack of adult support. Another study by McBrien (2006) found that refugee youth in the United States may find themselves in situations of peer violence, domestic violence, teen pregnancy (for which families may want to perform honor killings), and situations involving the juvenile justice system.

This review does not include an extensive critique of liaison program studies because there is no such body of literature. Using key words "refugee (or immigrant)" and "school" and "liaison" in six databases (EBSCO, ERIC, JSTOR, Wilson Web, Sociological Abstracts, and the Web of Science) resulted in not one article focused on a liaison service for refugee (or even, more broadly, immigrant) families. Some authors made mention of a liaison officer serving all of the refugee/immigrant school population (Mendoza, 2008; Short, 2002). Hones and Cha (1999) authored a book about one Laotian refugee and evangelical preacher who also served as a liaison at an elementary school. In Perry's (1997) report on the Migrant Education Program, a paragraph is devoted to explaining that liaison personnel can assist migrants with school and social services, but there is no research on the effectiveness.

Rah, Choi, and Nguyen (2009) examined practices of three school districts in Wisconsin that were designed to increase Hmong refugee parent involvement. They reported that one of the school strategies was to create a bilingual liaison position. These staff members answered phone calls from Hmong parents (the researchers estimated that over 50% of the parents were illiterate), helped families with food and clothing needs, and offered workshops for Hmong parents to learn more about the U.S. education system and to discuss their concerns. In their conclusions, they noted that "bilingual liaisons were the primary resource in creating a zone of comfort for refugee parents to be actively involved in school" (Rah et al., 2009, p. 363), and they "encourage school leaders to examine ways in which parent liaisons may create spaces of authentic interaction between school and refugee communities beyond mere translation of words" (p. 362). Clearly, there is a lack of research on what may be critical services for refugee parents and their children to negotiate vastly different educational practices from their homelands. Thus, this chapter, focusing on an agency liaison service, is greatly needed for teachers and administrators to understand ways to help refugee students and families.

THEORETICAL FRAMEWORK AND SOCIAL CONTEXTS

Globalization theory provides a justification for the present study. As Suárez-Orozco and Qin-Hilliard (2004) stated, "difference is becoming increasingly normative" (p. 3) as a result of globalization and rapid migration of people. Countries receiving people from other cultures must learn to negotiate differences. Suárez-Orozco and Qin-Hilliard (2004) recognized that educators in these countries "must develop an agenda to facilitate the incorporation of growing numbers of immigrant children worldwide and develop curricular and pedagogical programs to impart the cross-cultural skills children will need to thrive in their historical moment and emerge as agents of change to combat worldwide inequalities" (p. 16).

These researchers also note that globalization can generate anxiety about one's cultural placement, identity, and social practices. Because refugee youth and their families tend to be quickly immersed into two or more new geographical and cultural contexts during their flight and post-flight, they are disadvantaged when they do not have cultural brokers to help them negotiate both new contexts and the additional burden of healing from physical and psychological wounds resulting from the refugee experience. Additionally, refugee students need help to navigate complex cultural and academic contexts in order to build a positive identity and succeed in their new environment.

We located our study at a private refugee agency, Refugee Family Services (RFS), in the southeastern United States. This area was chosen as a relocation site for refugees during the time of the Vietnam War, due to low-cost housing and easy access to public transportation. It has remained the top resettlement site in the state; for instance, between 2003 and 2007, the county in which RFS is located resettled 5,500 refugees. Behind Miami, it is the second largest relocation site in the southeastern United States. Refugee populations in the schools range up to 32% (RFS, 2008). In 2008, RFS served 43 schools within a 10-mile radius of its headquarters (the schools with the highest refugee populations) and 24 schools 10–35 miles away from the RFS Center. Given budget cuts and some staff reductions, liaison staff were stretched to serve all of these schools. However, new schools could apply for assistance. RFS tried to help everyone who applied, but there were often waiting lists due to a limited budget and increasing needs. During the time of this study, RFS moved its offices approximately five miles to accommodate its growing needs. Both sites were near apartment complexes that housed many of the refugee families and the children's schools, making it easy for liaison staff to make home and school visits. Services provided by RFS included an after-school tutoring program, summer camp, individual tutoring, at-risk services, the liaison program, English lessons for adults, job counseling, and cultural information for the community and refugee families.

Our study focused on the key component of RFS, specifically, its school liaison program, started in the 1990s. Though there are no gender restrictions in hiring, all the liaison staff were women, and they represented the countries from which this US state was receiving refugees: Somalia, Sudan, Afghanistan, Iraq, Bosnia, Vietnam, and Ethiopia. Altogether, staff at RFS spoke 25 languages in addition to English. An important feature of the program was that the liaison staff were culturally and/or nationally matched to their clients. As a result, their refugee clients spoke the same language and shared similar experiences in their journeys to the United States. RFS was also sensitive to the fact that same nation does not necessarily mean same culture. For example, their program manual (RFS, 2008) states:

> Similar language does not necessarily mean similar understanding of a specific refugee community. If School Liaisons are from a region or country where citizens have been divided by tribe, religion, class, or ethnicity—and they are paired with clients from a similar area who belong to the "other" group—clients can feel uncomfortable, and sometimes threatened. (p. 27)

Hiring competencies for refugee liaison staff required that they be highly knowledgeable of the refugee population they served as well as being generally sensitive to all cultural backgrounds, able to interpret and translate between the refugee community language and English, write and speak well in English, demonstrate leadership and management skills, advocate for their community and for children, and exhibit strong interpersonal skills. Preferred competencies included experience with the American school system and prior work with refugee clients. Their primary goals were to increase parent involvement to help refugee children in schools and to educate school personnel about refugee experiences and needs. Secondarily, liaison staff worked as advocates regarding refugee policies, and they referred parents and students to appropriate external resources.

In orientation sessions, liaison staff explained to refugee parents what they could expect from U.S. schools, how they could create a home environment that supported learning, why to enroll their children in outside supports such as the RFS tutoring program and summer camp, how to understand specialized meetings at school, and why they needed to comply with U.S. laws regarding child abuse and neglect, as U.S. conceptions often differ from their own cultural dispositions. Liaison staff helped parents understand bus schedules, lunch programs, parent-teacher meetings, and report cards. They provided interpretation services for school meetings, social work, and doctor appointments. They also provided cultural presentations to school staff and social service providers to help them better serve refugee clients.

As explained below, there were several positive outcomes. Both refugee families and community members were better informed, and refugee students benefited academically and socially from programs, resulting in more positive identities and actions. Ultimately, the impact to the community was positive, in terms of better-adjusted refugee families who could help their children and native teachers who were more knowledgeable and empathetic to newcomer refugee youth and their families.

GOALS OF THE STUDY

The present study examined ways in which the liaison program for refugee families helped to overcome cultural barriers and misunderstandings involving school expectations. This study followed up on a previous two-year study in which McBrien (2009) examined the relationship between discrimination by U.S. students and teachers and academic motivation of 18 female adolescent refugees attending programs at RFS. Using interviews and observations, McBrien concluded that the girls encountered frequent instances of prejudice and discrimination, which caused them a short-term drop in academic motivation. However, in the long-term, nearly all of the participants maintained a GPA above 3.0 and had plans to attend college. Since the time of that study, at least nine have graduated and gone on to a university or community college. These somewhat surprising findings drew the researcher to explore a second question: What was it about the contexts of these refugee girls that resulted in such positive outcomes, in spite of discrimination?

Among several factors, one reason the participants gave for maintaining high motivation was the support they received through the programs at the refugee agency. Several of the young women progressed from being served there to working as volunteers helping younger refugee students after school and during summer camp. The girls also formed bonds with refugee staff. The current study more closely examines the agency programs and the attitudes of refugee students, parents, and teachers, primarily by use of survey instruments, but also by considering qualitative statements included by those who completed the surveys.

METHODS

The study took place over a two-year period and involved a combination of qualitative and quantitative approaches. A mixed methods study was important in addressing the three research questions. Both the agency and the researchers wanted to survey all new clients to gain a baseline understanding of their practices and challenges with their children's education, against which to measure their practices and concerns after working with liaison staff for a year. This was best accomplished with a Likert scale instrument developed by researchers and agency staff. This survey also addresses Q1 and Q2 of our research. Question 3, outcomes of the liaison program, was best addressed by open-ended interviews and focus groups among those targeted by the program: parents, teachers, and students.

Quantitative Methods

Survey instruments were created by the use of focus groups incorporating refugee liaisons, youth staff, and a teacher focus group. McBrien created draft parent surveys based on discussions with the RFS director and looking at funded grant proposals that indicated goals of the various programs. Focus groups with refugee liaison staff (who were refugee parents as well) from numerous countries examined the parent survey draft and made suggestions for changes that could be understood by refugee parents from diverse cultures. Thus, validity was increased by including refugees as collaborators on the survey creation. After two rounds of edits, the liaison staff translated the parent surveys into their native language so they had a standard protocol to ask each of their clients.

Youth staff provided similar feedback for the children's survey, and it was subsequently tested by three refugee youth who did not participate in the actual research sample. Children completed a one-time survey that measured beliefs, behaviors, and estimates of their academic competencies. Questions were taken from the Child Development Supplement (CDS–II) of the Panel Study of Income Dynamics (PSID) and from self-efficacy surveys.

Ultimately, however, the children's measurements were eliminated from the study. The original intent with children was to have them complete the same survey twice over a one-year time period in order to learn about their potential changes in attitudes and behaviors as a result of working with refugee liaisons and the children's programs. The second survey attempt was abandoned. Most children's answers from the first survey tended towards positive answers. Limitations arose regarding children's desire to please and their potential wariness towards authority figures or what they may have perceived as a "test." Because answers already tended towards highly positive responses, a repeated sample seemed unlikely to produce useful results that could indicate change.

The school personnel survey for teachers, administrators, and school counselors was critiqued by refugee staff and a focus group of middle and high school teachers, and it was revised based on their suggestions. Mc-Brien trained liaisons and refugee youth staff to administer the surveys. Ford administered the school personnel surveys.

A goal was to survey all of the parents and students who were new to RFS programs at the time of the study. The actual sample size was 65% of the students and 90% of the parents, determined by those who signed and returned informed consent forms. A beginning total of 87 parent surveys were conducted, with a repeated sample of 41 approximately one year after the initial survey round was conducted, to allow the parents time to work with liaisons. Much of the reduction in the second round of surveys was due to two reasons: First, the agency had to physically relocate five miles from its initial site. Although five miles may not seem far, it created considerable changes in the clients, because many refugees do not have their own transportation. Secondly, many of the families had moved out of the service area over the year between initial and repeated surveys.

Twenty-six parents who completed the surveys participated in focus groups. Twenty-eight school personnel (including four principals and five counselors) completed surveys that included both quantitative and qualitative questions. Research conducted on RFS's special services for at-risk refugee youth is discussed in a separate publication (McBrien, 2006), as are more detailed refugee mothers' discussions (McBrien, in press).

Qualitative Methods

To gain contextual information and rich description regarding the participants' attitudes towards RFS programs, and the liaison program in particular, we made use of focus groups and open-ended short answer survey questions. We conducted focus groups with adult participants who were selected at the recommendation of RFS staff and liaisons. In the spring of 2007, we conducted three focus groups of refugee parents: one group of Vietnamese refugees (seven women and one man), one Somali group (seven women one man), and one group of eight Iranian women and two Afghani women. The interview protocol included questions about the parents' backgrounds, education, and experiences prior to arriving in the U.S.; aid and services they received when they arrived in the U.S.; specific experiences with their U.S. communities and their children's schools; and their relationships and experiences with RFS and the liaisons to whom they were assigned. Interpreters were used in each session to translate for the interviewers. Each participant was given $10 for participating; however, two would not take the money, saying they were happy to have their voices heard. Because of the richness of the data and themes that emerged, we will report the findings from parent focus groups in a separate article (Mc-Brien, in press).

Qualitative data gained from teachers and school counselors were included as short written answers provided at the end of quantitative survey instruments. All focus groups, comprised of parents and interpreters (often a liaison), were tape recorded and transcribed. The researchers coded separately and discussed codes to reach inter-rater reliability. We looked for themes and patterns (Miles & Huberman, 1994) that would address our research questions. However, we were also mindful of Strauss and Corbin's (1990) open-ended coding approach, and we allowed additional themes to emerge.

We will begin the results section by providing the quantitative results, followed by qualitative information.

RESULTS

As mentioned, surveys were administered twice over a one-year time period to refugee parents to learn about changes of behavior over time as the parents worked with refugee liaisons. Teachers completed a one-time survey with statements about their understanding, attitudes, and behaviors with refugee students and families as a result of their work with refugee liaisons. We will address each group separately.

Parents

The parent survey consisted of 17 items, all using a 5-point Likert scale, with 5 = always, 4 = usually, 3 = sometimes, 2 = rarely, and 1 = never. A two-way within-subjects analysis of variance was conducted to evaluate the effects of participating in the liaison program with changes in refugee parent behavior that promote improved school strategies. The within-subjects factors were behaviors with two levels (prior to working with refugee liaisons and one year after working with the liaisons). Eleven of the 17 survey items demonstrated statistical significance over the one-year time period. An examination of Table 6.1 indicates that significant interactions between liaison interventions over time and behavior were found in responses to Questions 1, 2, 4, 6, 7, 8, 9, 10, 11, and 15, with effect sizes ranging from small (Questions 1, 4, 6, 7, 8, 9, 11, and 14) to moderate (Questions 2, 10, and 15).

TABLE 6.1 Parent Survey

Questions	Mean (1)	Mean (2)	F	d(f)	p	Partial eta squared
1. When my child is well, my child attends school.	4.32	4.84	5.735	1, 36	.022	.137
2. I contact the school when my child stays home due to illness.	3.2	4.11	37.197	1, 34	.000	.522
3. I attend parent–teacher conferences.	2.7	2.63	3.603	1, 34	.066	.096
4. I understand information my child brings home from school.	2.65	3.24	7.432	1, 33	.01	.184
5. I know how to get help understanding information from school when I do not understand it.	3.57	3.69	2.53	1, 34	.619	.007
6. I make sure my child attends an after-school program if enrolled.	2.96	1.89	7.364	1, 27	.011	.214
7. I ask my child about his/her school day.	3.18	3.76	5.23	1, 33	.029	.137
8. I make sure my child has time and space to do homework.	3.71	4.4	20.315	1, 34	.000	.13
9. I check to see if my child has done his/her schoolwork.	3.38	3.85	4.923	1, 33	.033	.13
10. I read with my child (or my child reads to me).	1.91	3.14	25.597	1, 34	.000	.43
11. My child attended summer camp or summer school last year.	1.12	2.18	12.109	1, 33	.001	.268
12. I think my child spends too much time watching TV or playing video games.	3.0	3.32	2.685	1, 37	.11	.068
13. I make sure my child gets at least 8 hours of sleep at night.	4.24	4.05	1.144	1, 36	.292	.031
14. I call the RFS caseworker when my child needs help with school work.	2.5	3.24	8.841	1, 33	.005	.211
15. I call the RFS caseworker when other children are hurting my child at school or home.	2.15	3.41	38.497	1, 33	.000	.538
16. I am happy with my child's behavior at school.	3.89	3.82	.117	1, 37	.734	.003
17. I am happy with my child's behavior at home.	3.92	4.05	.802	1, 37	.376	.021

School Personnel

The school personnel survey consisted of 10 items, or five paired questions, using a 5-point Likert scale. This survey was different in that it included five sets of statements about before and after working with RFS liaisons and staff (something we determined we could not do with parent surveys due to either cultural or developmental considerations). The questions were developed based on the goals of RFS's liaison services to assist with communications between refugee families and schools. Survey questions evaluated whether school personnel's knowledge and beliefs about refugee students changed after they worked with RFS liaison staff. Five specific variables were tested in the context of (1) before working with RFS liaison staff and (2) since working with RFS staff, as can be seen in Table 6.2.

A two-way within-subjects analysis of variance was conducted to evaluate the effects of working with RFS liaisons with changes in school personnel's attitudes, beliefs, and behaviors in school. The within-subjects factors were behaviors with two levels (prior to working with refugee liaisons and after working with the liaisons). All five of the measures demonstrated statistical significance, as can be seen in Table 6.2. The effect size was small for pairs 3 & 4, 7 & 8, and 9 & 10, and moderate for pairs 1 & 2 and 5 & 6.

School Personnel Comments

Major themes could be categorized into two patterns: school personnel's impressions of the service itself (31 comments), and specific behaviors related to the liaison service (43 comments). Regarding impressions, remarks referred to positive attitudes of the liaison staff and their willingness to help (described by six participants), the "invaluable service" they provided (described by 14), and thanks (mentioned by eight respondents). For instance, one school counselor wrote,

> RFS's liaison staff is an invaluable resource for me. They are effective, committed, and caring. They have made tremendous differences in the lives of families whose students attend our school. Our students and their families are in good hands when RFS is involved, and we can have confidence that those students will succeed in school. Thank you for providing this wonderful service to our refugee community!

Other comments included, "I don't know what we would do without them," "the service you offer to our school is priceless," and "they [RFS liaison staff] are always courteous and go out of their way to be helpful." Two teachers specifically mentioned names of liaison staff and the excellent work they were doing. This positive regard for the liaison providers and their services contributes to the overall school environment for refugee students.

TABLE 6.2 Survey for Teachers, School Counselors

	Mean (1)	Mean (2)	F	d(f)	p	Partial eta squared
1. Before working with RFS, I was well-informed about refugees.	2.52		31.638	1, 26	.000	.549
2. Since working with RFS, I am well-informed about refugees.		3.78				
3. Before working with RFS, I made a conscious effort to make my classroom friendly for refugee students.	3.79		11.441	1, 27	.002	.298
4. Since working with RFS, I make a conscious attempt to make my classroom friendly for refugee students.		4.32				
5. Before working with RFS, I had successful ways of working with refugee parents.	2.67		25.852	1, 26	.000	.499
6. Since working with RFS, I have successful ways of working with refugee parents.		3.96				
7. Before working with RFS, I expected refugee students to graduate from high school.	3.65		9.848	1, 25	.004	.283
8. Since working with RFS, I expect refugee students to graduate from high school.		4.15				
9. Before working with RFS, I expected refugee students to attend college or a technical school.	3.65		11.04	1, 26	.003	.298
10. Since working with RFS, I expect refugee students to attend college or a technical school.		3.78				

Specific behaviors described involved partnerships between schools and parents and between parents and liaison staff (described by 13 participants), increased parent involvement (described by eight), and improved student performance (described by eight participants). The following quotes are representative of the responses:

> The administrators, staff and faculty at _____ School feel very fortunate to have the support and assistance of RFS. The assistance provided by RFS staff has helped tremendously increased parental involvement, student achievement and overall a better partnership between parents, community, and school. We hope for continued support of the RFS staff. (a principal)

The principal's comment suggests exactly the goal of the liaison program: a family/school/community partnership that results in increased refugee parent involvement and student success.

The next quote from a special education teacher also suggests ways in which interventions by liaison staff increased opportunities for success:

> They have provided more than interpretation support. They have helped the family complete school documents and get necessary medical documentation completed. I especially like the way the same person continues to work with the family; therefore, a level of trust is developed. I consider them an invaluable asset to our community. (special education teacher)

In these responses, school personnel note that the specific services offered have increased family involvement and partnerships. They also indicate the importance of RFS liaison staff for their work at school and a desire for these services to continue. In fact, the only negative comments addressed an absence or reduction of involvement with RFS. Eight comments came from personnel at one school in which five of the staff perceived a reduction in their contact with RFS. Each of these teachers expressed concern about the reduced partnership. The following quote is representative:

> At one time our school was very involved with RFS and we had a great deal of success with our refugee families. It appears that the services are not as available and this has been detrimental to our refugee children and families in relationship to school. You do a wonderful job and I have appreciated your involvement with our school.

Two teachers suggested that the reduction in services was a result of RFS's relocation, and they expressed regret about the move. Two other teachers indicated that they were not aware of RFS but that they would like to learn about the services.

The teachers who specifically mentioned liaison staff they worked with also described specific ways in which these liaison personnel facilitated their teaching:

> "Linda" is a wonderful addition to your program. She has helped my families communicate with school. My students have been able to complete projects that required parent support due to Linda's contact with them. My Spanish speaking parents are more involved in school activities because Linda has made information available to them.

The comment about Linda alludes to the value of hiring liaison staff who are culturally similar to the clients they serve. Because Linda was a native Spanish speaker, she was able to engage the Cuban and Colombian refugees with whom she worked.

> Our ability to work successfully with refugee children and parents has completely changed since I began working with "Halwa." She has been invaluable in our work with parents and children. Having her assist with our program has enabled us to serve our refugee families in the same ways that we do for our non-refugee population. I believe that this has greatly enhanced the education of our students. Our refugee families were completely underserved before we became aware of RFS.

The latter quote suggests that the liaison service can bring the level of communication with refugee families on par with non-refugee families. Since communication is so important between schools and families and language/cultural barriers can greatly diminish communications, this teacher's observation is an important recognition of what a well-tailored service can make possible for supporting schools and refugee families.

DISCUSSION

This study was undertaken to discover whether or not a unique refugee liaison program, in which refugee parents themselves were trained to become cultural brokers for other refugees from their own nations and/or cultures, was successful in increasing refugee parent involvement with schools and with strategies for helping their children succeed. Additionally, the study sought to determine whether or not the liaison program made a difference in teacher attitudes, beliefs, and behaviors; and whether it aided refugee families involved with the RFS liaison program.

Data gathered from parent and teacher surveys indicated significant positive changes in attitudes, beliefs, and behaviors as a result of working with the RFS liaison program. Those statements indicating clear positive changes in refugee parents included understanding information from the school, insuring children's attendance at an after-school program, providing time and space for children's homework, children's attendance at summer camp, and contacting the liaison provider when children needed help at school or as a result of being hurt or teased at school or in the home environment. All of these measures are goals of the liaison program to help increase children's potential for academic success. They also indicate that the liaison service is welcomed by both the school and refugee communities.

It is also important to note those areas where there was not significant improvement. Areas in which liaison staff might provide more assistance included attendance at parent–teacher conferences and the perception that the children are watching too much TV or playing too many video games. Other questions may have had other factors affecting the results. For instance, in the first round of surveys, parents already had a high incidence of believing their children received adequate sleep (statement 13), so there was not much opportunity for improvement at a statistically significant level. The same is the case with the last two items, parents' satisfaction with their children's behavior at school and at home. Statement 5, about knowing how to get help understanding information from school, could have been skewed by the numbers of parents who answered the preceding statement (I understand information from school) at a high level. Overall, the quantitative portion of the liaison evaluation with refugee parents indicates the program's success.

Teachers who worked with RFS liaison staff were more likely to do the following: (1) report that their knowledge of working with refugees increased, (2) engage in more conscious attempts to make their schools refugee-friendly, (3) devise more successful ways of working with refugee parents, and (4) exhibit higher expectations about both the graduation rates of refugee students and the chances of refugee students attending college or technical schools. Every teacher respondent included additional qualitative comments that offered high praise for the work of RFS and its liaison staff.

The Ruddie Memorial Youth Foundation Grant enabled a thorough evaluation of the RFS liaison program to determine the value of the service to refugee clients. The research indicates a remarkably successful program worthy of being detailed for replication in other locations. Strongest results came from teacher surveys, indicating a transformation in school staff understanding, awareness, and positive attitudes as a result of working with RFS liaisons. Because there is little education and professional development to help U.S natives understand profound differences between refugees and other immigrants, services such as those provided by RFS could meet a critical need for information in order to help refugee students and families thrive. Repeated measures from the parent survey indicated more positive practices by parents to support their children's academic needs after they had an additional year of liaison support. A major limitation of the study and, therefore, caution concerning generalizing results is indicated by the small size of the sample.

Because of the success in providing assistance and education not only to the refugee community but also to local schools and social assistance agencies, programs such as the RFS liaison program need to be strengthened with greater funding in order to extend their services. One serious shortcoming in governmental funding is that it allows agencies such as RFS to provide assistance only to those refugees who have been in the United States for five years or less. The agency must rely on private funding sources to help those who have been here longer. Thirty of the original parents, and 13 out of 41 who completed the repeated surveys, had lived in the United States for over five years. It is clear that many refugee families and their children need support beyond the artificial marker of five years.

Programs such as the RFS Liaison Program need to be replicated in areas throughout the United States where there are resettled refugees. California, Minnesota, Florida, Texas, Washington, New York, Arizona, Georgia, Wisconsin, and Ohio are the top 10 states for refugee resettlement, at 63% of the total. Still, over one-third are settling in the remaining states. Even the top ten often lack services such as those provided by RFS.

School districts that do not have a resource such as RFS can increase their success with refugee students and families by considering the following recommendations suggested by this research. They can contact local agencies serving refugee families and request to work with adult refugees who speak English and who are interested in working with schools to provide liaison services. They can involve these refugee adults to create workshops to help school personnel better understand the refugee families' cultures and challenges in their new environment. They can also invite refugee adults to speak in classrooms in order to educate U.S. students about the refugee students among them. Such small steps can go far in reducing misunderstandings and increasing expectations for refugee students.

ACKNOWLEDGEMENTS

This study was generously funded by a grant from the Ruddie Memorial Youth Foundation. We also want to acknowledge the staff at RFS, without whose help this study could not have occurred.

REFERENCES

Birman, D., Trickett, E. J., & Bacchus, N. (2001). *Somali refuge youth in Maryland: A needs assessment.* Maryland Office for New Americans, Maryland Department of Human Resources. Retrieved from http://63.236.98.116/mona/pdf/somali.pdf

Boyden, J., de Berry, J., Feeny, T., & Hart, J. (2002). *Children affected by conflict in South Asia: A review of trends and issues identified through secondary research.* Refugee Studies Center, RSC Working Paper No. 7, University of Oxford. Retrieved from http://www.rsc.ox.ac.uk/PDFs/workingpaper7.pdf

Bridging Refugee Youth and Children's Services. (2007). *Clearinghouse.* Retrieved from http://www.brycs.org/brycs_clearinghouse.htm

Hones, D. F., & Cha, C. S. (1999). *Educating new Americans: Immigrant lives and learning.* Mahwah, NJ: Erlbaum.

McBrien, J. L. (2005). Educational needs and barriers for refugee students in the United States: A review of the literature. *Review of Educational Research, 75,* 329–364.

McBrien, J. L. (2006). Serving the needs of at-risk refugee youth: A program evaluation. *Journal of School Public Relations, 27,* 326–341.

McBrien, J. L. (2009). Beyond survival: School-related experiences of adolescent refugee girls in the United States and their relationship to motivation and academic success. In G. Wiggan & C Hutchison (Eds.), *Global issues in education: Pedagogy, policy, school practices and the minority experience* (pp. 294–330). Lanham, MD: Rowman & Littlefield.

McBrien, J. L. (2011). The importance of context: Vietnamese, Somali, and Iranian refugee parents discuss their resettled lives and school involvement in the United States. *Compare, 41*(1), 75–90.

Mendoza, V. P. (2008). Fostering an inclusive environment. *Diverse Issues in Higher Education, 25*(8), 9.

Miles, M. B., & Huberman, A. M. (1994). *Qualitative data analysis: An expanded sourcebook* (2nd ed.). Thousand Oaks, CA: Sage.

Mosselson, J. (2006). *Roots & routes: Bosnian adolescent refugees in New York City.* New York, NY: Peter Lang.

Office of Immigration Statistics, U.S. Department of Homeland Security. (2010). *2010 yearbook of immigration statistics.* Retrieved from http://www.uscis.gov/graphics/shared/aboutus/statistics/2003Yearbook.pdf

Perry, J. D. (1997). *Migrant education: Thirty years of success, but challenges remain.* New England Desegregation Assistance Center for Equity in Education, Brown University. U.S. Department of Education (DED #5004D3006).

Portes, A., & Rumbaut, R. G. (2001). *Legacies: The story of the immigrant second generation.* Berkeley, CA: University of California Press.

Rah, Y., Choi, S., & Nguyen, T. S. (2009). Building bridges between refugee parents and schools. *International Journal of Leadership in Education, 12*(4), 247–365.

Refugee Family Services. (2008). *School liaison program manual.* Stone Mountain, GA: Author.

Short, D. J. (2002). Newcomer programs: An educational alternative for secondary immigrant students. *Education and Urban Society, 34*(2), 173–198.

Strauss, A., & Corbin, J. (1990). *Basics of qualitative research: Grounded theory procedures and techniques.* London, UK: Sage.

Suárez-Orozco, M. M., & Qin-Hilliard, D. B. (2004). Globalization: Culture and education in the new millennium. In M. M. Suárez-Orozco & D. B. Hilliard (Eds.), *Globalization: Culture and education in the new millennium* (pp. 1–37). Berkeley, CA: University of California Press.

United Nations High Commissioner for Refugees. (1951/1996). *Convention and protocol: Relating to the status of refugees.* Retrieved from http://www.unhcr.ch/html/menu3/b/91.htm and http://www.unhcr.ch/html/menu3/b/93.htm

UNICEF. (2007). *Will you listen? Young voices from conflict zones.* Co-conveners of the Machel Study, Children and conflict in a changing world. Paris, France: Author.

United States Refugee Assistance Program (USRAP). (2010). Information sheet: Refugee resettlement in the United States. Retrieved from http://www.egypt.iom.int/Doc/Attachment%202010-06%20Final%20USRAP%20information%20sheet%20April%2030%20%282%29.pdf

Zhou, M. (2001). Straddling different worlds: The acculturation of Vietnamese refugee children. In R. G. Rumbaut & A. Portes (Eds.), *Ethnicities: Children of immigrants in America* (pp. 187–227). Berkeley, CA: University of California Press.

CHAPTER 7

SCHOOLS AT THE CROSSROADS OF COMPETING EXPECTATIONS

Linda Silka
University of Maine

ABSTRACT

Schools are at the crossroads of competing expectations about their core duties and responsibilities. Educational systems are on the frontlines of demographic changes as well, having to balance multiple and competing demands on them. Among all community systems, the schools are often the first to be affected by a swelling of the ranks of refugees and immigrants. Furthermore, although the ostensible mission of schools is to deliver education, they are often assigned a much larger role in their community: to prepare immigrant children and their families to live and work in the country they have entered and in some way accommodate to its culture. This chapter uses a midsized community in the United States to explore the issues that schools around the globe are facing as they wrestle with the dual roles imposed upon them. The chapter ends with a call for a focus on how schools can better integrate and advance their dual roles of educator and acculturator, providing education to all children as well as promoting social inclusion of immigrant youth and their families.

Refugee and Immigrant Students, pages 127–142
Copyright © 2012 by Information Age Publishing
127

Educational systems are on the frontlines of demographic change. Among all community systems, the schools are often the first to be affected by a swelling of the ranks of refugees and immigrants. Although the ostensible mission of schools is to deliver education, they are often assigned a much larger role by their communities: Schools are expected not merely to educate immigrant children but also to prepare them and their families to participate actively in the daily life and culture[1] of their adopted country. Young people are expected to come out of school knowing certain basics about the version of U.S. culture that is dominant in the region where they live. This dominant culture defines which behaviors are appropriate, how differences are settled, what rights people have, and how people can contribute responsibly in their communities. For the schools, ensuring that students are prepared with these skills is a very different proposition from ensuring that students know how to read, write, and do arithmetic. Yet both forms of knowledge are essential: Schools must support both academic and broader learning. No attempt to think about immigrants and schools can be successful without considering how to integrate both academic and cultural knowledge to ensure equity for immigrant students.

The tasks of both educating immigrant students and preparing them to be part of their new culture are confronting schools with daunting new challenges. Schools often have students from many different immigrant backgrounds, and the standardized high-stakes testing now in place makes it difficult to customize education in ways that are responsive to wide differences in the cultural backgrounds of incoming students. While it has always been assumed that schools transmit the dominant culture, the mantle of providing acculturation sits uneasily on the shoulders of educators. Conflicts between these two roles lie at the heart of many of the difficulties schools now struggle with as the demographics of their student bodies are transformed.

Too often the problems schools face have been considered only at the level of abstract statistical snapshots. From such a "three miles up" perspective, the everyday experiences of schools in immigrant communities flatten out and seem unexceptional. If the complex mixing of education and culture is to be understood in ways that will lead to solutions, this interweaving needs to be examined at close range. This chapter will illustrate the complexities that schools face through an examination of a midsized community in Massachusetts in the United States. This context is particularly appropriate for bringing into focus many of the challenges that communities in the U.S. are facing as they attempt to come to terms with these competing roles. This community, Lowell, Massachusetts, is now home to refugee children from many countries with cultures that differ greatly from that of the United States. Many of these youth have experienced interrupted educations and most have experienced educational systems in which the role of parents was different from parents' roles in the U.S. or, in important ways, was sharply constrained. Over the last decade, the schools in Lowell have invested in local, place-based partnerships to strengthen education while remaining attentive to the culture from which students come. Researchers and activists are increasingly focusing their attention on developing programs and practices that are "place-based" in the sense that they draw from and fit the local context. This is in contrast to a "best practice" or generic approach that assumes that one size fits all. Information on place-based approaches can be found in Schneekloth and Shibley (1995) or at www.promiseofplace.org.

The partnerships in Lowell involve students in learning the skills they need to succeed in the new culture in which they find themselves. The combination of problems they represent and the solutions they require are highly instructive.

The chapter first presents a brief overview of the growth of immigrant populations and their impact on local systems such as schools. This overview is followed by a critical examination of one city's encounters with and approaches to these competing expectations as the schools work to improve educational attainment of all students regardless of their past educational experiences. The chapter concludes by considering the questions that are raised by this example in relation to how the integration of the dual roles of educator and acculturator can be achieved without sacrificing equity or shortchanging either of these crucial roles.

THE GROWING NUMBERS OF IMMIGRANTS AND THEIR IMPACT ON COMMUNITIES

Many countries and regions, including the United States, Canada, Europe, and Australia, are undergoing rapid demographic changes with the arrival of large numbers of immigrants and refugees (Cornelius, Tsuda, Martin, & Hollifield, 2004). Consider the United States, for example: during the 1990s the immigrant population grew by more than 50% (Singer, 2004). Since 1970, the number of immigrants living in the U.S. has more than tripled, from 9.6 million to 28.4 million (Camarota, 2001). Moreover, over 70% of the annual population increase is now attributable to growth in immigrant populations, whether from newcomers or from the expansion of existing immigrant populations (Bean & Stevens, 2003).

The impact of these changes is being felt most dramatically at the local level (Zuniga & Hernandez-Leon, 2005). To a large extent the actions that people take—immigrants and non-immigrants alike—occur in local communities and are therefore place-based (Hamin, Geigis, & Silka, 2007; Portes & Rumbaut, 2006; Waldinger, 2001). Most people carry out their daily activities as part of community systems: Children are educated there, families seek their health care there, and police and law enforcement operate there. The housing, parks, and neighborhoods where people carry out their daily routines are all in the community, as are the public transportation people use and the jobs that immigrants fill (Grey, 2000; Santiago, Jennings, & Carrion, 2005; Silka & Tip, 1994).

These systems are the locations where the presence of new immigrants is profoundly felt and where those working in these systems are confronted—often on an almost daily basis—with the limits of approaches that were successful in the past (Iowa State, 2001; Turcotte & Silka, 2007). Local health centers have been overwhelmed with different diseases and shifting expectations about health care. Law enforcement agencies have had to reevaluate many of their practices so that they can ensure that all newcomers have equal access to the law. Furthermore, local schools have been especially influenced by these changing demographics (Darder, 1995; Portes & Rumbaut, 2006). New immigrant youth entering a local school system might come from many different educational systems (or sometimes no education system at all) and might speak any of dozens of different languages. Immigrant students enter schools that hold very clear expectations for their students: The young people are expected to respond to the educational opportunities in particular and prescribed ways. Expectations also exist for their parents: It is widely assumed that the parents will be knowledgeable about their responsibilities for encouraging their children and for interacting with their children's teachers.

It is within these various local systems that community leaders struggle to find ways to adapt their practices. All of this has proved challenging for schools. If refugees come from war-torn countries, the parents may have had interrupted educations themselves and may be ill-equipped to enter into the educational "contract" set out for them by schools. Or, the parents may not speak English or be unable to read the messages that are sent home. Parents may then need to rely on their children to translate or interpret messages or information about school practices. Parents may come from traditions in which it was deemed inappropriate for an "uneducated" parent to offer an opinion to the child's teacher on educational practices. In short, local schools feel the impact of immigrant youth coming into the system, and schools are places where immigrant families are made acutely aware of the extent to which they differ from other parents who grew up within the system (Kiang, 1992, 2006; Rumbaut & Kenji, 1988; Suarez-Orozco & Suarez-Orozco, 2002).

To fully understand the complex interweaving of education and culture at the community level—both in terms of the challenges and possible solutions that can be found to them—it is useful to examine one community's experience with and attempts to meet the needs of a highly diverse and ever changing student population. The chapter considers the immigrant city of Lowell, Massachusetts and how this city illuminates responses to these challenges through attempts to expand approaches to education by building on local resources and indigenous experiences.

THE FORM THAT COMPETING PRIORITIES TAKE: A CONSIDERATION OF ONE CITY'S PLACE-BASED INTERVENTIONS

Lowell, Massachusetts, a working class former mill town located thirty miles north of Boston in the Merrimack River Valley, has experienced a rapid influx of new immigrants and refugees. According to the most recent census, one third of Lowell's population of 105,000 is composed of immigrants and refugees. Cambodian refugees surviving the Khmer Rouge holocaust are among those who have come to Lowell seeking to create new lives. Cambodians now represent over a quarter of Lowell's population, and Lowell's Cambodian community is the second largest in the United States and the third largest in the world. The diversity of Lowell goes well beyond the Cambodian community: There are growing Brazilian, Columbian, Dominican, Laotian, and Puerto Rican communities, and every African country is now represented among the estimated 6,000 African immigrants and refugees living in Lowell.

As a result of the demographic changes, Lowell's high school has become a high school in which over half of the students are the children of immigrants or are immigrants themselves. In all, 29% of the young people in Lowell are from Asian immigrant families, and 21% are from Latino immigrant families. Furthermore, these school numbers are far from static: Every week the Lowell School system's Parent Information Center places children from newly arrived immigrant families in Lowell's schools.

In the face of this latest wave of migration to Lowell, the local schools have struggled to adapt and be responsive to the needs of newcomers. Early in the 1980s, lawsuits were filed against the school system because classes for new immigrant children were sometimes relegated to substandard conditions such as in school basements. Immigrant teachers with credentials from their home countries found themselves losing their temporary American teaching positions because they were unable to pass licensure tests. In addition, standard bilingual education programs that addressed the needs of children from immigrant families were targeted for elimination across the state. At the same time, high-stakes testing had been introduced, placing teachers under increased pressure to ensure that every student made significant educational progress toward standardized educational goals. In addition, nonimmigrant teachers continued their existing approaches to teaching and applied their well-honed but ill-adapted theories to working with very new populations:

Parents were, therefore, expected to attend parent–teacher nights, ensure that their children did their homework, and create learning spaces in the home that would foster education. Immigrant parents were expected to join school organizations and to show their involvement in their children's education in other ways. If immigrant parents did not behave like American parents, they were sometimes assumed to be uncommitted to the educational enterprise. Only rarely was the hypothesis entertained that cultural barriers might stand in the way of involvement by immigrant parents in the schools.

For the immigrant families themselves, the transition to an American school system has also been complicated. Some refugee families—perhaps many—have had troubling prior experiences with education. For example, during the Pol Pot years, educated Cambodians were among the chief targets of the Khmer Rouge for elimination. As a result of the killing fields, becoming educated was fraught with danger. When Cambodian refugee parents in Lowell have been asked to take on roles at the schools such as becoming involved as volunteer parent-leaders, they have hesitated. What is more, there are further cultural differences in expectations about schools. Cambodian parents often remark that they learned in their home country that their parental duty was essentially to turn their children over to the schools to be educated. For an "uneducated" parent to get involved and interfere with the educational process would not be right or respectful.

These challenges in Lowell mirror those faced by many communities across the U.S. What is perhaps unique about Lowell is the ways in which these challenges have been turned into opportunities by the schools. The Lowell schools have created extensive partnerships aimed at improving educational prospects for immigrant youth and their families. These partnerships show first-hand the intertwining of the two complicated, ambitious, but sometimes incompatible goals of strengthening educational achievement and assisting newcomers to accommodate to their new culture by building on the strengths they bring from their home countries. In the next section, five partnership examples—Partnership for College Success, GEARUP, Project Splash, New Ventures, and CIRCLE—will be used to illustrate the complex and interwoven nature of the challenges and solutions that arise in the context of immigrant education.

FIVE EXAMPLES OF THE CHALLENGES AND SOLUTIONS TO STRENGTHENING IMMIGRANT EDUCATION

Partnerships Aimed at Strengthening Academic Skills

In their efforts to strengthen academic skills, schools often begin by introducing generic programs designed to create new opportunities for all students. In the U.S., such efforts are often designed to prepare students for college. Lowell's Partnership for College Success Program[2] illustrates how generic programs of this sort, created with the best of intentions, can end up inadvertently reinforcing inequity in the lives of immigrant youth. What looks likes it would work for all students can sometimes simply end up making more apparent the formidable obstacles that stand in the way of immigrant youth fully entering their new culture with all of its attendant opportunities.

In Lowell, a new partnership was begun—the Partnership for College Success—that had as its goal the identification of ways to increase the likelihood that students, particularly first-generation students and those from refugee and immigrant backgrounds, would be academically prepared for college. With significant outside funds, this partnership created avenues for outside partners, especially from the local university, to come into the schools to promote academic achievement and strengthen the college preparation of Lowell's students. All elements of the program were focused on promoting tertiary education as the ultimate academic goal. The idea was to help students understand why attending college or a university is a critical stepping stone to an American middle-class life. In this program, faculty at the high school and college levels worked together to coordinate their courses and curricula so that the gaps between high school and higher education would not lead to a lack of preparedness for students as they enter college. Guidance counselors redesigned their approaches for helping high school students understand how their high school class choices would limit their college opportunities. College students mentored high school students so that they would know what to expect in college in terms of academics and college life. High school students worked with college students to use media in creative new ways to publicize the importance of a college education.

The emphasis throughout the Partnerships for College Success (PCS) was a generic one under the assumption that the most equitable strategy would be one that delivered exactly the same message to every student, and in which all students were equally encouraged to aim for college. What quickly became clear, however, were the stark differences in students' prospects. If young people were ineligible for citizenship (that is, if they were undocumented), they were generally also ineligible to apply for college in the American public higher education system. The many undocumented immigrant students in Lowell—often students who had lived most of their lives in America—were being repeatedly told by PCS that higher education was essential to a middle-class life, yet the very avenue that was being promoted was often closed off for some immigrant youth.[3] The generic PCS was inadvertently encouraging students to look to the very kind of future that might well be unavailable to them.

This PCS experience began to open the eyes of school personnel and their university partners to the cavernous differences in immigrant and nonimmigrant prospects. It became increasingly clear that the emphasis on introducing immigrant students to cultural expectations by heightening college aspirations raised many questions beyond the realms of academia. Aspects of students' lives having little to do with academic ability might pose even greater obstacles to their success than did the level of their academic skill; the issue of documentation status is an important example. As it turned out, these issues that emerged in PCS presaged what would be repeatedly seen across multiple initiatives and programs. It became apparent that educational achievement needed to be considered in relation to a range of other issues that were bound up in complex ways with immigrant students' old and new cultures. The GEARUP program described next suggests some of these possibilities.

Education Partnerships Encountering Culture

When other academic partnerships were introduced into the Lowell schools, we began to see yet more ways in which culture and education could not be disentangled, demonstrating that customization was in order. The intertwining was far from limited to a single program or a single educational level; it was pervasive. Gaining Early Awareness and Readiness for Undergraduate Programs (GEARUP)[4] was federally funded and designed to enlist the help of outside partners, including universities and community organizations, in bringing new approaches to local schools to strengthen academic achievement in low income communities. Lowell's GEARUP worked toward increasing educational achievement by introducing key elements for educational improvement, including teacher training, student tutoring, and after-school and summer support programs at the middle school and high school level. Customization became a central aspect of the program. In particular, this initiative (now in its ninth year) was focused on finding effective ways to collaborate with immigrant and refugee parents, with the recognition that they were often working multiple jobs and in many cases found it difficult to engage with the schools in the ways that the school might expect.

Although GEARUP's ultimate goal was to improve academic achievement, it very quickly became clear that progress in education simply could not be achieved in the absence of the schools developing a deep understanding of immigrant lives and using this understanding to guide the design and delivery of the educational programs in ways that linked them to American culture. Always there was the challenge of how to engage immigrant parents. Straightforward attempts to provide immigrant parents with information about what they could expect of the schools were rarely successful. It was quickly found that parents were struggling with too many challenges of their own to be receptive. Many newly arrived immigrant parents, for example, were finding it difficult to make headway in the local job market because they did not have the technical computer skills needed to thrive in the new society they found themselves in. In order to succeed in involving immigrant parents, it was necessary to find a solution to this problem. As part of GEARUP, we had created computer labs for GEARUP students to use in after-school activities. We realized these same computers might be used with parents to meet their need to become computer literate. This, however, needed to be done in a way that would focus the learning of computer skills on examples that were all about education and the schools. Additionally, immigrant and refugee parents could be hired to serve as coaches and resource leaders for the activities. These activities succeeded in bringing immigrant parents into collaboration with schools in ways that were responsive to the needs of the immigrant parents. The lesson the partnership began to draw from this experience is that it is often necessary to approach problems in new, sometimes roundabout ways that are guided by the lives of immigrant families in their home countries and their new countries. Still other new efforts in Lowell deepened this understanding of the links between specific areas of education and culture.

Combining Education with Culture to Advance Science Achievement

Other projects in Lowell struggled with the thorny problem of how academic achievement in the area of science could be improved among youth; here too, efforts came up against cultural differences that in the end offered opportunities to enrich science education in new ways. Consider the example of Lowell's Project Splash,[5] an informal science education program that used aquaculture as an innovative way to engage students in science by using cultural experiences brought to Lowell by immigrant families.

Students in Lowell were seriously underperforming in all of the sciences, and this gap in achievement was becoming a source of great concern because many of the jobs being created in the Lowell economy were science-based and would call for science training. Simply increasing the number of hours invested in teaching young people about science had not achieved sufficient progress; something different was needed. The goal of Project Splash was to test out innovative ways of increasing science understanding in the middle schools and beyond. The question was whether there might be ways to increase academic achievement by tapping into the partnership resources of the university that could help integrate culture and science.

Once again, efforts were made to combine the academic and the cultural in innovative ways. Project Splash came about because the schools and their partners started to learn about experiences of immigrant parents now living in Lowell who, in their home countries such as Cambodia, had had considerable experience with aquaculture (i.e., raising fish under controlled circumstances). By focusing on aquaculture—which calls for the integration of many areas of science—it became possible to introduce science in ways that captured the interest of diverse students. Here the students' home cultures and their new culture could be integrated, with the students learning from American teachers as well as from elders from immigrant cultures who brought experiences with aquaculture to the United States. This opened new perspectives on what the industry might look like in America. The students began to learn science in the context of what it means to be a productive, contributing member of the American culture. In this pilot program, schools became places of integration where students saw how their culture of origin and science were linked. Project Splash as well as other programs (see below) began to reinforce the lesson that education and culture of origin can sometimes be productively joined.

Combining Culture and Science in Other Ways

As noted above, in Lowell it was apparent that standard approaches to teaching science were not succeeding in increasing academic achievement among immigrant youth. The problem of how to improve academic achievement needed to be approached in new ways. We began to think about combining culture and science, to show how science is linked to culture rather than science being something foreign to or outside it. The science education programs for youth that we designed with funding from the National Institute of Environmental Health Sciences and the Environmental Protection Agency[6] provide a useful illustration. In these partnership programs, we worked with immigrant and refugee young people to increase their knowledge of the science of environmental health. Many initiatives were undertaken: for example, we asked Cambodian and Laotian youth to interview their elders about Buddhist approaches to protecting the environment. The partnership developed an initiative on environmentally healthy homes that taught students about environmental health, but organized the learning in terms of immigrant home examples. We involved youth in a "Year of the iPod" as a way to pique their interest in the fact that their home countries have become the sites of electronic waste disposal from iPods and other electronic equipment, creating tremendous environmental health problems, and how their countries were coping. We created a cable television show in which immigrant youth taught their parents about environmental health science and its link to culture. The partnership brought many of these ideas together in a Southeast Asian water festival that focused on environmental issues and culture. An important result of the Lowell New Venture Partnership was that it enabled explorations of the integrative possibilities of linking education, immigrant cultures of origin, and American cultures.

Drawing on the Strengths and Leadership Skills of Immigrant Parents

A final example points to the integrative possibilities that emerged in Lowell as schools struggled with the dual goals of educating immigrant youth and preparing them and their families for becoming active members of their new culture. The Lowell Center for Immigrant and Refugee Community Leadership and Empowerment (CIRCLE)[7] educational leadership training for new immigrants encouraged immigrant parents to serve as agents of change, who would work with schools to integrate and advance the linking of education and culture for immigrant and refugee youth and their families. CIRCLE is example of school–parent partnerships that showed how the dual emphases of education and culture might be combined.

CIRCLE included educational leadership training for immigrant parents in its portfolio of training. This training in Lowell emphasized two goals: assisting immigrants in learning about the schools and also ensuring that immigrants shared best practices about education and communication between schools and families from their home country. Often, the parents' own educational experiences did not prepare them to understand what their children were likely to encounter in U.S. schools. At times parent leaders expressed concern that the process of becoming educated would distance children from their cultural and family traditions, or would expose them to the risks educated people faced in Cambodia under the Khmer Rouge. The result of CIRCLE was the successful training of adult immigrant leaders who combined an understanding of American schools with an understanding of how to help the schools understand immigrant culture and traditions.

As the examples in this section illustrate, Lowell schools repeatedly found themselves confronted by ever-changing cross-currents of educational and cultural differences and expectations. This section has highlighted some of the conundrums one community faced as it struggled with new demographic realities and with the additional demands placed on schools by changing student populations. This chapter has illustrated how this community attempted to marshal its place-based resources to turn problems into integrative opportunities to enhance educational equity. The broader question then is: given the common cross-currents described here, what needs to be done if schools everywhere are to pursue paths towards their own place-based approaches to ensuring equity for immigrant and refugee children and their families? The final section considers some general lessons, issues, and next steps.

ACHIEVING EQUITY THROUGH INTEGRATING COMPETING EXPECTATIONS: WHAT NEEDS TO CHANGE

Schools are at the crossroads of competing expectations and, as we have seen, nowhere is this more apparent than when students are from refugee and immigrant families. Here schools are expected to be forces for acculturation *and* education. The demands that schools prepare students to achieve high levels of academic proficiency may compete with the expectation that they will prepare immigrant children to become members of their new culture. Everyone wants children to learn and to succeed, to perform well, and to complete their education, but having schools continue to be a primary locus for acculturation is an increasingly complex proposition. As noted throughout this chapter, the important question becomes how schools can make progress in the face of these complexities to ensure equity of educational experience for refugee and immigrant youth.

One solution that might at first blush seem appealing is that schools focus their efforts entirely on education and leave to others the preparation of immigrant children to become members of their new culture. This is not a viable solution. As front-line institutions having daily contact with immigrant families, schools will be placed in this role of cultural mediator and disseminator whether this is planned or not. If immigrant students receive academic education without acculturation to the local social context, they will be poorly prepared to thrive in the new culture. Conversely, if their cultures of origin are not represented within the curriculum, the educational experiences of immigrant youth will be seriously disconnected from the lessons they are learning from their parents and their immigrant community. In short, rather than eliminating these competing expectations of schools, there needs to be recognition that familiarization with both the culture of origin and the dominant culture are essential to achieving equity in education for refugee and immigrant students. The better solution is to explore how the roles can be enacted in a deliberate and thoughtful manner rather than occurring simply by happenstance; the real task ahead is finding innovative ways to integrate the two so that neither suffers.

As we found in Lowell, opportunities for changing education are likely to come from unexpected directions, and we need to be open to these possibilities. They need not start with an educational focus. Opportunities can begin with a cultural focus and then incorporate education. The Angkor Dance Troupe, a nationally acclaimed Khmer youth dance organization that makes its home in Lowell, is an example: It started integration from the cultural rather than the educational end. The premise behind the Angkor Dance Troupe was that there is an urgent need to stem the loss of cultural understanding among youth whose families are refugees from Cambodia, a loss that was one of the perverse legacies of the Cambodian holocaust. Although traditional formal dance was long central to Cambodian culture, this form of cultural expression was nearly wiped out by Pol Pot. The goal of the Angkor Dance Troupe was to train new generations of Lowell's Khmer youth in this traditional dance form as a way to help them understand their cultural heritage. It quickly became apparent that education could be tied to this teaching of culture. The local university became involved in helping the troupe find ways to use youths' interest in learning about traditional dance to increase educational achievement. This was accomplished by building education activities into the training itself. Immigrant and refugee youth began to see that education and culture were not incompatible.

The above example illustrates the importance of looking for available but untapped avenues that will encourage the integration of culture and education. It is equally important to recognize the unexpected places where our assumptions about cultural uniformity prevent us from redressing educational barriers. An example is our experience in Lowell as we sought to address the problem many urban school systems are facing: high rates of lost school days among students, which result from high rates of pediatric asthma. In many urban communities, asthma now accounts for perhaps the largest number of missed school days among youth, with predictable deleterious effects on student learning. Something needed to be done in Lowell to reduce asthma by reducing youth exposure to asthma triggers in their homes—for example, mites in beds and indoor smoking. Yet a focus on the home is problematic. It is essential to be attuned to cultural differences in habits and practices in the home that may influence the effectiveness of interventions for reducing asthma. We failed at this. Standard asthma interventions often target children's bedrooms, so in Lowell, mattress covers were given to immigrant families to reduce childhood exposure to asthma triggers during sleep.[8] Adult smoking in the home, however, was perhaps an even greater contributor to asthma: Outsiders to the culture told parents that they should keep smoke out of the child's bedroom. But many of the assumptions turned out to be incorrect. Children in immigrant families in Lowell were not necessarily sleeping on traditional-sized beds for which the mattress pads would be suitable, so these devices did not work as barriers to asthma triggers such as mites. Furthermore, children and young people were not necessarily sleeping in their own rooms and so there was little opportunity to isolate children who were sleeping from adults who were smoking. Whether it is sleeping spaces or some other aspect of the home that might be expected to affect learning, outsiders—including the schools—may not know enough to make appropriate recommendations. Cultural practices need to be understood and taken into account.

Engagement with immigrant communities may well provide some of the best opportunities now available for rethinking and redesigning approaches to integrating education and culture. Schools with immigrant youth have an opportunity to approach their tasks differently so that the diverse needs of all children are met. Consider innovations needed around the key task of how schools contact and engage parents. Schools have traditionally made contact with parents through sending written notes home. As in Lowell, where many immigrants experienced war-interrupted educations, parents may not be literate, and so written materials (even in the home language) may be unsuccessful communication strategies. U.S. schools have also long depended on parent–teacher conferences and parent–school organizations as ways to communicate and build partnerships. Yet when immigrant parents are working multiple jobs at nontraditional hours, such approaches rarely succeed. Furthermore, if immigrant parents hold the view that it is disrespectful to directly engage with or question teachers and other education authorities, limited communication will result from the standard approaches relied upon by schools. These challenges, made salient by large numbers of immigrant families in a district, are in fact challenges that schools face with many parents, immigrant and nonimmigrant alike. The shifting demographics provide schools with an impetus to test out new strategies for communication with all parents in ways that integrate education and acculturation.

Ultimately we need to be ever vigilant in terms of our assumptions. It might be "normal" if teachers were to conclude that immigrant parents are uninterested in schools, given their lack of participation in traditional school opportunities. But as Chath pierSath, a Cambodian community leader and others have argued, what is needed is a new dialogue about engagement. In the "old" Cambodia, parents were not expected to be involved in the schools. He argues that now we need a new set of traditions that work in this new country (personal communication, 2009). These new traditions would be about immigrant parents engaging with the schools in new ways. PierSath is making a point about change and tradition: Tradition can be honored at the same time that change is introduced to reflect new conditions and new opportunities.

ACKNOWLEDGEMENTS

This chapter could not have been written without the years of collaboration with friends in the African, Caribbean, South American, and Southeast Asian immigrant and refugee communities in Lawrence and Lowell, Massachusetts. Thank you for helping all of us learn to create better, more inclusive communities that meet the needs of families and children.

NOTES

1. The term culture is used here and in the remainder of this chapter in an anthropological sense to refer to all of the activities, habits, expectations, and assumptions that are a part of daily life in a particular country or region.
2. Lowell's Partnership for College Success was funded by the Nellie Mae Educational Foundation.
3. Detailed information on this barrier and the resulting challenges it creates is available at websites such as www.immigrationpolicy.org/just-facts/dream-act.
4. GEARUP Lowell was funded by the U.S. Department of Education.
5. Project Splash was funded through the U.S. National Science Foundation's Informal Science Education Program.
6. The New Ventures program was funded through the U.S. National Institute for Environmental Health Sciences and the U.S. Environmental Protection Agency.
7. The Center for Immigrant and Refugee Community Leadership and Empowerment was funded through a grant from the U.S. Office of Refugee Resettlement.
8. This intervention was carried out through the Southeast Asian Environmental Justice Partnership through funding from the National Institute of Environmental Health Sciences.

REFERENCES

Bean, F. D., & Stevens, G. (2003). *America's newcomers and the dynamics of diversity.* New York: Russell Sage Foundation.

Camarota, S. A. (2001). *Immigrants in the United States 2000. A snapshot of American's foreign-born population.* Center for Immigration Studies. Retrieved from http://www.cis.org/articles/2001/back101.html

Cornelius, W., Tsuda, T., Martin, P., & Hollifield, J. (2004). *Controlling immigration: A global perspective.* Stanford, CA: Stanford University Press.

Darder, A. (Ed.). (1995). *Culture and difference: Critical perspectives on the bicultural experience in the United States.* New York, NY: Bergin & Garvey.

Grey, M. A. (2000). Marshalltown, Iowa and the struggle for community in a global age. In T. W. Collins, & J. D. Wingard (Eds.), *Communities and capital: Local struggles against corporate power and privatization* (pp. 87–100). Athens, GA: University of Georgia Press.

Hamin, E., Geigis, P., & Silka, L. (Eds.). (2007). *Preserving and enhancing communities: A guide for citizens, planners and policymakers.* Amherst, MA: University of Massachusetts Press.

Iowa State University Extension (2001). *The impact of immigration on small- to mid-sized Iowa communities: A citizens' guide to change.* Retrieved from http://www.extension.iastate/publications/pm1879.pdf

Kiang, P. N. (1992). Issues of curriculum and community for first generation Asian Americans in college. *New Directions for Community Colleges, 20*(4), 97–112.

Kiang, P. N. (2006). Policy challenges for Asian Americans and Pacific Islanders in education. *Race, Ethnicity, and Education, 9*(1), 103–115.

Portes, A., & Rumbaut, R. G. (2006). *Immigrant America: A portrait* (3rd ed.). Berkeley, CA: University of California Press.

Rumbaut, R. G., & Kenji, I. (1988). *The adaptation of Southeast Asian refugee youth: A comparative study.* San Diego, CA: San Diego State University.

Santiago, J., Jennings, J., & Carrion, L. (2005). *Immigrant homebuyers in Lawrence and Lowell Massachusetts: Keys to the revitalization of cities.* Malden, MA: Immigrant Learning Center. Available at http://www.tufts.edu/jjenni02/pdf/homebuyers-lawrence-lowell.pdf

Schneekloth, L. H., & Shibley, R. G. (1995). *Placemaking: The art and practice of building communities.* New York, NY: John Wiley & Sons.

Silka, L., & Tip, J. (1994). Empowering the silent ranks: The Southeast Asian experience. *American Journal of Community Psychology, 222*, 497–529.

Singer, A. (2004). *The rise of new immigrant gateways.* The Living Cities Census Series. New York, NY: The Brookings Institute.

Suarez-Orozco, C., & Suarez-Orozco, M. M. (2002). *Children of immigration (The developing child).* Cambridge, MA: Harvard University Press.

Turcotte, D., & Silka, L. (2007). Reflections on the concept of social capital: Complex partnerships in refugee and immigrant communities. In J. Jennings (Ed.), *Race, neighborhoods, and misuse of social capital* (pp. 109–132). New York, NY: Palgrave-Macmillan.

Waldinger, R. (Ed.). (2001). *Strangers at the gates: New immigrants in urban America.* Berkeley, CA: University of California Press.

Zuniga, V., & Hernandez-Leon, R. (2005). *New destinations of Mexican immigration in the United States: Community formation, local responses, and intergroup relations.* New York, NY: Russell Sage.

PART III

SYSTEMIC ISSUES AND POLICIES FOR REFUGEE
AND IMMIGRANT EDUCATIONAL EQUITY

CHAPTER 8

AUSTRALIA'S NEW ARRIVALS POLICY AND THE NEED TO REFORM REFUGEE EDUCATION PROVISION

Florence E. McCarthy and Margaret H. Vickers
University of Western Sydney

ABSTRACT

This chapter provides a critical overview of current educational provisions in Australia for students with refugee backgrounds. Across Australia's states and territories, the Commonwealth New Arrivals Program (NAP) provides a common funding base for the initial education of these young people. It is argued that the NAP is premised on an outmoded model that ignores the reality that currently arriving groups of refugee newcomers have qualitatively different pre-settlement experiences from those who arrived in the past. Although the level of support provided through NAP was improved marginally in 2007, the program does not adequately meet current needs. It imposes substantial limits on the capacity of the school systems to provide adequately for the personal and academic needs of refugees whose pre-settlement experiences may have involved limited or disrupted schooling, or no schooling at all. Moreover, more comprehensive implementation of existent antiracist

Refugee and Immigrant Students, pages 145–165
Copyright © 2012 by Information Age Publishing
145

policies is needed to ensure that schools provide inclusive, safe learning environments for all students. In the field of teacher education, there is also a lack of broadly conceived programs adequate to prepare beginning teachers for the challenge of responding to students with refugee backgrounds. Some universities are instituting changes to ensure that new teachers will have the experience of working with and developing relationships with young people from refugee backgrounds. However, across the board, more consistent efforts need to be made to ensure that all teachers achieve the flexibility, sensitivity, and understanding required to meet the educational challenges of this increasingly diversified student population.

Contemporary Australia represents a diverse, multilingual, multicultural society in which slightly more than one in every four persons was born outside the country (Australian Bureau of Statistics, 2010). Notwithstanding the cultural diversity of its population, the society itself is fraught with deep divisions. Strong currents of racialization, exclusion, and disparity mar the lives of countless numbers of its citizens (Jakubowicz, 2009). Nowhere is this more apparent than in the complex array of policies and practices surrounding refugees and their settlement in the country (McCarthy, 2011). Like many controversial subjects, that of "refugees" engenders strong divergent opinions, and is often politicized.

Of particular concern in this chapter is a critique of educational provision and the factors shaping the experience of children with refugee backgrounds as they negotiate their way through Australian schools. While the pre-settlement experiences of refugees are critically important in shaping the identities of humanitarian entrants who arrive in Australia, post-settlement issues have a complexity of their own. A focus on the individual and personal adjustment of students with refugee backgrounds in schools is essential. However, in the long run, successful settlement requires a broad, inclusive approach that goes beyond the school to include accommodation for families, assistance with labor market entry, and health services. Overall, it is generally recognized that support for new arrivals needs to ensure the social integration and personal well-being of students with refugee experience, in addition to their academic accomplishments (Christie & Sidhu, 2006; Matthews, 2008).

This chapter provides a critical overview of issues related to educational provisions for students with refugee backgrounds. These include (1) a lack of consistent, long-term Commonwealth policies for the education of refugee students, premised on an outmoded model of who refugee newcomers are; (2) limits on the capacity of the system to provide for the complex learning needs of acute refugees, as educational policies and practices developed by the school systems (both public and Catholic) are constrained by the funding provided by the Commonwealth; and (3) the lack of broadly conceived teacher preparation programs able to meet the ongoing challenge of responding to students who do not fit the mainstream definition of "student." Some universities are instituting changes in their teacher preparation programs to ensure that new teachers will have experience working with and developing understanding for children with refugee backgrounds. However, more consistent efforts need to be made to ensure new teachers achieve the flexibility, sensitivity, and understanding required to meet the complex learning needs of an increasingly diversified student population.

REFUGEE POLICIES AND PROGRAMS IN AUSTRALIA

Australia is one of nineteen countries that participate in the resettlement program of the UNHCR, and generally has had one of the highest per capita rates of refugee reception in the world (Pittaway & Muli, 2009). During 2008–2009, 11,010 humanitarian refugees were accepted by Australia through the UNHCR resettlement program (known as the Offshore program) out of the total of roughly 13,500 refugees accepted that year (UN High Commissioner for Refugees, 2010). The remaining 2,497 persons were granted visas under the Onshore program. Refugee and other humanitarian entrants represented only 7.4% of all settler arrivals during that year. Australia accepts roughly equal numbers of refugees from Asia, Africa, and the Middle East, including the countries of Sudan, Ethiopia, Congo (DRC), Somalia, Liberia, Sierra Leone, Iraq, Afghanistan, Burma/Myanmar, and Bhutan (Department of Immigration and Multicultural and Indigenous Affairs, 2009). While the numbers accepted by Australia appear small, Australia is (on a per-capita basis) third among the countries in the world that accept refugees for resettlement (UNHCR, 2010).

Australia's migrant arrivals numbered 168,700 in 2009 (Australian Bureau of Statistics, 2009); compared with this the refugee and humanitarian program represented only 6.6% of the overall migration program, close to its lowest level in 35 years (Refugee Council of Australia, 2010). The fact that humanitarian refugees account for such a small portion of the immigrant population may help to explain why the settlement of refugees is largely incorporated within overall federal and state programs, and why so little attention is paid to developing settlement policies that are specifically designed to meet their needs.

The treatment of refugee newcomers to Australia is established within the framework of Commonwealth policies found in the Humanitarian Protection Program. Each year the total intake of newcomers is divided among the various categories of applicants: refugees; special humanitarian persons being sponsored by family members, NGOs, or businesses; On-shore Protection visas given to people who arrive in Australia as asylum-seekers by boat or air and are found eligible for refugee status; and people of temporary humanitarian concern (DIAC, 2009).

General Commonwealth support for newcomers is found in the Integrated Humanitarian Settlement Strategy (IHSS), which was introduced in 1997 as a national framework for improving the humanitarian services provided to newcomers (Community Relations Commission [CRC] Report, 2006). The IHSS was based on partnerships with community organizations and improved linkages between settlement planning activities and service delivery (DIMIA, 2006). IHSS services are now delivered by contractual service providers, many of which are nongovernmental organizations (NGOs). Basic services include on-arrival support such as meeting newcomers at the airport and taking them to temporary housing. Other supports include a basic pre-departure orientation to the country, initial food and household supplies, information regarding available services, and assistance with immediate emergencies. Also provided are accommodation services, case coordination, information and referrals, and short-term counselling.

Many of these services are only available for the first six months after the newcomer's arrival. However, many of the problems faced by refugee families persist well beyond the initial period of assistance. Given the changing nature of the current refugee population, the IHSS program has been heavily criticized for not being properly sensitive and supportive of these newcomers (CRC, 2006).

COMMONWEALTH EDUCATIONAL POLICIES
FOR ACUTE REFUGEE STUDENTS

The Commonwealth government provides financial support to the state and territory departments of education and the nongovernment school systems to cover the costs of initial intensive English language learning and transition programs to mainstream schools. The content and enactment of these policies are critical in establishing the social context for initial refugee settlement in primary and secondary schools across Australia. As the Community Relations Commission (2006) has argued, these policies are no longer meeting the needs of refugee newcomers arriving in Australia.

The issue is that the nature of Australia's refugee intake has changed fundamentally in the past 15 years, while Commonwealth policies and programs for refugee settlement and education have hardly changed at all. Unlike traditional refugees coming to Australia, currently arriving refugees are what McBrien (2005) refers to as "acute" refugees. These are different in that they are likely to have suffered the effects of war and violence that drove them from their homes, of walking long distances to relative security, of perhaps being separated from family members, and of seeing loved ones killed or raped. Additionally, young people with refugee backgrounds may have been born in or spent considerable time in refugee camps, and may have limited, interrupted, or even no education.

In contrast, traditional new arrivals, for whom the Commonwealth program was originally designed, most often were literate in a first language, had prior experience in schools and some education, and were often of similar cultural backgrounds to local Australians. These newcomers included immigrants and refugees, and it was assumed that they would rapidly adjust to life in Australia, hence the short-term provisions for settlement and education. These kinds of assumptions have, until recently, provided the basis for the 50-year-old New Arrivals Program (NAP).

Funds from the Commonwealth provide financial support for all NAP educational programs, through grants to the states and territories. Such grants are made to state public education systems as well as to the Catholic education systems. The systems then establish policies for the expenditure of these funds.

Based on concerns about the inadequacy of the NAP, the Ministerial Council on Education, Employment, Training and Youth Affairs (MCEETYA) established the Schools Resourcing Taskforce (SRT) in 2006 to survey all government school systems in Australia and the two largest Catholic dioceses. The taskforce found that (1) the expenditure on each humanitarian refugee student by state for ESL services was nearly $11,000 on average while Commonwealth funding provided only $5,039, and (2) funding for humanitarian refugee students was falling behind funding for adult learners (210 hours and 510 hours for primary and secondary students respectively depending on language ability in contrast to 910 hours for adults) (MCEETYA, 2006).

In late 2007, Commonwealth funding available for all newly arrived humanitarian students of refugee background in all school sector ESL programs was doubled (DEEWR, 2009). The amounts were increased from a one-off payment of $5,039 per eligible ESL-NAP student to $11,572 per student for humanitarian entrants and $5,786 for other ESL-NAP students (Department of Education, Employment and Workplace Relations, 2009). Essentially, the increase in funds enabled schools to improve services provided to students with refugee experience and other newcomer students (including full-fee international students and migrant children) through the NAP programs. Generally NAP money is used in order to (1) hire ESL teachers based on the annual school census and index of students qualifying for ESL instruction; (2) run NAP schools and intensive English or English language centers, and/or (3) fund "transition to work" programs and other special initiatives. Decisions on how NAP funds are used are often left to the schools, provided they conform to the guidelines set within each state or territory.

These adjustments to government funding for the most recent refugee new-comers are welcome. However, fundamental policy changes across all systems are necessary to match the changing conditions shaping refugee lives abroad and to meet the changing needs of humanitarian entrants as new groups are resettled in Australia. The possibility of students with refugee experience "fall-ing through the cracks" (MCEETYA, 2006) as a result of insufficient and in-consistent support once in Australia suggests that new collaborative initiatives are needed that encourage Commonwealth as well as multi-sectoral govern-ment, state, school and community participation (Vickers, 2011).

SCHOOLS, SCHOOLING, AND EDUCATIONAL POLICIES FOR HUMANITARIAN ENTRANTS

The role of education as an essential ingredient in social stability and per-sonal development is widely recognized. For example, education has been identified as being fundamental in promoting the wellbeing (Gilford, Cor-rea-Velez, & Sampson, 2009; Matthews, 2008) and social inclusion (Pinson & Arnot, 2010) of migrants and newcomer children with refugee experi-ence. It has also been identified as a critical factor in stabilizing political and social environments in conflict-afflicted and fragile states (Barakat, Karpinska & Paulson, 2008; Eschenbacher, 2009; Tebbe, 2009). Whether in Western countries (Kanu, 2008; McBrien 2005; Portes & Rambault, 2001) or in countries in Africa (Brown, 2010; Chelpi-den Hamer 2009), the Mid-dle East (UNHCR, 2009), Asia (van der Stouwe & Oh, 2007), or the Pacific, educational policy and the delivery of educational services are key factors in social stability and security.

Australia's educational system confronts difficult issues as it attempts to meet the educational needs of students with acute refugee experiences. These young people often challenge established definitions of who a "stu-dent" is, and present teachers and school administrators with patterns of learning and reactions to the established cultural norms and practices of lo-cal schools that are unfamiliar, or even alarming (Ferfolja, Vickers, McCar-thy, Naidoo, & Brace, 2011; Vickers & McCarthy 2010). It would under any circumstances be difficult for schools to manage this degree of diversity. Un-fortunately, the recent tendency of the Commonwealth government to cen-tralize control over what schools do through increased reliance on teacher accountability, standardized testing, and the publication of comparative data on school performance makes the task even more difficult (Ferfolja et al., 2011). Contradictory pressures are being created for schools, particu-larly those with significant numbers of refugee and immigrant students, as they attempt to meet the broad and complex needs of refugee students, while at the same time dealing with an increase in centralized government controls and a corresponding increase in the standardized auditing of student performance.

State-Level Provision for Humanitarian Entrants

Based on an analysis of the documentation available from different state departments of education, it is apparent that the different states and territories receive support from the federally funded New Arrivals Program, and follow essentially similar procedures in allocating funds for programs such as refugee support. However, at the school level, there is no uniform approach to educational support for children and families with refugee backgrounds. ESL instruction, for example, may vary by school; however, in most cases the New Arrivals Program funding covers the employment of ESL teachers or teacher aides who work with newcomer students to develop their vocabulary, language skills, and background understandings related to curriculum subjects. Unlike the U.S., there is no separate "track" for ESL students. At the primary school level they are generally integrated into mainstream classrooms and attend ESL classes as part of a regular schedule. At the secondary level they attend a separate Intensive English center for one year and are then integrated into mainstream classrooms. Moderate differences have emerged in provisions for the education of students with refugee backgrounds in South Australia, Victoria, and New South Wales. These illustrate the degree of variation in new arrivals support across Australia.

South Australia

South Australia, a relatively small state of some 1.6 million people, and recently experiencing a growth in newcomers by 33% in the last ten years, assumes a flexible and holistic approach to the inclusion of immigrant and refugee students in its schools. The Department of Education and Community Services (DECS) advocates that schools adopt the "learner wellbeing framework" that involves creating a whole-school approach that works to dismiss "discrimination, prejudice, or harassment towards people of diverse cultural, linguistic or religious backgrounds" (Government of South Australia, 2010, p. 21). Within this broad whole-school approach, specific resources are devoted to creating partnerships with parents, communities and outside agencies, and ensuring the wellbeing and support of teachers and staff as well as focusing on the educational needs of all children (DECS, 2007). Language learning occurs as part of a pedagogical approach that features multicultural education and culturally inclusive classrooms and emphasizes social and cultural learning among all students about all other students. It also encourages humanitarian refugee students to acquire the linguistic and cultural understandings necessary to function successfully in

Australian society. Similar to other states, South Australia has new arrivals programs and school-based centers that provide language instruction and cultural orientation, as well as transition programs to mainstream schools and ongoing ESL and other special provisions for newcomer students.

Victoria

From 2003 to 2007, some 17,000 humanitarian entrants settled in the state (Department of Education and Early Childhood Development, 2008), with roughly 30% of them being of school age. New entrants came primarily from African countries during 2003–2005; however, the balance has shifted recently to entrants coming from Afghanistan and from Burma/Myanmar (DEECD, 2008). Of the approximately 3,000 school-aged entrants who arrive each year, over 2,000 students who require English language learning enroll directly in mainstream schools (DEECD, 2008).

The approach to providing relevant education to students with refugee backgrounds is an extensive mix of special English language schools and centers; ESL classes in primary and secondary schools for students who directly enroll; and transition programs for students as they move from small, specialized classrooms to mainstream schooling. Support for these efforts is provided by the ESL unit of the Department of Education and Early Childhood Development, which generates and coordinates supports for schools and provides state-wide learning activities for teachers engaged with students with severely interrupted schooling and literacy learning needs (DEECD, 2008). Additional funding from the Commonwealth and state government has made it possible to reduce class sizes in the English language schools and newcomer centers and to extend the stay of new arrivals for up to 12 months (DEECD, 2008). Other funding has made it possible to provide extended ESL tuition for immigrant and humanitarian students.

Transition officers have been appointed in eleven schools to help students make the transition to mainstream schools. These officers assist students and teachers in classrooms; link parents with schools and teachers; and connect teachers, parents, and students to community support services that are designed to help meet the settlement as well as educational needs of humanitarian and immigrant students. Particular foundations and organizations provide important assistance to classroom teachers and to students with refugee backgrounds.

Victoria differs from the other states by providing two versions of the Year 12 graduation certificate. Alongside the standard Victorian Certificate of Education, there is the Victorian Certificate in Applied Learning (VCAL), which has been designed for students 15 years and older, many of whom have experienced severe disruptions in their past educational experiences. Students with refugee backgrounds represent a clear example of VCAL's target client group. Specialized re-entry or developmental programs are also offered, providing the necessary knowledge and skills that enable older students to successfully transition into mainstream VCAL or other senior-secondary programs (DEECD, 2008).

New South Wales

New South Wales (NSW) is home to roughly a third of Australia's total population, and within its huge public educational system, a targeted-school approach to providing educational services to students with refugee backgrounds has been adopted. Each year between 1,100 and 1,500 newly arrived humanitarian students enroll in public schools. In 2009, there were a total of approximately 12,000 humanitarian entrants in public schools. However, the distribution of refugee families and their children is not evenly dispersed throughout Sydney or the state as a whole. Immigrant and humanitarian families and children tend to be concentrated in the Greater Western Sydney (GWS) area, and it is these schools that are targeted and carry the prime responsibility for providing education to newcomer students. GWS is a region where one third of the population is overseas born, where half the world's languages are spoken, and where approximately 80% of all humanitarian refugees arriving in NSW were settled from 2001–2006 (Vickers & McCarthy, 2010).

Educational assistance for humanitarian students is delivered through specific support to targeted schools that have large enrollments of humanitarian students or that qualify for special support programs (New South Wales Department of Education and Training, 2009). Such schools may qualify for additional ESL staff and are supported by regionally based Refugee Student Support Officers. These officers are to provide in-school support and professional learning for teachers (New South Wales Department of Education and Training, 2009). The English as a Second Language (ESL) program is the broadest of all NSW programs as it provides English language learning in primary and secondary schools (K–12), in intensive English centers (IECs) and in the Intensive English High School (IEHS). There are 14 IECs and one IEHS. While many of the students in the IECs are students with refugee backgrounds, in some high schools an increasing proportion of the places in IECs are being taken by migrant or full-fee-paying international students who are aiming to improve their English language competencies (MCEETYA, 2006).

Principals are responsible for the effective management and operation of the ESL programs in their schools. At the secondary school level, ESL instruction tends to focus on specific subject matter areas so that students become acquainted with the concepts and language associated with each subject. While newcomers need help to gain an understanding of the cultural context of schools and the wider community in which they live, this is unlikely to happen in mainstream classrooms. It is more likely to occur within the IECs where class sizes are small and instruction is individualized as much as possible. Until very recently, the number of ESL teachers was quite limited, and provision of adequate ESL instruction outside the IECs was problematic in many schools.

From this brief summary, it is apparent that each state follows somewhat different approaches to educational provision for students with refugee backgrounds within the overall guidelines set by Commonwealth funding. However, there is as yet no substantive Commonwealth program of learning support for humanitarian students within a larger rubric of programs for disadvantaged students.

Critically important is the issue of how adequately any of these existing initiatives are likely to meet the needs of students who experienced disrupted schooling or no schooling at all during the pre-settlement phase. While it may take many years for students from refugee backgrounds to achieve oral and academic proficiency in English (Miller, Mitchell, & Brown 2005), it is also evident that refugee students are likely to exhibit considerable variability in their language learning abilities, in part because the nature of their pre-settlement experiences can vary so greatly. However, important aspects of student wellbeing, the acquisition of social capital, and identity formation are also deeply affected by student encounters with racialized behavior and alienating institutional practices in schools and surrounding communities (Arzubiaga, Noqueron, & Sullivan, 2009).

Across Australia, refugee students at the secondary level make the transition from IECs to mainstream classrooms after 12 months. Under exceptional circumstances, they may remain in the IEC for an additional term. Their transition into mainstream classes in not based on when they have acquired proficiency in English. Rather, limits to the time spent in IECs are based on funding allocations and set time frames (Garcia, 2000). Brown, Miller, and Mitchell (2006), Collier (1995), and others maintain that general policies for newcomers, such as the length of targeted support for English language learning, were initially established on the assumption that students had significant prior educational experience. While it is the case that some of the recently arrived students with refugee backgrounds have had prior educational experience, there are many others for whom literacy in even their first language is missing.

Moreover, when it is recognized that the prior experiences of most humanitarian students involves trauma from conflict situations, life in refugee camps, and loss of and separation from family member among other issues, it would not be untoward to argue that more time is required to enable almost all of them to develop trusting relationships with teachers, mentors, and other students, and to acquire the social capital, general knowledge, and literacy and numeracy skills necessary to adequately function academically and socially in Australian schools. In addition, without consistent efforts being made to counter bullying and to create more inclusive and secure schools, it is likely that the school environment itself may become a major obstacle in the successful acculturation of refugee students in Australia.

SPECIALIZED TEACHER EDUCATION PROGRAMS: UNIVERSITY, COMMUNITY, AND SCHOOL CONNECTIONS

Recognizing the importance of classroom teachers in mediating the educational experiences of young people with refugee backgrounds, a number of universities have developed programs that aim to increase the awareness of pre-service teachers in relation to the kinds of individualized support these students require. Such initiatives are critically important in helping schools respond to the challenges of working with the more recent cohorts of acute refugees whose pre-settlement experiences disrupt the traditional assumptions about who a student is.

Most mainstream primary and secondary schools constitute well-established, institutionalized cultures dictating the behavior and normative expectations that govern the activities of all who participate in school life and create a tacit but common understanding of what it means to be a student. Everyone knows the rules. They have clear ideas about how teachers, students, and staff are to behave, and there are common views about how classroom teaching and learning should occur. When students with refugee backgrounds who do not understand this culture and the behaviors expected of them enter mainstream classrooms, they often disrupt the normative assumptions and practices that are taken for granted by everyone else. This situation can create a difficult classroom environment for students, for teachers, and especially for pre-service teachers. Conventional teacher education programs may be effective in establishing skills in classroom management and knowledge transmission, but they often fail to encourage the kinds of creativity, flexibility, and improvisation that are evident among experienced teachers who know how to work effectively with non-mainstream students such as humanitarian or newly arrived students (Dudderar & Stover, 2003; Gallego, 2001; Vickers, 2007).

Institutional constraints tend to restrict what pre-service and beginning teachers can learn about young people's lives, the communities in which they live, and the nature of their lives outside of school (Cochran-Smith & Zeichner, 2005). Boyle-Baise and Sleeter (2000) argue that when beginning teachers first encounter students whose cultural backgrounds are different from their own, their experiences may reinforce their pre-existing stereotypes about the "difficulties" of working with these students, rather than leading to a disruption of such stereotypical thinking. Gallego's (2001) research, which contrasted the experiences of trainee teachers in classroom-based practica and community-based small-group settings, found that pre-service teachers became aware of the limitations of the standard practicum and particularly the confining nature of standard classrooms in reaching culturally diverse students. Vickers (2007) also contrasted the narrow kinds of learning that occur in the traditional practicum with the learning that occurs when pre-service teachers are able to work directly with young people in more natural community settings.

Brief descriptions of university–school–community partnerships are provided here in order to illustrate some of the alternative pathways that are being created through which higher-education students engage with young people with refugee backgrounds. All of these programs depend on non-government organizations to train the tutors and/or organize the homework centers. Tutors in these programs may be university students or community volunteers. In some situations student-tutors gain course credit for their participation, and in other cases they function as volunteers. Sometimes the state department of education pays coordinating teachers and provides school classrooms for the homework centers, but in most cases the homework centers are run in out-of-school settings. Assistance for some programs comes from the state offices of Commonwealth departments such as the Department of Families, Housing, Community Services and Indigenous Affairs (FaHCSIA), or the Department of Education, Employment and Work Place Relations (DEEWR). The following programs are merely indicative of the range of initiatives operating across Australia.

New South Wales: The Refugee Action Support program (RAS)

The Refugee Action Support (RAS) program is a joint initiative of the NSW Department of Education and Training, the Australian Literacy and Numeracy Foundation (ALNF) and the UWS School of Education. Through this initiative, refugee students in secondary schools receive in-school assistance and after-school tutoring aimed at developing their literacy skills and improving their participation and engagement in schooling (see Vickers & McCarthy, 2010; Ferfolja et al, 2011 for more extended accounts).

Within the secondary teacher-education program at the University of Western Sydney, a for-credit subject known as Professional Experience 3 (PE3) is a required component of the Master of Education (secondary) degree. PE3 represents a third practicum that differs from the two conventional classroom-based placements known as Professional Experience 1 (PE1) and Professional Experience 2 (PE2). These two conventional four-week block-placement practica focus on the preparation and delivery of classroom lessons in the disciplines in which teaches aim to qualify (for example, mathematics, science, English). In contrast, PE3 introduces beginning teachers to the broader professional responsibilities carried out by public schools in Greater Western Sydney. Through PE3, beginning teachers provide 60 hours of service to targeted groups of young people. The RAS option in PE3 provides beginning teachers with opportunities to forge personal relationships with and expand their understanding of the complex histories of refugee students.

RAS provides 12 weeks of one-on-one tutoring for refugee students. It focuses on helping refugee students to improve their English language and literacy skills, meet assessment requirements in particular subject areas, and develop the confidence to participate in classroom activities. RAS assists students in making the transition into mainstream schools and helps them gain generic institutional understandings such as how to prepare an assignment for submission. Implicit in the RAS relationship is the assumption that small-group tutoring increases the cultural and educational capital of young people with refugee backgrounds, while at the same time improving the understanding and empathy of the RAS tutors for these young people.

The initiative was initially proposed by the Australian Literacy and Numeracy Foundation. It began in four schools in 2007 and expanded to nine secondary schools in 2008 and 2009. To date, approximately 260 refugee students have participated in the program in the GWS region (Brace, 2011). ALNF is now taking this initiative to other universities, including Charles Sturt University.

Through RAS, beginning teachers work as tutors in small-group situations with supervision and assistance from coordinating teachers and community liaison officers (CLOs). All RAS tutors participate in twelve hours of intensive training provided by the ALNF at the beginning of each semester. During their placement, ALNF also provides the tutors with online access to resources and support. In-class tutoring is provided for three hours each Thursday afternoon and is followed by two hours of after-school tutoring, with the coordinating teacher assisting. During the after-school sessions, tutors provide 1.5 hours of face-to-face tutoring: They assist students with different aspects of language acquisition, help them understand the content of different subjects, or help them work through assignments. The last half hour is a debriefing session with the coordinating teachers where the tutors discuss the events of the session and receive feedback on their own interactions with students.

Data from Brace (2011) indicate that students participating consistently and continuously in RAS show marked improvement in academic skills such as comprehension and writing English, and more actively understand and participate in classroom activities such as preparing assignments. For RAS mentors, the experience sharpens their understanding and awareness of the unusual histories of students with refugee backgrounds, and sensitizes them to being aware of all the students they are likely to find in their classrooms.

Victoria: Learning Beyond the Bell (LBB)

La Trobe University supports eight learning support programs for primary and secondary age students in Melbourne's Northern and Western suburbs. Through these programs, beginning teachers who are completing their diploma in education work in out-of-school homework clubs organized through Learning Beyond the Bell (LBB). This initiative is, therefore, based on a partnership between the La Trobe University School of Education and a nongovernment community organization, the Centre for Multi-Cultural Youth (CMY).

The CMY originally created LBB as one of its core initiatives. Funded by the Department of Education and Early Childhood Development, the mission of LBB is to provide coordination and support for out-of-school-hours learning support programs (also known as homework clubs) across Victoria. The goal of these clubs is to increase the connectedness of young people with refugee and migrant backgrounds to their schools and to their communities, and contribute to improving their educational outcomes.

Beginning teachers participating in LBB are expected to attend training workshops, commit to regular weekly tutoring in the learning support programs, and document their students' progress and the pedagogies they use, wherever possible (Naidoo, 2011). The initial training of the beginning teachers is supported by LBB staff and the focus is on helping beginning teachers to understand tutoring responsibilities and strategies and to learn about how refugee experiences can make it difficult for young people to accommodate to the local school system (Naidoo, 2011). Workshops on literacy scaffolding techniques and digital story-telling are also conducted by a part-time La Trobe University lecturer and by an e-learning consultant.

In 2009, 40 pre-service teachers were involved in the program with twelve homework support program staff and forty refugee and ESL students. The homework coordinators monitor the beginning teachers' and school students' attendance, participate in research interviews, liaise with parents/guardians to assist with recruitment of student participants, advise on content and translation of project information for students and parents/guardians, and liaise with researchers and students in the arrangement of interviews and observations (Naidoo, 2011). School students attending the out-of-school-hours learning support programs (OSHSLPs) include both recent migrants and refugees.

LBB operates across Victoria, so the La Trobe partnership is just one node in a quite extensive network. As of May 2009, the LBB's database recorded the existence of 138 active out-of-school-hours learning support programs, with 10 operating at more than one site. Of the 138 programs, 32 were coordinated by schools and 64 by community organisations, 11 were school/community partnerships and eight were community/local government partnerships. The remainder were corporate/online programs or combinations of the above (Tribe, cited in Bond, 2009, p.7).

Perhaps the most significant difference between the UWS Refugee Action Support program (RAS) and the La Trobe Learning Beyond the Bell program is that the latter takes place outside of schools. It follows that the La Trobe beginning teachers are not in a position to work with refugee students in classrooms and cannot observe first-hand how these students relate to the demands of the curriculum. Nevertheless, the La Trobe program provides valuable tutoring support in out-of-hours settings, in collaboration with community volunteers.

South Australia: Inspire Peer Mentor Program

The Inspire Peer Mentor program is a partnership among Flinders University, the Department of Family and Community Affairs (FaCS), now known as Families, Housing, Community Services and Indigenous Affairs (FaHCSIA) Mentor Marketplace program, and schools and community organizations in Southern Adelaide. Funding is provided through the FaCS Mentor Marketplace program which is a Commonwealth initiative (Inspire mentoring program, 2010). Inspire is focused on providing mentoring to at-risk and disadvantaged students, including humanitarian students, living in the southern suburbs of Adelaide. It seeks to increase participation and engagement with learning among children and young people considered unlikely to complete their education (Inspire mentoring program, 2010). Inspire acts as an umbrella organization as it coordinates and funds projects from schools and community organizations that have applied for peer mentors. Funds are made available from the Mentor Marketplace initiative (Inspire, personal correspondence). Currently, mentoring projects have been negotiated with over 30 primary and secondary schools and alternative education programs in the southern suburbs of Adelaide. With a focus on disadvantaged children and youth, students with refugee experience are among the mentees participating in the program. However, to date, the exact numbers of these students are not available, as each project is tailored to meet the specific needs of the local learning environment.

Inspire mentors can belong to any department of Flinders University, and if they are enrolled in an education degree program, they can apply their mentoring experience in Inspire towards academic credit for their degrees. Students from disciplines other than education serve in a voluntary capacity as mentors. In the School of Education, a teaching practicum elective topic was included in the education degree programs in order to expand the teaching experience of new teachers so that they can serve as mentors and receive recognition for their work (Koerner & Harris, 2003). Education academics recognized that if pre-service teachers could observe experienced teachers carrying out many different aspects of their roles, and if they could participate in the full range of school activities, this would provide them with a far broader preparation than could be achieved through the standard curriculum-based practicum (Koerner & Harris, 2003).

In order to be a mentor, all university students must obtain a national police check and attend compulsory training sessions held at the beginning and during the program. Throughout their participation in the program, mentors receive supervision by staff from partner organizations. In the case of the education students, a representative from the education faculty also tracks their progress by regularly visiting the schools. Mentors are expected to spend two hours per week in mentoring activities for at least one semester, if not two. They are encouraged to be "co-learners" in their learning environments, to listen to and interact with their mentees both inside and outside the traditional classroom (Inspire website, 2009).

Inspire mentors who are education students are awarded a non-graded pass upon successful completion of their mentoring experience, and upon submitting a reflective journal or a 1,000-word reflective essay on what they have learned and how being a mentor has influenced their ideas about teaching. A report for the school is also required. Currently, about 120 university students are recruited and trained for placement as mentors each semester.

Anecdotal evidence suggests that Inspire projects are largely successful in meeting youth development and local community needs in a number of ways. These include, for instance, developing young people's skills, self-esteem and engagement in education, training, and employment (Wilczynski, Ross, Schwartzkoff, Rintoul, & Reed-Gilbert, 2004). In addition, Koerner and Harris (2003) suggest that new teachers acting as mentors develop more confidence about being teachers and have greater insight into professional aspects of teaching than do pre-service teachers who have not served as mentors.

CONCLUSION

There are few national policies, other than the funding for the New Arrivals Program, that provide consistent support for refugee students in Australia. Moreover, the current levels of funding are not adequate to meet the long-term, complex educational needs of most students with refugee backgrounds. State policies mostly provide one year of English language instruction and cultural orientation in new arrivals centers, based on Commonwealth funding. Exceptionally, South Australia provides up to two years of support. However, the tendency to push newcomer students into mainstream classrooms, without adequate English-language preparation and without the cultural knowledge or social capital required to negotiate the complex learning environments of classrooms and schools, puts many of them at risk of failure.

A more serious problem is the absence of concerted policies at all levels, but particularly at the school level, to actively transform schools into more equitable and inclusive learning environments where the abilities and knowledges of students with refugee experience can be recognized and celebrated, and where the differences caused by refugee status, race, gender, and religion are not minimized, but are accepted and incorporated as normalized facets of learning environments (Green & Luke, 2006).

For the education sector, the pressure from the Commonwealth government to privilege teacher accountability, standardized testing, and outcome-based assessments means schools and teachers largely have to struggle on an individual basis to address the personal and academic needs of their refugee students. It is evident as well that in each state and territory there are local initiatives and partnerships among schools, universities, government agencies, community organizations, and NGOs to create new generations of beginning teachers who have had first-hand experience in mentoring and assisting students with refugee backgrounds. In critically important ways, these initiatives help schools to compensate for the fact that the level of governmental support is not adequate to meet the educational needs of students with refugee experience. Such initiatives also create awareness and open-mindedness among new teachers. This has the potential to improve the learning environment for all students as these teachers move into their careers and implement what they have been learning.

What is lacking, however, is a commitment on a national level to create policies that ensure adequate funding and long term support designed to give refugee students every opportunity for social and academic success. Without this kind of commitment, it is likely that the long-run costs to the nation will escalate, as numerous students with refugee backgrounds find that they are unable to access the standard pathways that lead to successful employment and secure lives. The danger is that many will instead become dependent on institutional welfare supports or enter the criminal justice system. Considering the promise that students with refugee backgrounds offer to Australia, this outcome is both tragic and avoidable.

REFERENCES

Australian Bureau of Statistics. (2009). (Cat. No 3218.0). Canberra: Author.

Australian Bureau of Statistics. (2010). Australian Demographic Statistics (Catalogue No. 3101.0) Canberra: Author.

Arzubiaga, A. E., Nogueron, S.C., & Sullivan, A.L. (2009). The education of children in im/migrant families. *Review of Research in Education, 33,* 246–271.

Barakat, B., Karpinska, Z., & Paulson, J. (2008). *Desk study: Education and fragility.* Conflict and Education Research Group. Geneva, Switzerland: Inter-Agency Network for Education in Emergencies.

Bond, S. (2009). *Learning support programs: Education reform beyond the school.* Fitzroy, Victoria, NSW: Brotherhood of St. Laurence.

Boyle-Baise, M., & Sleeter, C. (2000). Community based service-learning for multicultural teacher education. *Educational Foundations, 114*(2), 33–50.

Brace, E. (2011). Crossing borders to create supportive educational spaces for refugee youth. In T. Ferfolja, M. Vickers, F. McCarthy, L. Naidoo, & E. Brace (Eds.), *Crossing borders: African refugees, teachers and schools* (pp. 91–113). Canberra, ACT: Australian Curriculum Studies Association.

Brown, J., Miller, J., & Mitchell, J. (2006). Interrupted schooling and the acquisition of literacy: Experiences of Sudanese refugees in Victorian secondary schools. *Australian Journal of Language and Literacy, 29*(2), 150–162.

Brown, T. (forthcoming). Education dilemmas in protracted refugee situations in Africa. In F. McCarthy & M. Vickers. (Eds.), *Achieving equity in education for immigrant and refugee students* (pp. 189–203). Charlotte, NC: Information Age.

Chelpi-den Hamer. (2009). Educational attainments of Liberian refugees in Cote d'Ivoire (1992–2007): Reflections on certification, equivalence and informal schooling for refugees. In J. Kirk (Ed.), *Certification counts: Recognizing the learning attainments of displaced and refugee students.* Paris, France: UNESCO International Institute for Educational Planning.

Christie, P., & Sidhu, R. (2006). Governmentality and 'fearless speech': Framing the education asylum seeker and refugee children in Australia. *Oxford Review of Education, 32*(4), 449–465.

Cochran-Smith, M., & Zeichner, K. (Eds.) (2005). *Studying teacher education: The report of the AERA panel on research and teacher education.* Mahwah, NJ: Lawrence Erlbaum.

Collier, V. (1995). Acquiring a second language for school. *Reading Rockets.* Washington, DC: U.S. Department of Education, Office of Special Programs.

Community Relations Commission. (2006). *Investigation into African humanitarian settlement in NSW.* Sydney, NSW: NSW Community Relations Commission.

Department of Education and Early Childhood Development. (2008). *Strengthening outcomes: Refugee students in government schools.* Melbourne, Victoria: Government of Victoria.

Department of Education, Employment and Workplace Relations. (2009). Retrieved from http://www.deewr.gov.au/Schooling/Programs/EnglishasaSecondLanguageNewArrivalsProgram/Pages/Arrangements2009

Department of Education and Training. (2009). *Key Initiatives, 2009.* Sydney, NSW: Government of New South Wales.

Department of Immigration and Citizenship. (2008). *New beginnings: Supporting new arrivals on their settlement journey 2006–07.* Canberra, ACT: Australian Government.

Department of Immigration and Citizenship. (2010). *Annual report 2008–2009.* Commonwealth of Australia. Retrieved from www.immi.gov.au/about/reports/annual/2008-2009/pdf/outcome/pdf.

Department of Immigration and Multicultural and Indigenous Affairs. (2006). *Australia's support for humanitarian entrants 2004–2005.* Canberra: Australian government.

Dudderar, D., & Stover, L.T. (2003). Putting service learning experiences at the heart of a teacher education curriculum. *Educational Research Quarterly, 27*(2), 18–32.

Eschenbacher, H. (2009). INEE guidance on education in conflict-affected countries: Responsive education from project to system. *Journal of Education for International Development, 4*(1), 1–11.

Ferfolja, T., Vickers, M., McCarthy, F., Naidoo, L., & Brace, E. (2011). *Crossing borders: African refugees, teachers and schools.* Canberra, ACT: Australian Curriculum Studies Association.

Gallego, M. (2001). Is experience the best teacher? *Journal of Teacher Education, 52*(4), 313–325.

Garcia, G. (2000). *Lessons from research: What is the length of time it takes limited English proficient students to acquire English and succeed in an all-English classroom?* Issue and Brief No 5. Washington DC: The National Clearing House for Bilingual Education.

Gilford, S., Correa-Velez, I., & Sampson, R. (2009). *Good starts for recently arrived youth with refugee backgrounds. Promoting wellbeing in the first three years of settlement in Melbourne, Australia.* La Trobe Refugee Research Centre, La Trobe University and the Victoria Foundation for Survivors of Torture. Melbourne, Victoria: Foundation House.

Government of South Australia. (2010). South Australia's curriculum portal. Transition for New Arrival Program students. Retrieved from http://www.decs.sa.gov.au/curric/pages/ESL/transition

Green, J., & Luke, A. (2006). Rethinking learning: What counts as learning and what learning counts. *Review of Research in Education, 30*(1), xi–xvi.

Inspire Mentoring Program. (2010). *INSPIRE.* Retrieved from http://www.flinders.edu.au/careers/services/mentor/inspire.cfm and http://www.flinders.edu.au/business-community/community-engagement/education

Jakubowicz, A. (2009). *Cultural diversity, cosmopolitan citizenship and education: issues, options and implications for Australia.* A discussion paper for the Australian Education Union. Unpublished. Sydney, NSW: University of Technology Sydney.

Kanu, Y. (2008). Educational needs and barriers for African refugee students in Manitoba. *Canadian Journal of Education, 31*(4), 915–940.

Koerner, C., & Harris, J., (2003). Inspired learning: Creating engaged teaching and learning environments for university and school students through university to school mentor programs. *International Education Journal.* http://iej.cjb.net.

Matthews, J. (2008). Schooling and settlement: refugee education in Australia. *International Studies in Sociology of Education, 18*, 31–45.

McBrien, J. L. (2005). Educational needs and barriers for refugee students in the United States: A review of the literature. *Review of Educational Research, 75*(3), 329–364.

McCarthy, F. E. (2011) Crossing borders: Policies that shape refugee life. In T. Ferfolja, M. Vickers, F. McCarthy, L. Naidoo, & E. Brace (Eds.), *Crossing borders: African refugees, teachers and schools* (pp. 15–32). Canberra, ACT: Australian Curriculum Studies Association.

Miller, J., Mitchell, J., & Brown, J. (2005). African refugees with interrupted schooling in the high school mainstream: Dilemmas for teachers. *Prospect, 20*(2), 19–33.

Ministerial Council on Education, Employment, Training and Youth Affairs [MCEETYA]. (2006). Schools resourcing task force. *Funding for English as a Second Language for New Arrival Students, 8*(2), 354–364. Discussion Paper.

Naidoo, L. (2011). School–university–community partnerships. In T. Ferfolja, M. Vickers, F. McCarthy, L. Naidoo, & E. Brace (Eds.), *Crossing borders: African refugees, teachers and schools.* Canberra, ACT: Australian Curriculum Studies Association.

New South Wales Department of Education and Training. (2009). *Refugee support strategy key initiatives, 2009.* Sydney, NSW: Department of Education and Training.

Pinson, H., & Arnot, M. (2010). Local conceptualisations of the education of asylum-seeking and refugee students: from hostile to holistic models. *International Journal of Inclusive Education, 14*(3), 247–267.

Pittaway, E., & Muli, C. (2009). 'We have a voice—Hear us': The settlement experiences of refugees and migrants from the Horn of Africa. Sydney, NSW: Horn of Africa Relief and Development Agency.

Portes, A., & Rambault, R. G. (Eds.). (2001). *Legacies: The story of the immigrant second generation.* Berkeley, CA: University of California.

Refugee Council of Australia. (2010). *Australia's refugee and humanitarian program 2010–11: Community views on current challenges and future directions.* Surry Hills, NSW: Author.

Tebbe, K. (2009). Global trends for education to support stability and resilience: Research, programming and finance. *Journal of Education for International Development, 4*(1), 1–12.

United Nations High Commissioner for Refugees. (2009). *Refugee education in urban settings. Case studies from Nairobi, Kampala, Amman and Damascus.* Operational Solutions and Transition Section, Division for Programme Support and Management. Geneva, Switzerland: United Nations High Commissioner for Refugees.

United Nations High Commissioner for Refugees (2010). *2009 Global Trends: Refugees, Asylum-seekers, Returnees, Internally Displaced and Stateless Persons.* Paris, France: United Nations High Commissioner for Refugees.

Van der Stouwe, M., & Oh, S.-A. (2007). Educational change in a protracted refugee context. *Forced Migration Review, 30*, 47–49.

Vickers, M. H. (2007). Reversing the lens: Transforming teacher education through service learning. In S. Billig & S. Gelmon (Eds.), *From passion to objectivity:*

International and cross-disciplinary perspectives on service learning research. Charlotte, NC: Information Age Publishing.

Vickers, M. H. (2011). Teachers Crossing Borders. In T. Ferfolja, M. Vickers, F. McCarthy, L. Naidoo, & E. Brace (Eds.), *Crossing borders: African refugees, teachers and schools* (pp. 49–72). Canberra, ACT: Australian Curriculum Studies Association.

Vickers, M. H., & McCarthy, F. E. (2010). Repositioning refugee students from the margins to the center of teachers' work. *International Journal of Diversity in Organizations, Communities & Nations, 10*(2), 199–210.

Wilczynski, A., Ross, S., Schwartzkoff, J., Rintoul, D., & Reed-Gilbert, K. (2004). *Evaluation of the Mentor Marketplace Program.* Report prepared by Urbis Keys Young. Canberra, ACT: Commonwealth Department of Family and Community Services.

Youth Mentoring Network. (2010). INSPIRE peer mentor program. Retrieved from http://www.youthmentoring.org.au/program_details.php?id=63

CHAPTER 9

EQUITY IN EDUCATION FOR MIGRANT AND REFUGEE CHILDREN

Issues from the United Kingdom

Jill Rutter
Institute for Public Policy Research, London, UK

ABSTRACT

This chapter reviews equity in education for migrant and refugee children in the United Kingdom. It argues that governmental and nongovernmental organizations involved in planning interventions to support greater equity in education need to reframe they way they see migrant and refugee children and pay greater attention to broader measures of equality, including income equality and maternal education.

My little girl, me and my husband are just staying in one room. Someone asks me "just cover this job for me, at the end of the week I will pay you £40, I will pay you like £60." That is how I have been surviving. It is hell, I know what I am talking about. It's getting harder by the day, harder by the day. Because what I learn here, when you have

Refugee and Immigrant Students, pages 167–188

kids here, kids come first—in all parts of Europe. But when you don't have the right to stay, it's difficult to give your children things that everyone else has.

—Irregular migrant from Nigeria who is the mother of a six year old girl, interviewed in London in 2010

Although international migration has always been a feature of national life, this aspect of UK population change has increased over the last 20 years, mostly as a result of asylum arrivals in the 1990s, and more recently, migration from the new member states of the European Union. While many migrant children have successful school careers in the UK, there is evidence of substantial educational underachievement in some communities. Poverty and low levels of maternal education are two factors that impact on migrant children's achievement, as well as factors that may be more specific to particular migrant groups, such as an interrupted prior education. However, interventions to secure greater equality of outcome in relation to children's schooling rarely address employment, poverty, and maternal levels of education.

This chapter reviews equity in education for migrant and refugee children. It argues that governmental and nongovernmental organizations involved in planning interventions to support greater equity in education need to reframe the way they see migrant and refugee children and pay greater attention to broader measures of equality, including income equality and maternal education.

WHO ARE MIGRANT AND REFUGEE CHILDREN IN THE UK?

The UN definition of migrants is that they are people who reside outside their country of birth. In the UK, many migrants have British citizenship and have been resident in the UK for many years and are more usually described as members of minority ethnic communities. This chapter uses the term "new migrants" in a qualitative sense to describe those new to the UK. Most migrant children arrive in the UK with families. However, unaccompanied or separated children also arrive in the UK, often as asylum-seekers, but sometimes through other routes.

Today an estimated 11.5% of the total population of the UK is foreign-born, a figure that rises to one in three in Greater London.[1] The proportion of migrants in the total population is similar to most western European countries, but less than the United States, Canada, and Australia. Migrants from European Union (EU) states comprise the largest group of migrants resident in the UK. They include migrants from pre-2004 EU states such as Ireland, France, and Portugal, as well as those from the new member states, of whom the largest number are from Poland. Table 9.1 presents data on

TABLE 9.1   Country of Birth Estimates for UK, Quarter 4 2010

Country	Population estimate from Labour Force Survey, Q4 2010	Percent of population arrived since 2006	Arrival routes
Afghanistan	37,500	9	Almost all as asylum-seekers including large numbers of separated children
Australia	104,100	15	As British citizens, with ancestry visas, work and student visas
Bangladesh	180,100	9	Through student and work migration routes and for family reunion
Brazil	36,300	26	As visitors and then overstayers and through student and work migration
Bulgaria	53,600	49	Mostly as EU nationals, but with smaller numbers coming as studens
Canada	75,200	13	As British citizens, with ancestry visas, work and student visas
China (inc HK)	196,200	32 Mainland China, but 13 HK	Mostly through work and student visa routes including previous (pre 1960s) favouring Commonwealth citizens, with a significant number of asylum applicants
Cyprus	63,700	7	Mostly through work and student visa routes including previous ones favouring Commonwealth citizens, a few refugees and recently as EU nationals
Czech Republic	38,000	48	As EU nationals
France	116,800	23	As EU nationals
Germany	279,900	8	As EU nationals, but also the German born children of military personnel
Ghana	91,600	10	Mostly through work and student visa routes including those favouring Commonwealth citizens
Hungary	53,700	57	As EU nationals
India	672,400	18	Mostly through work and student visa routes including previous (pre 1960s) routes favoring Commonwealth citizens and for family reunion.
Iran	65,900	12	Mostly as asylum-seekers with a small number of students
Iraq	64,700	15	Mostly as asylum-seekers
Ireland	362,900	5	Irish nationals have always had full right to live and work in the UK
Italy	114,300	20	As EU nationals

(continued)

TABLE 9.1   Country of Birth Estimates for UK, Quarter 4 2010 (cont.)

Country	Population estimate from Labour Force Survey, Q4 2010	Percent of population arrived since 2006	Arrival routes
Jamaica	146,700	3	Mostly through work and student visa routes including those favouring Commonwealth citizens, with a small number of asylum applicants
Japan	47,900	39	
Kenya	102,200	1	Through work visa routes and as refugees, but also as British citizens.
Latvia	74,700	47	As EU nationals
Lithuania	102,500	46	As EU nationals
Malaysia	61,200	16	Mostly through work visa and student visa routes
Mauritius	40,600		Mostly through work visa and student visa routes
Nepal	44,700	50	As army personnel and through family reunion and work visa routes
Netherlands	70,800	13	As EU nationals
New Zealand	58,200	9	As British citizens, with ancestry visas, work and student visas
Nigeria	160,700	12	Mostly through work and student visa routes including previous (pre 1960s) favouring Commonwealth citizens and for family reunion, with some recent refugee migration
Pakistan	403,700	11	Mostly through work and student visa routes including previous (pre 1960s) favouring Commonwealth citizens and for family reunion, with some recent refugee migration
Philippines	123,600	24	Mostly through work visa routes
Poland	552,500	34	Previously as refugees, students or visitor overstayers and more recently as EU nationals
Portugal	90,500	22	As EU nationals
Romania	79,200	63	As asylum-seekers and more recently as EU nationals
Russia	52,500	27	Through work visa and student visa routes, with some migration as EU nationals from Baltic states
Singapore	40,300	3	Mostly through work and student visa routes including previous (pre 1960s) favouring Commonwealth citizens

TABLE 9.1 Country of Birth Estimates for UK, Quarter 4 2010 (cont.)

Country	Population estimate from Labour Force Survey, Q4 2010	Percent of population arrived since 2006	Arrival routes
Slovakia	45,200	46	As EU nationals
Somalia	104,700	16	Mostly as asylum-seekers, but also as onward migrants from other EU countries
South Africa	224,200	11	As British citizens, with ancestry visas, work and student visas
Spain	66,700	28	As EU nationals
Sri Lanka	121,300	15	As asylum-seekers and students
Tanzania	37,400		Through work and student visa routes with some asylum migration
Thailand	52,200	32	Through work and student visa routes
Turkey	87,900	6	As asylum-seekers and though work and student visa routes
Uganda	52,700	4	As asylum-seekers and through work and student visa routes, as well as those with types of British nationality
USA	189,100	25	Through work and student visa routes and as military personnel
Zimbabwe	133,300	8	As British citizens, asylum-seekers and through work and student visa routes
UK	54,205,500	—	

Source: Labour Force Survey, Quarter 4, 2010, author calculations.

the size of the main country-of-birth groups resident in the UK. European Community law gives them freedom of movement within Europe and the right of residence as European Economic Area (EEA) workers, providing they remain in employment.

In the last five years, too, there has also been a significant onward migration of migrant communities from other EU countries to the UK. Significant numbers of Somalis, Nigerians, Ghanians, Sri Lankan Tamils, and Latin Americans have moved to the UK from other EU countries. While many of these onward migrants have secured EU citizenship or refugee status elsewhere in the EU, some are irregular migrants (Koser, 2005). Many of these onward migrants have experienced forced migration from their country of birth, and their backgrounds are often similar to refugee populations in the UK.

Labor migrants also come from outside the EU. In 2010, some 162,450 work visas were granted from outside the EU (Home Office, 2010). The work visa system has seen considerable change over the last five years, and routes in to the UK for unskilled or semiskilled workers have all but ended. Skilled migrants are now subject to a new cap on numbers, and those who wish to bring their dependents have to show savings to indicate they can support their children.

About 40,000 dependent spouses, spouses, children, and civil partners were admitted to the UK in 2010. The numbers of overseas students from outside the EU has gradually increased in the last 15 years, with 311,111 admitted to the UK in 2010 (Home Office, 2010). While most overseas students are young and do not have dependent children, a portion do.

Asylum-seekers comprise another migratory movement. Although the numbers of asylum applications have decreased since a peak in 2002, some 17,790 asylum applications were lodged in the UK in 2010, with Iran, Afghanistan, Zimbabwe, Pakistan, and Sri Lanka being the top five countries of origin of asylum-seekers (Home Office, 2010). Of those who received an initial decision on their asylum applications in 2010, 17% were granted refugee status and another 8% were either granted discretionary leave or humanitarian protection and were allowed to remain in the UK. In 2010, 75% of asylum applicants were refused asylum after an initial decision. While over a quarter of those refused asylum are subsequently successful in their asylum appeals[2] or are removed from the UK, the vast majority of those refused asylum are neither successful appellants nor are they removed. Instead they remain and comprise a significant component of the UK's irregular migrant population.

Over the last 20 years, significant numbers of unaccompanied asylum-seeking children have arrived in the UK. In 2010, 1,595 asylum applications were received from children, of whom about 30% were Afghan nationals, mostly boys. For children whose initial asylum claims are refused—the majority—most are given discretionary leave to remain in the UK until they are 17.5 years old. After this they have to make a further claim for asylum. The treatment of unaccompanied asylum-seeking children has been subject to longstanding criticism from refugee and human rights organizations; their ages are often disputed, they receive little support from local government social services, and most cannot access legal advice to help them make an asylum claim (Refugee Council, 2011; Stanley, 2002).

The UK also admits a small number of program refugees whose status has been determined abroad. In 2010, some 715 program refugees were admitted to the UK through the offices of UNHCR. Many families admitted through the UK's two programs have been long-term residents in refugee camps.

A further group of international migrants comprise British nationals returning to the UK as well as those with ancestry visas. Research suggests that in 2009 there were 5.4 million British nationals living abroad, including nearly one million UK nationals living in Spain (Finch, Latorre, & Andrew, 2010). They include those returning to the UK after short periods working abroad, and long-term migrants who have maintained their British passports and are now faced with changed circumstances necessitating a "return" to a country with which they may have few connections. Some 84,000 UK nationals migrated to the UK between June 2009 and June 2010, including a large number of children.

There are also an unknown number of irregular migrants in the UK, and in many of the UK's cities, "undocumented" children comprise a sizable proportion of children living in poverty. The irregular migrant population mostly comprises visa overstayers, including visitor visa overstayers, and asylum overstayers, but it also includes smaller number of clandestine entrants. Recent population estimates put the irregular migrant population in the UK at between 373,000 and 719,000 people at the end of 2007, with a central estimate of 533,000 people (Greater London Authority Economics, 2009). Using the same methodology to estimate population size, a recent study suggested that at the end of 2007 there were 104,000–216,000 children who have no permission to remain in the UK whose numbers include overstayers, but also include the UK-born children of irregular migrants. This research gives a middle estimate of 155,000 undocumented children, with 85,000 children born in the UK (Sigona & Hughes, 2010).

ENTITLEMENTS, STRUCTURES AND ORGANIZATIONS IN THE UK

Immigration control is the responsibility of the UK Border Agency, a government agency that is accountable to the Home Office. Education is now a devolved power in the UK, and the Welsh and Scottish governments and Northern Ireland Assembly formulate their own educational law and policy (as well as their own migrant integration policies). Despite the devolution of powers, broad trends in the direction of educational policy are similar in all the constituent nations of the UK, as are many of the issues facing migrant children.

In all parts of the UK, overseas-born children can attend state schools until the end of compulsory education and afterwards with the permission of the head teacher. Despite this right, many migrant children face long delays in finding a school place. Policy is also very unclear about the rights of undocumented children to attend school. Many do, but undocumented children are a group that falls between two conflicting policy agendas: the universalism of children's rights, as enshrined by the UN Convention on the Rights of the Child and articulated by nongovernmental agencies working with children, and the desire by governments to promote border security.

Generally, in England, central government coordination of refugee and migrant integration policy, including children's education, has been further weakened as a consequence of the change of government in summer 2010 and continuing public spending cuts. Arguably, the controversial nature of migration into the UK, including asylum migration, has resulted in central government ministers and their civil servants being unwilling publically to advance migrant integration policies for fear of an anti-migrant backlash in the print media (Rutter, 2006). At the time of writing there were only two staff with a brief for refugee and migrant children's education within the central government in England. No guidance or evaluation of migrant children's experiences has been published by the English central government since 2007.

Nongovernmental organizations (NGOs) and local governments have stepped into this policy vacuum and they are the ones that have largely defined what is "good practice" to support refugee and migrant children (Pinson, Arnot, & Candappa, 2010; Rutter, 2006). This good practice has been conceptualized as:

- induction and welcome into new and often unfamiliar education systems
- English-as-an-additional-language teaching and support for those with limited fluency in English
- measures to challenge racism and hostility to new migrants and to build cohesive schools that can manage diversity
- counseling and other forms of psychosocial support for children who have experienced organized violence, loss of key carers, or other forms of trauma
- partnership work with other organizations able to support refugee and migrant children (Bolloten & Spafford, 1998; Ingleby & Watters, 2005; Rutter, 1994).

Among NGO actors, it has been the national refugee organizations and the large national children's NGOs that have been most involved in policy advocacy for refugee children, and in constructing a discursive hegemony about children's needs. Significant NGOs include the Refugee Council, the Children's Society, and the Medical Foundation for the Care of Victims of Torture. Many of these organizations also advocate for refugees' rights and have thus been forced to mobilize humanitarian discourses, mostly the discourse of refugee trauma, to argue for the sympathetic treatment of asylum-seekers. Additionally, the language of trauma has been invoked as an argument for greater healthcare and welfare resources for this group. It is also worth noting that there is a much weaker lobby for the rights of labor migrants' and their families in the UK, and very few national organizations are willing to advocate for children who are irregular migrants.

Within local government, there has been a long tradition of supporting the education of migrant children. From the late 1960s onwards, local governments employed teams of English-as-an-additional-language teachers in many parts of urban England (less so in Scotland and Wales). These teachers often worked in a number of schools and were partly supported by a direct grant from central government (Klein, 1993). By the 1970s, many of the same local government staff began to espouse policies that were described as "multiculturalist." Although lacking in a coherent agenda, advocates of multicultural education sought to improve provision for children from minority ethnic and migrant groups by ensuring the maintenance of their home languages and cultures. Multicultural education also aimed to prepare children from the majority community for life in a multiethnic society.

Asylum arrivals increased significantly starting in 1989, and in 1990, three local government areas in London set up teams of teachers or advisors whose job was to support refugee children in schools and in some cases to develop school and local government policy on refugee education. Later, many other local government areas followed, appointing refugee support teachers or "new arrivals teachers," partly funded by the same government grant that funds English-as-an-additional-language teaching in schools. But since 2005, the numbers of refugee support teachers or new arrivals teachers has decreased in all parts of the UK. This is a consequence of public spending cuts, but it is also the result of a policy shift in central government. Prior to 2005, there was still an acceptance by ministers and civil servants that a central government should fund some of the interventions to meet the additional and specific needs of migrant and refugee children. Since 2005 central government has advocated a policy to "mainstream" these children's educational support. Guidance issued by the English central government in 2007 argues that schools must use their general budget to meet most English-as-an-additional-language learning costs. In 2011, the central government grant that had supported English language learning for migrant children was abolished, and schools were informed that they must meet most of the additional learning needs of these children from their general funds.

Generally, new arrivals with limited English are placed straight into a mainstream classroom and may receive some additional help in the classroom from a classroom assistant. Specialist English language teachers generally do not give much direct classroom support; instead, they are generally involved in initial assessments, teacher training, and helping children who are struggling. Research has highlighted the decreasing amount of English language learning support given to migrant and refugee children, particularly those in secondary education (see Rutter, 2006). Many migrant children arriving in London secondary schools receive no additional language support at all.

There are also a number of school-based interventions run by NGOs that are largely targeted at refugee children—for example, psychotherapeutic counseling, youth groups, and befriending projects for young refugees.

THE EDUCATIONAL EXPERIENCES OF MIGRANT CHILDREN

As Table 9.2 indicates, migrant children come from many different countries of origin and move to the UK for many different reasons. Children's prior length of residence in the UK varies widely. In a school, some migrant children may have moved to the UK as very young children and spent most of their lives in the UK, with others being more recent arrivals. Within different communities there is also considerable diversity within families in

TABLE 9.2   GCSE Performance by Ethnic Group, 2003

Ethnic group	Mean % difference in proportions of children achieving five A*-C grades at GCSE relative to mean for England, 2003
Chinese	+11.0
Sri Lankan	+8.0
Indian	+7.0
Iranian	+5.0
Irish	+4.5
Filipino	+4.5
French	+3.0
Nigerian	+1.5
White British	+1.0
Ghanaian	−0.8
Italian	−1.0
Cypriot	−5.5
Bangladeshi	−9.3
Pakistani	−11.3
Jamaican	−15.3
Somali	−22.8
Turkish	−23.6
Portuguese	−32.3

Source: Department for Education and ippr calculations originally cited in Rutter et al, 2008. GCSEs at examinations taken at the end of compulsory education.

relation to their class origins, parental levels of education, children's prior experiences of schooling, as well as the families' experiences of integrating into the UK. Apart from the need by many, but not all, migrant children to learn English, there is a considerable heterogeneity of needs and experiences among new migrant children in the UK. This diversity is not always acknowledged by those researching migrant children or advocating for their rights.

So what are the experiences of migrant and refugee children in the UK? How able are they to secure equal educational outcomes with non-migrant children and with settled members of minority ethnic communities? What interventions work in the UK, and what social issues do we need still need to solve?

Education departments in all parts of the UK collect neither country-of-birth data nor data on specific migrant groups such as refugees, so it is very difficult to analyze how well migrant children are doing at school. In England, data on school achievement are analyzed using broad ethnicity categories, although local authorities can collect more nuanced data by using "extended ethnicity codes." This system allows broad ethnicity categories—for example, white UK (WTUK), black African (BAFR)—to be refined using extended categories. BNIG and BSOM are extended ethnicity codes for Nigerians and Somalis, respectively.

Some local authorities have used extended ethnicity codes to look at the achievement of specific groups of migrants. Table 9.2 presents data on GCSE performance by ethnic group in 2003, for the local authorities who collected these data. It should be noted that the central government is extremely reticent to carry out a national analysis of educational outcomes by extended ethnicity codes, and spending cuts mean that fewer local authorities are now undertaking such analysis.

Data presented in Table 9.2 highlight the differential levels of achievement among children from migrant and minority ethnic communities in the UK, with some children enjoying a measure of success, but also significant underachievement in some groups, including Somalis and Portuguese. Although these data were collected in 2003 and there have been improvements since then, this achievement gap between migrant/minority and non-migrant groups remain. Across the UK, groups at risk of underachievement include those of Albanian, Bangladeshi, Congolese, Pakistani, Portuguese, Somali, Turkish, and Caribbean origin, including children who have migrated, but also the UK-born children of these ethnic and national groups. Gender also affects achievement as girls in many ethnic groups perform better than boys (Department for Education and Skills, 2005). There are also considerable local differences in achievement, with groups who underachieve in one area sometimes securing rather better results in another part of the UK (Rutter, Newman, & Pillai, 2008).

There is an extensive body of research about the educational under-achievement of children from migrant and minority ethnic communities (Gillborn & Mirza, 2000; Tikly, 2005; Tomlinson, 2001). This literature highlights causes of educational underachievement that are common to all ethnic groups, of which growing up in poverty and low levels of maternal education have the biggest impact. There are also causes of underachievement that are specific to or more frequent among migrant children or particular migrant communities. Among Somalis, for example, an interrupted or non-existent education prior to migration to the UK is a significant cause of underachievement, as children arrive in the UK without age-appropriate skills. (The school system in southern Somalia has been destroyed, and some refugee children spend years out of school in their lengthy journeys to the UK.) The present levels of support for learning English are insufficient to develop high levels of academic literacy in children with an interrupted prior education. Mothers may also have limited literacy. The very high levels of worklessness among Somalis living in the UK also have a major impact on their children's educational outcomes (Rutter, 2006). Significantly, analyses of UK-born children of Somali origin indicate that they do not achieve better examination results than do Somali children who came to the UK as refugees. And while many Somali children do underachieve, there is also a confident and reasonably successful Somali middle class whose children do well at school (Rutter et al., 2008).

Among Portuguese migrant children, negative parental educational experience and a culture of early school leaving impact on their children's educational outcomes. In the UK, most newly arrived Portuguese migrants are from working-class origins in Portugal and are employed as low-paid workers in agriculture, food processing, or in the hospitality sector in the UK. Research on this community shows that low pay and parental absences from home due to shift work are significant causes of underachievement. Parents cannot afford enrichment activities such as music lessons, and their absence from the home in the evenings means that homework may not be completed. In the East of England, many Portuguese migrant workers are living in poor-quality or overcrowded housing, often of a temporary nature. This also makes homework difficult. Children who move home and school frequently are a group at risk of educational underachievement. A lack of English language support in schools is a further factor contributing to educational underachievement among Portuguese children (de Abreu, Cline, & Lambert, 2003).

Underachievement in migrant children has many causes. The limited UK research on underachievement in this group of children often fails to analyze the many, varied, and sometimes group-specific factors that cause underachievement. There are also migrant groups whose test and examination results are better than average. Again, there is little in-depth analysis about why some groups do well. Class differences in migrant and refugee communities are seldom mentioned, although social class, poverty, and maternal levels of education are the three factors most strongly associated educational achievement in the UK (Gillborn & Gipps, 1996).

CHILD POVERTY IN MIGRANT GROUPS

In both Somali and Portuguese migrant communities, average household income levels are much lower than the UK average, and rates of child poverty[3] are higher (Institute for Public Policy Research, 2007; Rutter, 2011). This is another manifestation of social inequality as it affects migrant and refugee children. Moreover, child poverty is strongly associated with educational underachievement (Lupton, Heath, & Salter, 2009). Children growing up in poverty are less likely to participate in enrichment activities or visit cultural sites—activities that improve educational outcomes. Poverty causes bad health and parental stress, which again impacts on children's schooling. Overcrowded housing makes homework difficult to complete.

While some migrant families are prosperous or have a secure income, there are a number of migrant groups where children are at higher risk of poverty. Table 9.3 presents data on the earnings and labour market experiences of selected country-of-birth groups for Quarter 4 of 2011. We need to be cautious about such figures as they are averages, and there are often significant differences in income *within* different groups. But some country-of-birth groups are disproportionally represented among the low-paid, particularly those from refugee-producing countries and from the EU's new member states, where many migrants work in agriculture, hospitality, and catering, all low-paid sectors of the economy.

As can be seen from Table 9.3, the employment status of different country-of-birth groups is also very varied. Broadly, the employment status of different migrant groups relates to their mode of entry into the UK. Newly arrived EU migrants and work-visa holders, who have essentially come to the UK to work, have high levels of employment. Those populations who have come to the UK as refugees tend to have much lower levels of employment—for example, just 32% of Somalia-born adults were employed in 2007. Research on barriers to labor market participation among refugees shows that that poor levels of fluency in English, employer prejudice, the absence of qualifications, the absence of UK work experience and references, child care obligations, and the fear of loss of benefits and social housing are major barriers to work.

Many migrant families have an additional demand on their income: remittance payments. Research with low-paid migrant workers in London indicated that they were sending home between 20 and 30% of their net

TABLE 9.3   Employment and Qualification Levels of Migrants by Country-of-Birth

Country	Proportion of working population earning less than £6.53 per hour (%)	Employment in proportion to the working age population (%)	Proportion of adult population possessing higher level qualifications, 2001[a] (%)	Proportion of adult population with no qualifications, 2001 (%)
Afghanistan	61	47	19.9	50.2
Australia	19	66	65.3	8.8
Bangladesh	36	72	14.7	54.0
Brazil	52	67	54.6	4.3
Bulgaria	41	78	55.3	3.1[b]
Canada	24	65	47.5	16.9
China (inc HK)	22	47	49.3	28.5
Cyprus		58	16.1	58.0
Czech Republic	21		39.3	20.8
France	8	61	60.4	12.1
Germany	17	65	53.1	11.3
Ghana	20	63	33.3	18.5
Hungary	38	64	45.2	22.6
India	24	67	37.7	34.2
Iran	19	60	50.3	16.0
Iraq	n/a	46	47.8	24.3
Ireland	12	52	20.5	53.1
Italy	12	42	40.1	29.0
Jamaica	20	50	18.4	44.4
Japan	0	69	61.4	21.4
Kenya	11	71	30.9	21.5
Latvia	53	75	45.5	23.3
Lithuania	59	68	30.4	31.9
Malaysia	23	69	58.6	10.4
Mauritius	13	76	33.8	22.2
Nepal	24	64	41.5	20.8
Netherlands	24	42	63.9	8.7
New Zealand	4	78	51.8	13.9
Nigeria	20	71	52.5	10.8
Pakistan	28	60	32.7	34.4
Philippines	16	69	38.9	33.9
Poland	30	74	45.3	19.1
Portugal	37	64	15.9	49.1
Romania	n/a	70	52.4	19.5
Russia	22	71	68.7	10.3
Singapore	6	86	50.1	8.8

TABLE 9.3 Employment and Qualification Levels of Migrants by Country-of-Birth (continued)

Country	Proportion of working population earning less than £6.53 per hour (%)	Employment in proportion to the working age population (%)	Proportion of adult population possessing higher level qualifications, 2001[a] (%)	Proportion of adult population with no qualifications, 2001 (%)
Slovakia	54	63	31.3	20.8
Somalia	30	32	12.1	49.4
South Africa	10	76	56.0	10.4
Spain	n/a	67	45.2	25.0
Sri Lanka	44	68	28.3	12.0
Tanzania	32	64	33.5	22.7
Thailand	52	64	39.0	34.5
Turkey	38	60	18.1	58.3
Uganda	17	76	32.8	24.5
USA	14	55	76.4	6.2
Zimbabwe	16	62	49.1	7.1
UK	19	48[c]	30.1	23.8

Source: Labour Force Survey, Census 2001 and author calculations.

[a] The ten yearly census is a much more accurate measure of qualifications among migrants in the UK than is the Labour Force Survey, as the Labour Force Survey designates all overseas qualifications as 'other qualifications'.

[b] The numbers of Bulgaria-born migrants without qualifications has increased since 2001, since Bulgaria joined the EU.

[c] The UK-born population has an older profile than migrants and has higher proportions of people in the 50s and 60s who may have left the labour market.

income and engaged in many different money-saving strategies to do this. Having more than one job and eating the cheapest food are common approaches, strategies that impact on children's well-being. Some migrant households also take in destitute co-nationals, who are often irregular migrants. Both remittance payments and generosity to co-nationals impact on migrant children in the UK (Evans, Herbert, Datta, May, McIlwaine, & Wills, 2005).

For migrants who cannot find work, the welfare state is meant to prevent a family from falling into destitution. However, many migrants have no entitlement to claim benefits—at present only those who have secured British citizenship, those who possess EEA worker status or settled status (indefinite leave to remain), and those who receive positive decisions on asylum applications can access the UK benefit system. Moreover, since the late 1980s, increasing proportions of migrants have seen this welfare safety-net removed. This is a trend across all developed countries, with constantly shifting boundaries between citizen, legal migrants, and outsiders.

Since 2003, new asylum-seekers have been unable to work legally in the UK. At the same time they are supported by a system that operates outside the mainstream welfare system and condemns many to ongoing poverty. A daily allowance for an adult is set at £6.50 per day. Those requiring accommodation are housed by the UK Border Agency outside Greater London and the South East, often far from support networks. Unsurprisingly, about 20% of asylum-seekers opt to live with friends and family and near support networks. Providing accommodation to co-nationals impacts on the host family, with more mouths to feed and less space.

Among migrants who are entitled to welfare benefits, their uptake is at a lower rate than the UK-born population. This is a consequence of a lack of awareness of entitlements among migrant communities, an inability to understand the application process, often as a result of limited English language fluency, and an inability to produce documentation to support a benefit claim.

Income inequalities caused by employment patterns, high levels of unemployment among refugee communities and among some longer settled migrants, a lower uptake of benefits, asylum support systems that cause destitution, and inadequate support for large numbers of irregular migrants are all factors that ensure that migrant children are overrepresented among those living in poverty. Newly arrived migrant children are also more likely to be housed in temporary and substandard private rental accommodation, again something that impacts on children's educational outcomes. Five groups of migrant children seem particularly at risk of poverty in the UK:

1. Children of low-paid migrant workers: This is a numerically large group. Many children are from the new member states of the EU, but this group also includes children from outside the EU whose parents entered with work visas and are working in low-paid jobs, for example, as care workers. Families in this group are often housed in the private rental sector, sometimes in very poor-quality and overcrowded accommodation. The nature of this accommodation means that families sometimes experience high levels of housing mobility, with children's schooling being interrupted. One study of low-paid migrant workers showed that nearly 40% did not have enough money always to pay for food for their children and over a third could not pay for children's clothes (Evans et al., 2005).

2. Children who are irregular migrants, or are undocumented because they are the UK-born children of parents who are irregular migrants. Again they are a large group of children, disproportionally settled in London: Research that has examined the survival strategies of

irregular migrants in the UK highlights shocking levels of household poverty and reliance on the informal sector for employment. Irregular migrants who are in work may be working at levels near to or below the national minimum wage, and fear of officialdom makes it difficult for them to seek redress for this. Those without work are reliant on charities such as the Red Cross. Informal sector working and the hidden nature of irregular migration may mean that data that are meant to capture patterns of poverty may be distorted because it does not account for irregular migrants

3. Asylum-seeking children in receipt of support from the UK Border Agency: This group of children presently numbers about 6,000 children who are dispersed around the UK
4. Children of refugees and some other migrants who are unemployed: As Table 9.3 shows, this is a significant group. Welfare-to-work initiatives have had limited success in getting families into work.
5. Children in low-income households supporting destitute co-nationals, where generosity to others impacts on family income and children's welfare. There is little research on this group, but they are likely to be a sizable community in London.

REFRAMING THE WAYS WE THINK ABOUT MIGRANT AND REFUGEE CHILDREN

If central and local governments and NGOs are to implement social interventions to improve the educational outcomes of underachieving migrant children, these organizations will need to focus on three areas of work:

- ensuring that children receive sufficient support for learning English
- challenging the economic issues associated with poor educational outcomes: poverty, low levels of maternal education, social segregation, and bad housing
- focusing on issues that affect specific groups of migrant children— for example, older separated children or those who arrive in the UK late in their educational careers.

But how do central and local governments and NGOs see migrant and refugee children's needs? Table 9.4 presents a thematic analysis of 38 reports about migrant and refugee children published in the UK in 2008 and 2009. All were press released and received national media coverage. Some 19 were published by NGOs, the remainder by central and local government.

TABLE 9.4 Thematic Analyses of Themes in Reports

Theme	Frequency of occurrence as a major theme
Child trafficking	8
Induction systems in schools to welcome new arrivals	7
Child detention	4
Treatment of separated asylum-seeking children by the UK Border Agency and by local government social services	4
The destitution of asylum-seeking families	2
Refugee trauma and generalized vulnerability	2
English language learning pedagogy	3
Specific groups of migrant children: Poles, Roma and Somalis	5
Community relations	1

In all of these reports, migrant and refugee children were implicitly portrayed as a homogenous group in relation to parental wealth and social class. Significant factors that were missing from these policy reports included the impact on children of parents' working conditions, including low pay, the nature of the lives of children who are irregular migrants, and the post-16-year-of-age experiences of children in post-compulsory education and in the labor market. As indicated in Table 9.4, migrant children's needs were largely seen through a rather sensationalized and simplified framework of refugee trauma and generalized "vulnerability" or as victims of trafficking. Such a construction has its origins in the need felt by refugee NGOs to mobilize public support for "deserving" victims in the face of governments whose policy agenda is to limit asylum applications. Arguably this construction of a "traumatized" or trafficked victim impedes a real analysis of migrant children's backgrounds and experiences as well as masking the significance of post-migration experiences, such as poverty and bad housing. This is not to deny the importance of working with those who have experienced trafficking, coerced labor, torture, or organized violence.

Arguably, if social interventions undertaken by governments and NGOs are to promote greater equity, the way that migrant and refugee children's needs are understood needs to be reframed. We need a much more detailed understanding of the specific pre-migration, migratory, and post-migration factors that impact on children's school experiences, and how events within the family, community, and national environment impact on children.

Policymakers and researchers working for governments and NGOs need to draw more from ecological models of child development[4] as well as ethnographic research, including studies that come from a phenomenological or ethnomethodological tradition. National quantitative datasets and local administrative data remain underutilized, yet these have potential to tell powerful stories about inequality—and policymakers need to get out and listen to migrant families in the environments where they live and work.

PRESENT SUCCESSES AND FUTURE CHALLENGES

The first policy challenge in the UK is to reframe the way we think about migrant and refugee children and ensure that interventions focus on the specific needs of groups and sub-groups. But there are other areas that need attention if this group is to secure equal outcomes. Ensuring a greater uptake of free early-years' provision for three- and four-year-olds is a policy priority, because high-quality nursery education means that children from migrant communities can start school speaking English. Local authorities have used "parent champions" drawn from migrant communities to disseminate information about free nursery provision and encourage uptake.

In the UK, NGOs supporting refugees also need to monitor the numbers of migrant children who face long delays in finding school places and pursue the application of equal opportunity legislation through the courts to ensure basic access to schooling. Within government, there needs to be a debate about the real costs of providing language support for children and the impacts of not doing this. In the UK, many migrant and refugee children leave school able to speak English, but with limited academic literacy. Funding for English-as-an-additional language support in schools must match demand.

We need to give greater support to children who arrive in the UK late in their educational careers, as well as those with an interrupted prior education. There have been some successful induction programs for these groups in different parts of the UK. One London local authority ran a 13-week induction program for teenagers with little prior education, a large proportion of whom were unaccompanied refugee children, while others were persistent truants or had a criminal record. Based in a secondary school, it was staffed by a teacher, a classroom assistant, and a part-time social worker. Children were part of a mainstream class for registration times and physical education but received their academic teaching in this small group. The social worker helped children with attendant social issues, such as acting as liaison with immigration lawyers, the health service, and so on. Although the outcomes of this program were excellent—in relation to later attendance, examination results, reoffending rates and progression into work—funding for it ceased, unfortunately, in 2009.

We need to work to improve the home learning environment for some migrant and refugee children. Some parents, particularly mothers, need greater support to learn English. At present, asylum-seekers, spouses from outside the UK, and those not actively looking for work are not usually qualified for subsidized English classes. Even if they are able to study, demand for these classes outstrips supply, and the quality of some teaching is poor. But without English, many parents do not feel confident to interact with their child's school or support their children's education. There have been some programs to improve the home learning environment of migrant and refugee families, using the skills of health visitors, outreach workers, and sometimes volunteers, but these projects need more rigorous evaluation, and the successful projects need wider replication.

Above all, we need to challenge child poverty. The causes of child poverty in poor migrant families are often the same as in the larger population, as are the solutions—solutions that include enabling parents to move into and stay in work, affordable childcare, ensuring that welfare benefit levels do not punish children, and supporting low-income families in work. But migrant families also face some specific issues in relation to child poverty. Many are starting again, but unlike others who are poor, they have no store of accumulated possessions. Support networks can also be severed by migration—networks that in other groups enable low income families to cope. Language barriers can impact on migrants' employment prospects and lead to a lower uptake of benefits. Remittance payments and support for destitute irregular migrants also impacts on family welfare.

We need a wider debate about in-work poverty. In the UK, faith groups, community organizations, and trade unions have come together to campaign for a living wage, at a level that is about 25% higher than the national minimum wage. Welfare-to-work programs for migrants need to be tailored toward their specific needs. It is meaningless to channel people into job search courses if they cannot read or write English.

We need to take a more realistic approach to irregular migration. Mid-range estimates suggest that there are around half a million irregular migrants in the UK, including over 100,000 children. Some families could go home, but many cannot or will not return. A significant proportion of irregular migrants are asylum overstayers in the UK. For them, in particular, forcible removal is hugely expensive: £12,000–£25,000 on average. Even if the UK Border Agency could locate more irregular migrants, it could not afford to remove them. Many individuals and organizations across the political spectrum argue for an earned regularization program for some irregular migrants, where law-abiding individuals are allowed to settle in the UK. Almost all undocumented children are living in poverty, and their immigration status prevents their parents from moving out of poverty. This is a fundamental inconsistency in a country that aims to eradicate child poverty. Without the support of powerful advocacy NGOs of the refugee sector, undocumented children emerge as a very vulnerable group in the UK.

Finally, we must also work to ensure that our schools are aware of the impact of poverty on children's lives. Teachers need to be more sensitive to the needs of children living in poverty—migrant and non-migrant. Greater understanding of this issue needs to be promoted through teacher education courses. In some parts of the UK, schools have become powerful local actors in campaigns and local programs to eradicate child poverty. We need to harness these local voices.

NOTES

1. Population estimate from the Labour Force Survey, Quarter 4, 2010
2. Home Office statistics indicate that 27% of appeals were upheld in 2010; among Somali nationals this figure was 50%.
3. In the UK, the Government defines child poverty as a child growing up in a household that has a disposable income below 60 per cent of the median income before housing costs have been taken into account and with equivilisation to account for differences in household composition.
4. See Hamilton and Moore, 2004

REFERENCES

Bolloten, B., & Spafford, T. (1998). Supporting refugee children in East London primary schools. In J. Rutter & C. Jones (Eds.), *Refugee education: Mapping the field* (pp. 107–123). Stoke on Trent, UK: Trentham Books.

de Abreu, G., Cline, T., & Lambert, H. (Eds.). (2003). *The Education of Portuguese children in Britain: Insights from research and practice in England and the Channel Islands.* Oxford, UK: Oxford Brookes University.

Department for Education and Skills (DfES). (2005). *Ethnicity and education: The evidence on minority ethnic pupils.* London, UK: Author.

Evans, Y., Herbert, J., Datta, K., May, J., McIlwaine, C., & Wills, J. (2005). *Making the city work: Low paid employment in London.* London, UK: Queen Mary, University of London.

Finch, T., Latorre, M., & Andrew, H. (2010). *Making the most of the British Diaspora.* London, UK: Institute for Public Policy Research.

Gillborn, D., & Gipps, C. (1996) *Recent research on the achievement of ethnic minority pupils.* London: Office for Standards in Education.

Gillborn, D., & Mirza, S. (2000). *Educational inequality: Mapping race, class and gender: A synthesis of research evidence.* London, UK: Office for Standards in Education, Children's Services and Skills (OFSTED).

GLA Economics. (2009). *The economic impact on the London economy of an earned regularisation of irregular migrants to the UK.* London, UK: Greater London Authority.

Hamilton, R., & Moore, D. (2004). *Educational interventions for refugee children.* London, UK: Routledge Falmer.

Home Office. (2010). *Control of immigration statistics, 2010.* London, UK: Author.

Ingleby, D., & Watters, C. (2005). Mental health and social care for asylum seekers and refugees: A comparative study. In D. Ingleby (Ed.), *Forced migration and mental health: rethinking the care of refugees and displaced persons* (pp. 193–212). New York, NY: Springer.

Institute for Public Policy Research. (2007). *Britain's immigrants: An economic profile*. London, UK: Author.

Klein, G. (1993). *Education towards race equality*. London, UK: Cassell

Koser, K. (2005). *Irregular migration, state security and human security*. Geneva, Switzerland: Global Commission on International Migration.

Lupton, R., Heath, N., & Salter, E. (2009). Education: New labour's top priority. In J. Hills, T. Sefton, & K. Stewart (Eds.), *Towards a more equal society* (pp. 71–91). Bristol, UK: Policy Press.

Pinson, H., Arnot, M., & Candappa, M. (2010). *Education, asylum and the non-citizen child*. Basingstoke, UK: Palgrave Macmillan.

Refugee Council. (2011). *Lives in the balance: The quality of immigration legal advice given to separated children seeking asylum*. London, UK: Author.

Rutter, J. (1994). *Refugees in the classroom*. Stoke on Trent, UK: Trentham Books

Rutter, J. (2006). *Refugee children in the UK*. Buckingham, UK: Open University Press

Rutter, J. (2011). Migration, migrants and child poverty. *Poverty, the Journal of the Child Poverty Action Group, 1*, 8–13.

Rutter, J., Newman, N., & Pillai, R. (2008). *Moving up together: Promoting equality among the UK's diverse communities*. London, UK: Institute for Public Policy Research.

Sigona, N., & Hughes, V. (2010). *Being children and undocumented in the UK*. Oxford, UK: Centre for Migration Policy and Society, University of Oxford.

Stanley, K. (2002). *Cold comfort: The lottery of care for young separated refugees in England*. London, UK: Save the Children.

Tikly, L. (2005, August). *The achievement of minority ethnic learners in the UK and a critical analysis of government initiatives to tackle underachievement*. Paper presented to Widening Participation Conference, London.

Tomlinson, S. (2001). Some success, could do better: Education and race 1976–2000. In R. Phillips & J. Furlong (Eds.), *Education, reform and the state: Twenty-five years of politics, policy and practice* (pp. 192–206). London, UK: Routledge.

CHAPTER 10

POST-PRIMARY EDUCATION DILEMMAS IN PROTRACTED REFUGEE SITUATIONS

Timothy Brown
UNESCO, Monrovia, Liberia

ABSTRACT

When people are displaced en masse to a neighboring country due to ongoing conflict at home, they often stay there for many years as refugees. In such protracted situations, when the initial emergency phase of the refugee crisis has long passed, funding for refugee assistance invariably diminishes. Given the inevitability of competing demands for scarce resources, budgetary allocations to education may be the first to suffer. In addition, allocations to primary education often compete with funds for post-primary education, which is more expensive to provide. This chapter highlights the dilemmas that arise as the result of this competition for funding. The case of the Sudanese refugees in Uganda from the mid 1980s up to the present is used to illustrate these dilemmas. It argues that post-primary education is vital for refugees' present and future needs, and for the reconstruction of war-torn countries.

This chapter considers some of the education challenges that arise when large numbers of people have fled to a neighboring country and remain

Refugee and Immigrant Students, pages 189–203

there as refugees for many years due to continued insecurity in their home country. In such protracted situations, longer-term needs, rather than immediate requirements for food and shelter, become more pressing. As refugees move on from managing their immediate circumstances and begin to plan for the future, education ranks high on their list of priorities (Corrigan, 2005). Primary education is essential for basic literacy and numeracy. Beyond this, however, post-primary qualifications, including secondary education, vocational skills training, and tertiary education, contribute significantly to refugees' future economic opportunities. For stakeholders, there is an inevitable competition between providing funds for humanitarian assistance and providing funds for longer-term development. Thus, international donors in the past have been inclined to reduce their assistance to refugees once the initial emergency phase is over. As the development agenda gains priority, new and additional forms of funding are required. If these are not made available, funding for education may suffer. Since many developing countries are unable to provide post-primary education to all their own citizens, the educational needs of refugees they host cannot be given priority. The resulting challenges that practitioners and policymakers are faced with in supporting post-primary education for refugees in protracted situations form the basis of discussion in this chapter.

Protracted refugee situations have become common in recent times. This chapter focuses on a particular example; that of the Sudanese refugees in Uganda from the 1980s up to the independence of South Sudan in 2011. The chapter considers the following dilemmas especially related to post-primary education that are exacerbated by the acute shortage of funding:

- How is support for post-primary education balanced with that for primary education, given their mutual importance?
- How can the available funding for post-primary education be distributed effectively to as many beneficiaries as possible?
- How can both the short-term and long-term educational needs of the refugees be satisfied?
- Given that there are insufficient funds to provide a full, free secondary education for all refugees, what are the most equitable and effective strategies for the selection of beneficiaries?

PROTRACTED REFUGEE SITUATIONS

The UN refugee agency, the United Nations High Commissioner for Refugees (UNHCR), was set up in 1950 in the aftermath of the Second World War. Its original mandate was to provide assistance to individual persons from Europe displaced by the war, who were in danger of persecution if they returned to their home countries. In the latter half of the 20th century, large-scale civil wars erupted in many parts of the world, especially in Africa in the wake of decolonization. These conflicts resulted in mass migrations of people fleeing their countries and seeking safety and shelter in neighboring states. The mandate of UNHCR evolved to regard these people as prima facie refugees as per the 1969 Organization of African Unity (OAU) Refugee Convention. UNHCR ensured the immediate provision of security and assistance to these large groups en masse, at the request of host governments, in collaboration with the international community and the refugees themselves. In these large-scale situations, UNHCR generally established camps and provided basic services such as education and health. In the early years, it was assumed that refugee situations would be short-term, leading to voluntary repatriation as soon as possible.

Unfortunately, many civil wars over the past few decades have not been of short duration, but have continued for long periods of time through seemingly unending cycles of conflict. As a result, refugees are left in a state of limbo, most often in marginalized border areas. During these protracted situations, the availability of humanitarian assistance may diminish once the emergency is over. Funding from UNHCR or other aid and development agencies is often insufficient to allow continued assistance to be provided, since emerging crises in other locations tend to compete for the same resources. As a result, refugees in protracted situations may be expected to become self-reliant. One option is integration with the local population if a host country is sympathetic and provides land for settlement and cultivation or provides economic support and entry to the business community. This was the case for the Southern Sudanese who fled to Uganda in large numbers from around the mid-1980s and stayed in refugee settlements well into the 21st century. During recent decades, Uganda has been very generous in hosting thousands of refugees from neighboring countries and providing them with land for self-reliance.

SUDANESE REFUGEES IN UGANDA

Many Southern Sudanese had already experienced a prolonged refugee life in Uganda in a 17-year civil war which ended with the signing of the Addis Ababa Peace Agreement in 1972. However, during the ensuing peace, there was instability in Uganda. This prompted Sudanese refugees to return home, and at the same time produced waves of Ugandans seeking refuge in Sudan, especially after Idi Amin was ousted in 1979. Merkx (2000) provides a discussion of the recent history of the region, and from this it is clear that during the late 1900s and early 2000s there was a context of recurrent and ongoing unrest, where Southern Sudanese people may migrate to Uganda in one period, and Ugandans may migrate to the Sudan in another period. At various times UNHCR worked on either side of the border, repatriating old refugees and receiving new ones. This is an example of regional instability, where refugee situations often do not occur in isolation. Host governments can be sympathetic to refugees in such cases—perhaps because they believe that their own citizens might become refugees in need of protection at some time in the future. This is formalized in Africa through the 1969 OAU Refugee Convention, which specifies that African countries have an obligation to accept refugees from neighboring countries.

The second Sudanese civil war was even longer, lasting 22 years from 1983 to 2005. It broke out after the government in Khartoum imposed Sharia Law in the north of the country and ended the autonomy of the Southern Region. As a consequence, the Sudan People's Liberation Army (SPLA) established itself in the south and operated outside the main garrison towns still controlled by the government. A change in education policy imposed by the Khartoum government required that school-going children learn in Arabic, but in the rural areas that were under the control of the SPLA, the curriculum could still be in English. However, the rural schools were full of able-bodied young people who provided soft targets for SPLA rebels aggressively searching for new recruits. Many secondary school students were, therefore, abducted and press-ganged into the SPLA, thus ending their educational aspirations. As a result, large numbers of Sudanese families and young people fled to Uganda or Kenya, in pursuit of an English-medium education and safe conditions.

From the mid 1980s, many Sudanese reached Uganda and immediately set up self-help primary schools while the various camps and settlements became established. In those early days, refugee leaders mobilized their people into collecting grass and sticks and building mud-walled structures as classrooms. The quality of these makeshift schools, including the physical structures, their ongoing maintenance, and tidiness of the school compounds, greatly depended on the leadership of the head teachers and their ability to motivate the surrounding communities. Teachers were identified and selected from those community members willing to help in the schools on a voluntary basis. Volunteer teachers could be former teachers from the Sudan, but most were unqualified and untrained individuals committed to helping their people, including stranded secondary school students who had been torn away from their studies because of the war. External organizations such as the UNHCR and nongovernmental organizations (NGOs) came in to support the schools by providing basic educational materials (such as textbooks, exercise books, and pens) and assistance to the teachers in the form of training, supervision, and monetary incentives. UNHCR also supported the construction of permanent school buildings, especially in locations where school facilities were shared with a sizable proportion of local children of the host country. In these places the new school buildings would still be used by the local communities for schooling or other purposes after repatriation of the refugees.

In the early years in Uganda, the standard of the refugee schools in terms of external examination results was often higher than that of the local schools, owing to the high motivation of the refugee teachers and pupils and the outside support they received. As a result, many local children would walk miles each day to attend schools in the refugee settlements, which were free and generally open to the locals. Before universal primary education was declared by the Ugandan government in 1997, local primary schools charged fees. Refugee primary schools, on the other hand, were supposed to be free, although many did charge the parent–teacher associations small amounts. Refugee schools opened their doors to local children partly in reciprocity for the kindness shown by the host population, and partly because the Southern Sudanese refugees and their Ugandan hosts had similar ethnic roots. As the situation became more prolonged, the Ugandan host government and local education authorities grew increasingly involved in the education of the refugees, in terms of registration and oversight of the refugee schools. This was part of a broader self-reliance strategy introduced by UNHCR, promoting the integration of refugee services into the district plans of the local authorities. Some refugee schools were converted into government schools and taken over by the local authorities. The idea was for the government eventually to take over the payment of teacher salaries from UNHCR. In this context, the ultimate objective was full integration of refugee schools into the local system.

Refugees are often located in remote border areas of a developing country where local schools and other services are well below national standards. UNHCR consequently developed a refugee-affected area policy in Uganda in the mid-1990s as the refugee situation continued (Sesnan, Brown, & Kabba, 1995). One outcome of this policy was the provision of direct UNHCR support to local schools in areas hosting refugees. This not only improved the quality of education for the indigenous populations, but also helped to ease tensions between the locals and refugees.

After the Comprehensive Peace Agreement in Sudan in 2005, many refugees started to return home. Some refugee schools in Uganda then closed down while others were consolidated and received refugees from a wider geographical area. As part of the process of integrating refugee schools into the local system, the Ugandan government deployed government-paid teachers in the remaining settlement schools. However, as of 2010, most of the settlement schools still did not have enough government-paid teachers. UNHCR has, therefore, continued to support these schools through payment of teacher salaries and provision of stationery. Local officers noticed that support from NGOs had fallen, and this adversely affected the performance of the settlement schools.

The above account suggests that education plays a major role throughout the refugee cycle. Lack of appropriate education can be a major cause of war itself or ensuing refugee crises (Wedge, 2008). Once refugees have settled in a host country and have overcome the initial shock of displacement, their thoughts quickly turn to education. The daily occurrence of children attending school helps to heal wounds by giving refugees a sense of normalcy and brighter prospects (Tebbe, 2009). As the refugee situation becomes protracted, education progressively takes on a more important role. Refugee youth, for example, need to be suitably occupied and stimulated so that they can start preparing for a better life. Education provides a constructive alternative to joining fighting forces or turning to substance abuse or crime (Buckland, 2005). Refugees themselves are well aware of the importance of education. Anecdotal evidence, for example, suggests some parents even sold part of their food rations in Uganda to raise enough funds for secondary school fees. In a camp meeting with teachers and parents, a Sudanese teacher told the author that education was the reason for their being refugees in Uganda.

IMPORTANCE OF POST-PRIMARY EDUCATION FOR REFUGEES

As increasing numbers of Ugandan and Sudanese students completed the primary level, the demand for continued education at the post-primary level grew. The refugees themselves set up secondary schools in strategic positions. These self-help schools benefited from limited outside support. The host population was also short of secondary schools, and there was a symbiotic relationship between refugees and locals with both populations benefitting from the presence of additional secondary schools.

For refugees in protracted situations, post-primary education is crucial for the following reasons:

- It can raise refugees' self-esteem and sense of worth when they possess little else.
- It empowers refugees by providing knowledge and skills to enable them to challenge their aggressors intellectually and fight for their rights both in the present and future.
- It encourages self-reliance and thereby hope for the future, constructively occupying youth when their morale is low.
- It helps refugee youth grow into adulthood by providing values and attitudes necessary to prepare them for their future role in rebuilding a peaceful society.

- It provides a "training ground" for future leaders and technicians who will be urgently needed for the reconstruction of their country when the conflict is over.

Adolescence is a critical age when young people's psychosocial needs are great, and they need crucial life skills to help them cope with refugee situations. Provision of post-primary education is a means by which the refugee community can protect their youth and shield them from exploitation and immediate dangers such as landmines, sexual and gender-based violence, and HIV/AIDS (Zeus, 2010).

In the developed world, education after the primary level is universally regarded as essential and compulsory. It benefits both individuals and society as a whole. Post-primary education can lead to a better quality life for individuals and helps to secure more interesting jobs with higher salaries. It also benefits society by providing the trained population needed for social and economic development. Higher-level cognitive skills that normally develop at the post-primary stage, such as critical thinking, solving complex problems, questioning, and not taking things at face value, are vital for surviving and thriving in a fast-changing world. Moreover, in developing countries where primary school enrolment and retention fall far short of 100%, the existence of opportunities for post-primary education can encourage children to complete primary school.

Gender considerations have provided another boost for the cause of secondary education. The third Millennium Development Goal requires gender parity at all education levels by 2015. However, gender disparities are much worse at the post-primary levels, especially for refugees. Specifically, far fewer girls are enrolled at the post-primary level than boys. Yet female youth need secondary education to become teachers and other role models who would attract more girls into school and help break the vicious cycle impeding girls' education. Donors now understand the importance of providing secondary education to girls. In Uganda during the early stages of the Sudanese refugee situation, an NGO gave secondary scholarships to promising girl students to fast-track their entry into teacher training institutions. Towards the end of the 1990s and during the 2000s, special scholarship programs were supported in Uganda focusing on secondary education for refugee girls.

How might gender parity be achieved, and how might affirmative action be taken when educational assistance is provided to girls? Refugee girls often lose out on schooling due to extra duties assigned to them at home, such as collection of water and firewood or taking care of younger siblings. Post-primary education provides a good entry point for tackling gender disparities. But if incentives are created and selection criteria for girls are lowered, it can cause resentment and backlash.

In the Djibouti refugee camps, the author has observed a successful education program run by UNESCO-PEER (Program for Education for Emergencies and Reconstruction) in which the parents of refugee girls have been provided with extra food rations by World Food Program (WFP) to improve girls' attendance at school. However, in Liberia, cases have been reported where girls have been victims of sexual and gender-based violence (SGBV) as a result of receiving extra incentives to go to school. This was in the context of limited food rations and a marked degree of corruption in food distribution. Sexual favors were traded in return for food, which signaled to the male students that SGBV was acceptable.

DILEMMAS IN THE PROVISION OF POST-PRIMARY EDUCATION

In view of the importance of post-primary education for refugees and the scarcity of funds to support it, practitioners and policymakers are faced with many challenges and dilemmas. The basic challenge is how to provide post-primary education when funding is so inadequate. This gives rise to further dilemmas, which are now described. These dilemmas constitute key issues on which hard choices must be made when planning or supporting post-primary education programs for refugees.

Primary Education versus Post-Primary Education

The global drive towards universal primary education (UPE) and education for all (EFA) means that most donors place priority on primary education. Indeed, free primary education is a basic human right, whereas secondary education is not. Secondary education is less popular with donors because it is far more expensive, per capita, than primary education. The salaries of secondary school teachers are higher than those of primary school teachers, pupil–teacher ratios are lower at the secondary level, and secondary schools require more expensive facilities and materials such as laboratories and science equipment.

However, if the education provided in a refugee camp or settlement terminates at the end of the primary years, the population of unemployed out-of-school youth rapidly rises. The swelling number of young people who are frustrated because they are unable to continue their education may endanger camp security. The recent brutal wars in West Africa have shown the havoc that can result when youth are denied education. Although the provision of secondary education has been somewhat neglected in the past, donors and other stakeholders are now beginning to provide educational opportunities for refugee youth after primary education. An example is provided by the Dadaab camps in Kenya where almost all children attend primary school but only a few can be admitted into the secondary schools. Youth programs such as the Youth Education Pack, with emphasis on vocational skills as well as computer literacy and life skills, have been developed and implemented for such situations.

As a result of tight budgets for refugee education, UNHCR has to balance how much of the available resources should be allocated to the respective education levels. In situations of limited funding, secondary education is often considered a luxury provided at the expense of primary education. The author has met some officials who even believed that secondary education was outside the mandate of UNHCR. These officials were therefore reluctant to provide assistance for this level of education because they thought they could be accused of misusing UNHCR's funds.

UNHCR itself has taken some initiatives in support of refugee secondary education during the last decade. Among the initiatives taken are the following:

- In the year 2000, on the 50th anniversary of UNHCR, the refugee agency established the Foundation for the Refugee Education Trust (RET) for refugee post-primary education. The RET is an independent organization committed to assisting communities to meet the educational needs, in the broadest sense, of young people made vulnerable by displacement, violence, armed conflict, and disasters (see www.theRET.org).
- A second initiative was the revision of the Education Field Guidelines in 2003 (UNHCR, 2003). In these guidelines, UNHCR guaranteed to provide eight years of education to all refugees. In many countries, the first eight years of education includes a few years of secondary education.
- A third initiative was the formulation of an Education Strategy (2007–2009) in which UNHCR states it will ensure a common understanding of its definition of basic education as including lower secondary education in addition to primary education. Partnerships with international NGOs (such as RET) and other UN agencies will also be strengthened to address gaps in post-primary education (UNHCR, 2007).

Focus versus Spread

Limitations on funds for refugee education have significant impacts because post-primary education is relatively expensive. This leads to the dilemma of how to reach the maximum number of beneficiaries with the funding available. Should support be spread thinly to as many refugees as possible? Or should programs focus on individual "gifted" refugees so that they can continue up the education ladder to become fully qualified and hopefully reach a position to help their community in a professional or leadership capacity? To what extent is an elitist approach justifiable in a refugee context? How, moreover, does one balance the needs, desires, and rights of the refugee community with those of an individual refugee? For example, when selecting individual refugees for tertiary scholarships, should one require that courses benefit the community as a whole (e.g., nursing, teaching), or is it more important to encourage refugees to follow courses in which they might have a strong personal interest (e.g., fine art, pure mathematics)?

One way to spread refugee education assistance widely is to support a whole school—be it a refugee school or a host school admitting refugees—instead of giving scholarships to individual refugees. The support given to a school might be in the form of renovation of school buildings, construction of a laboratory or library, or the provision of materials, textbooks, and equipment. Many beneficiaries may benefit from this support. In the 1990s, UNHCR made contracts with various Ugandan schools in which the schools agreed to admit a number of refugee students in return for identified capital support provided by UNHCR. The number of students admitted to each school was limited in order to minimize the burden on the schools' recurrent costs.

Competitive scholarships for secondary and vocational education were one form of assistance that enabled some refugees to attend high-quality Ugandan institutions throughout the country. In the 1990s, when the Sudanese refugee crisis was considered an emergency, and humanitarian aid flows were therefore relatively high, many qualified and highly performing refugees, including women and girls, benefited from scholarships provided by UNHCR and other NGOs. In the late 1990s, as aid diminished, the number of scholarships was reduced. The dwindling number of scholarships for secondary education increased competition and had an unexpected and undesirable side effect: Some Sudanese refugee boys continually repeated their final year at primary school in order to boost their rankings and scholarship prospects. Teachers observed that girls were harassed, some getting pregnant and dropping out of school, due to the presence of these over-aged boys.

UNHCR then developed a three-pronged approach to its secondary education strategy in Uganda:

- Limited provision of scholarships for high achievers and a quota for refugee girls
- Support for refugee self-help secondary schools
- Support for local secondary schools which admitted refugee students

Another way to spread limited funds more widely is to give partial scholarships to refugees rather than full scholarships that cover every requirement of an individual learner. Partial scholarships can encourage refugee initiative, self-reliance, and an appreciation of the importance of education. However, there needs to be a support structure to ensure that refugees can cope and that money is not wasted on "dropouts." Should refugee students be encouraged to seek support from several sources or sponsors? In which case, how do we prevent the possible duplication of funds, which is an unfair and wasteful use of resources?

Short-term versus Long-term Programs and Issues of Repatriation

In protracted refugee situations, it becomes difficult to identify the most appropriate type of post-primary education for refugees. Should education be for settlement in the country of asylum, or for repatriation to the country of origin? Skills training relevant to a host country may help refugees become self-reliant in the short term but may detract from the preferred durable solution of voluntary repatriation to the home country. Post-primary education may therefore become a factor inducing people to stay in the host country. In 2010, five years after the Comprehensive Peace Agreement, Sudanese refugees were still benefiting from scholarships for post-primary education in Uganda. Although most Sudanese refugees had repatriated, about 30,000 remained in Uganda, according to UNHCR figures.

A short-term response is to provide skills training, livelihood skills, or apprenticeships to give refugees the tools to earn a living, attain self-reliance, participate in the social life of the community, and become active productive members of that community. Short-term, non-formal skills training courses are often cheaper and have a quick impact when compared with longer-term formal education courses. Such short-term responses can also have positive long-term repercussions. The skills refugees learn and practice in exile could be used to aid recovery if they return to their home country. In Southern Sudan, as of 2010, there was an urgent need for practical skills such as construction, plumbing, and mechanics. Recently, the amount of building in Juba (Southern Sudan) was phenomenal—mostly carried out by Ugandan and Kenyan builders because Sudanese refugees were returning without the appropriate skills. However, these short-term courses generally lack official accreditation from recognized institutions. Such lack can pose problems when refugees repatriate or wish to continue their education in the future.

Formal secondary education, on the other hand, is a multi-year developmental process that promotes the gradual overall growth of young people, enabling them to acquire knowledge, attitudes, and skills in preparation for further education, employment, and self-reliance in future life. It also contributes to the future development of the country of origin if refugees return. In specific refugee situations, a balance between short-term and long-term responses should be found that depends on particular circumstances such as availability of funding and willingness of host governments to allow refugees to earn a living. However, due to limited funding, relatively small numbers of refugee youth are able to benefit from either form of post-primary education. In the UNHCR Education Strategy (2010–2012) it is stated that 69% of children aged 12–17 from 92 refugee camps are not enrolled in secondary education (UNHCR, 2009a).

The division that donors make between short-term relief and long-term development is itself a cause of funding deficiencies. For example, how should refugee secondary education be funded—by relief or development donors? Relief donors may say that they do not fund secondary education because it is not life-saving, whereas development donors might say that they do not fund refugees because it does not fit into the development picture that normally operates through a host government justifiably reluctant to include non-nationals. As a result, refugee secondary education falls between the two and often goes severely underfunded.

While working for UNHCR in Kampala, the author once visited the British High Commission (BHC) and asked the Secretary for Aid if they would support refugee education in Uganda to enable refugees to integrate with the nationals. He replied: "It is difficult because we have two 'pots' of money—one for development and the other for relief. Refugee education is not covered by either pot." It is important to recognize that refugees have both protection and developmental needs, both of which should be addressed. One solution might be to allocate part of the development budget for a country of origin to the corresponding refugee program in the host country. The gap between relief and development was also evident when refugees returned to Southern Sudan in great numbers (Brown, 2006).

Selection of Beneficiaries

Post-primary education is important for refugees but expensive to provide, and therefore, available funds are not always sufficient to cover the needs of all refugees. Only a few can be chosen, leaving many refugees frustrated without post-primary education. Identifying and selecting beneficiaries for refugee post-primary education programs is therefore a critical and sensitive task. How does one make hard choices and reach fair decisions? The selection of beneficiaries involves many important issues around equity and other factors such as cost-effectiveness, probability of success, human rights, corruption, and capacity building.

Education is an important ingredient for a refugee youth's development and survival, but it could also be a factor that attracts a large number of refugees into a country. How can governments establish policies to distinguish between refugees who are genuine and migrants who are drifting between different countries looking for subsidized education? Some refugees have genuine needs, while others may be trying to "beat the system" by falsifying their circumstances in order to attract unwarranted sympathy and funds.

Should priority be given to camp-based refugees who might be rather neglected? Urban refugees are often more eloquent and better placed to visit UNHCR and other offices to look for a scholarship and secure admission into a host school. According to UNHCR's 2009 report on Refugee Education in Urban Settings, the number of urban refugees is steadily increasing, with about half of the world's refugees residing in cities or towns (UNHCR, 2009b). If refugee students are encouraged to leave the camps for the main cities, they are at risk of greater exploitation, but, on the other hand, they may have better options for high-quality education.

Refugees may need extra support because they may lack the legal status and social networks that local citizens have. How are refugees to be supported so that they are not seen as more privileged than the local population? There is a danger of resentment and conflict building up between the two communities. Since the host population is carrying the additional burden of the refugees and is often equally needy, local citizens should also be able to benefit in one way or the other from educational support given to refugees.

CONCLUDING REMARKS

In considering the dilemmas surrounding the provision of post-primary education in protracted refugee situations, a number of points have been raised. Between Southern Sudan and Uganda, for example, there has been an ongoing and complex exchange between the refugee populations, the governments, and the organizations that support refugees. Given intermittent conflict affecting both countries, each country relies on the other for accepting and supporting refugees in times of strife. As these situations of hosting refugees become long-term, post-primary education plays an important role in shaping the refugee experience. The growth in the numbers of young people eligible for education beyond the primary years puts increasing pressure on the UNHCR, NGOs, and governments to provide suitable education for them. Refugee post-primary schools funded by the UNHCR and operated by refugees are opened to local students to attend.

Local schools may accept limited numbers of refugee students, and in some cases these schools are supported by UNHCR or other organizations. These kinds of agreements are likely to ameliorate tensions that may arise because of perceptions of advantage one segment of a population thinks another group is enjoying. Ongoing problems of the recruitment, training, and retention of teachers affect the quality of instruction that students receive, as do the costs associated with providing different kinds of post-primary courses. Machinery, equipment, higher salaries, and fewer students per dollar of investment all contribute to make post-primary education expensive. The need, however, for people with post-primary qualifications, especially in post-conflict situations, is of paramount concern in reconstruction efforts to rebuild the economy, provide a qualified work force, and contribute to the social and physical infrastructure of the country.

There are a number of "push–pull" factors that also influence the demand for post-primary education in protracted situations. The opportunity for post-primary education in Uganda, for example, can operate as a reason for young Sudanese refugees to opt to remain in Uganda and resist repatriation to Sudan. The quality of schooling also creates an incentive for many Sudanese youth to continue in post-primary institutions in Uganda as the Southern Sudanese education system rebuilds itself in the aftermath of the war. Opportunities for girls' education may be greater in Uganda than in Southern Sudan, and this too may encourage families to seek educational opportunities in Uganda. The content and focus of existing curricula also play an important role. Curricula that are perceived to be current and useful can encourage students to seek further education in one country rather than another, thus furthering contributions to the local work force.

While there is no denying the importance of primary education in generating literacy and numeracy, the very success of these basic inputs highlights the need for further investment in post-primary education as the numbers of young people increase who are seeking additional education. Most importantly, post-primary education offers refugees a lifeline of hope during long years of displacement. It equips them with skills and attitudes needed for a better life in future when the conflict is finally over.

ACKNOWLEDGEMENTS

I am especially indebted to Pamela Baxter, Martha Hewison, Eldrid Midttun, Barry Sesnan, and Jürgen Wintermeier for detailed comments on later drafts of this article. I am also grateful to Ann Avery, Br Stan Goetschalck, Atle Hetland, Myriam Houtart, Brian Kavanagh, Susanne Kindler-Adam, Marina Lopez Anselme, Jozef Merkx, Unny Mundarath, Anna Obura, Veton Orana, Kenyi Paulino, Margaret Sinclair, Hans Thoolen, Sallie Wareing, and Julian Watson for their valuable suggestions.

I am indebted to my former employers UNHCR, RET, UNICEF and UNESCO for my experiences in refugee and post-conflict education. The views presented in this article, however, do not necessarily reflect the views of those organizations.

Finally, and not least, I am indebted to the many refugees I have known for their inspiring example.

REFERENCES

Brown, T. (2006). South Sudan education emergency. *Forced Migration Review* (Supplement. Education & conflict: Research, policy & practice), July, 20–21.

Buckland, P. (2005). *Reshaping the future: Education and postconflict reconstruction.* Washington, DC: World Bank.

Corrigan, S. (2005). *Beyond provision: A comparative analysis of two long-term refugee education systems.* Toronto, ON: Ontario Institute for Studies in Education at the University of Toronto.

Merkx, J. (2000). *Refugee identities and relief in an African borderland: A study of northern Uganda and southern Sudan.* Geneva, Switzerland: United Nations High Commissioner for Refugees (UNHCR).

Sesnan, B., Brown, T., & Kabba, M. G. (1995). *Education in the refugee-affected areas of northern Uganda.* Unpublished. Kampala, Uganda: United Nations High Commissioner for Refugees (UNHCR).

Tebbe, K. (2009).Global trends for education to support stability and resilience: research, programming and finance. *Journal of Education for International Development, 4*(1), 1–12.

United Nations High Commissioner for Refugees. (2003). *Education field guidelines.* Geneva, Switzerland: United Nations High Commissioner for Refugees (UNHCR).

United Nations High Commissioner for Refugees. (2007). *Education strategy 2007–2009.* Geneva, Switzerland: United Nations High Commissioner for Refugees (UNHCR).

United Nations High Commissioner for Refugees. (2009a). *Education strategy 2010–2012.* Geneva, Switzerland: United Nations High Commissioner for Refugees (UNHCR).

United Nations High Commissioner for Refugees. (2009b). *Refugee education in urban settings.* Geneva, Switzerland: United Nations High Commissioner for Refugees (UNHCR).

Wedge, J. (2008). *Where peace begins: Education's role in conflict prevention and peace building.* Geneva, Switzerland: International Save the Children Alliance.

Zeus, B. (2010). *Whole people, holistic approaches: Cross-sectoral action and learning. Framing Paper 3.* Interagency Network for Emergencies in Education (INEE) 2010 Policy Roundtable—An Enabling Right: Education for Youth Affected by Crisis. Geneva, Switzerland: Interagency Network for Emergencies in Education (INEE).

CHAPTER 11

LEARNING FROM THE EDUCATION PROGRAMS FOR SRI LANKAN REFUGEE STUDENTS IN INDIA

K. C. Saha
Indian Civil Servant

ABSTRACT

Ethnic violence against Tamils in Sri Lanka has resulted in a large influx of Sri Lankan Tamil refugees to the state of Tamil Nadu in southern India since 1983. Presently, over 100,000 refugees are living in 113 refugee camps in different parts of the state and outside the camps on their own. This chapter first discusses India's refugee assistance policy and then examines the education program being run by the Organization for Eelam Refugees Rehabilitation (OfERR) for the Sri Lankan refugees in light of this policy. The lessons that may be learned from the education program of OfERR have also been highlighted in this chapter.

Ethnic violence against Tamils in Sri Lanka has resulted in a large influx of Sri Lankan Tamil refugees to the state of Tamil Nadu in southern India since 1983. The refugees arrived in four phases: the first phase from 1983 to

Refugee and Immigrant Students, pages 205–225
205

1987 (134,053 refugees), the second from 1989 to 1991 (122,078 refugees), the third from 1996 to 2003 (22,418 refugees), and the fourth from 2006 to 2010 (24,518 refugees) (South Asian Human Rights Documentation Centre, n.d.). Following the Indo-Sri Lanka Peace Accord in July 1987, about 30,000 refugees were repatriated to Sri Lanka (SAHRDC, 1997). Continuing ethnic violence, however, resulted in further influxes of refugees in later years. After the signing of the peace accord between the Liberation Tigers of Tamil Eelam (LTTE) and the government of Sri Lanka in February 2002, some refugees living in India started returning to Sri Lanka. However, from January 2006 onwards, Tamils began to flee their homeland once more; there had been many ceasefire violations on the part of the LTTE and the government forces (OfERR, n.d.d). Some of the refugees were fleeing to India for the second, third, and fourth times.

Presently about 73,251 refugees are living in 113 refugee camps set up in 24 regions of Tamil Nadu (Human Rights Law Network, 2007). In addition, about 32,242 refugees are living outside the camps on their own (HRLN, 2007). Two thirds of the refugees are Hindu and the remainder Christian (Saha, 2004). Almost all are from the conflict-affected areas of Sri Lanka's northern and eastern provinces. Before fleeing into India, most of the refugee families were agricultural laborers or fishermen (Saha, 2004). Many refugees living outside the camps in Tamil Nadu are economically and socially better off than other Sri Lankan refugees. Many of them are supported by relatives in western countries who send remittances. These refugees are mostly living in rented accommodation in big cities. Some of them have established businesses.

This chapter first discusses India's refugee assistance policy and then, in light of this policy, examines the education program being run by the Organization for Eelam Refugees Rehabilitation (OfERR) for Sri Lankan refugees. A case study approach has been adopted to describe this education program and is based on interviews conducted in 2009 with the team members of OfERR, government functionaries, and the Sri Lankan refugees (Saha, 2009). The chapter will consider the organization of OfERR, the education program being run by OfERR, the impact of the education program on the refugee community, and the lessons that may be learned for other refugee situations.

INDIA'S REFUGEE ASSISTANCE POLICY

India is not a signatory to the 1951 UN Refugee Convention relating to the Status of Refugees or the 1967 Protocol on the Status of Refugees. India also does not have a cohesive national policy on refugees, and the admission of refugees is generally assumed under the Foreigners Act of 1946

(SAHRDC, 1997). India has, however, handled many important refugee situations involving Tibetan refugees, refugees from former East Pakistan (now Bangladesh), as well as Sri Lankan and Chakma refugees. While these were formally recognized as refugees, Afghan and Bhutanese refugees have not been recognized as such, but are being treated as foreigners temporarily residing in India. Recognition of refugee status in India has been based on political expediency (HRLN, 2007).

Recognition of refugee status is a precondition for refugee assistance. As such, no refugee assistance is being provided to the Afghan and Bhutanese refugees. India's refugee assistance policy is based on humanitarian considerations. The Indian government regards the stay of refugees as a temporary phase and expects them to go back to their country of origin when it returns to normalcy. In general, the need for shelter is met in temporary camps, temporary structures, and government buildings. Drinking water, sanitation facilities, and medical facilities are also provided (Valatheeswaran & Rajan, 2011). In the emergency phase, refugees are provided with free rations and other essential requirements like clothing, utensils, and blankets. Refugees are also provided with cash doles, and are not permitted to work.

In the federal organization of government in India, the entire expenditure of setting up camps, and the provision of relief and assistance to the refugees, is met by the Indian government. State governments, on behalf of the Indian government, are responsible for actually setting up camps and making the necessary arrangements for the distribution of relief and assistance to the refugees out of funds provided by the Indian government (Valatheeswaran & Rajan, 2011). The nature of the assistance offered varies both qualitatively and quantitatively from one refugee situation to the other (Bose, 2001). In reality, much depends on the initiative of the respective state governments. It may be useful to consider briefly the assistance provided in different refugee situations in the past.

Tibetan Refugees

In the case of the 56,000 Tibetan refugees who entered India in 1959, a comprehensive rehabilitation package was provided. Tibetan refugees were given agricultural land and provided with all other infrastructure including roads, water supply, and educational and medical facilities (SAHRDC, 2008). The government also provided Tibetan refugees with cottage industries, particularly, the manufacture of handloom and handicraft products. The Tibetan refugee society has set up various educational institutions, and the government provides annual grants to them. Symptomatic of the generally insecure status of refugees, however, is the fact that Tibetan refugees arriving in India since the 1980s have not been necessarily afforded the same recognition and support as the earlier Tibetans (SAHRDC, 2008).

Refugees from Former East Pakistan

In the case of the 10,000,000 refugees from erstwhile East Pakistan who came to India in 1971, the government established 1,200 camps in the border states of West Bengal, Assam, Meghalaya, and Tripura in Eastern India. Arrangements were made for the provision and distribution of food, drinking water, and medical care. As the refugees were staying in India for a temporary period and were eventually to return to Bangladesh, it was not considered necessary to provide any elaborate schooling for them in India. Normally, the Indian government does not accept help from other countries when providing assistance to refugees, but in this case, considering the magnitude of the problem, it appealed to the international community. Immediately after the surrender of Pakistani forces and the inauguration of the Republic of Bangladesh, the refugees returned after a stay of more than ten months in India.

Chakma Refugees

In the case of the 57,000 tribal Chakma refugees from Bangladesh, six camps were established in the State of Tripura in Eastern India. Living conditions in these camps were so poor that the National Human Rights Commission (NHRC) had to intervene (Bose, 2001). Even the distribution of food and other relief materials was irregular. Proper arrangements for education had not been made. It was only after the intervention of the NHRC that conditions in the camps and distribution of food improved.

Sri Lankan Refugees

Sri Lankan refugees were first received in two transit camps: one located at Mandapam in Ramanathapuram district and the other at Kottapattu in Trichirapalli district in the state of Tamil Nadu. The Mandapam camp sets the standard for the other refugee camps and is spread over about 295 acres of land. There are 827 cottage-type old buildings and 1,200 semi-permanent buildings. It has good sanitary facilities, water, and electricity supplies. Adequate educational facilities with primary, middle, and high schools are available in the camp. There is also a twenty-bed hospital, and banking facilities are available. Food is distributed through fair-price shops located in the camp (Saha, 2009).

On arrival, refugees are screened for registration. Those who wish to stay in camps are dispersed to the camps throughout the state. Each of the families living in one of these camps is issued a family identity card. As of January 2010, about 19,916 families, comprising 73,251 persons, were living in camps (OfERR Database, 2006). In addition, 11,478 families comprising 32,242 persons were living on their own outside the camps and were not entitled to any relief assistance (HRLN, 2007). The OfERR maintains a database on refugees living in camps. Births, deaths, marriages, camp transfers, and other developments are constantly updated. This database is of great benefit to new refugees who can locate camps where persons they know are accommodated, which facilitates the reunion of families and friends. The database also helps in reconciliation of records with the Rehabilitation Department of the government of Tamil Nadu.

Two special camps have been set up at Poonamallee in Thiruvallur district and Chengalpattu in Kancheepuram district for refugees suspected of having links with militant groups. As of January 2010, 53 refugees are lodged in these two special camps. In 1992, 1,629 militants were living in special camps of this kind (SAHRDC, 1997). Militants against whom there were no specific charges were permitted to leave the country.

Camps were formerly located in coastal areas, but the Indian government did not want the refugees to go fishing at sea in case of infiltration of militants among them. Later the camps were relocated to the mostly rural interior area. Most of the camps are located at distances between ten and twenty kilometres from the local Taluk headquarters. A Taluk in Tamil Nadu is a revenue administrative unit with a population of about 50,000. There may be one or two other small towns in a Taluk. A Taluk normally has good educational and medical facilities and a few markets. Some of the camps are located very close to big towns.

The camps used to be located in government buildings, huts, community centers, temporary sheds, cyclone shelters, and rented buildings. Most are now on government land or in warehouses of the regulated market committees (RMC). A one-room row house of ten feet by ten feet, with brick walls, mud floors, and roofs made of asbestos sheets, constructed on government land, was allotted to each family. Similarly, in RMC warehouses, a space of the same dimensions was allotted to each family, although without any partitions between them (Saha, 2009). Several families lived together in a warehouse. Individual families constructed kitchens of their own in the adjoining space next to the houses/warehouses, and in some of the camps, individuals constructed dwelling units at their own cost on vacant land. Some camps have been established in areas where unused Public Works Department accommodations were available. The camps have common sanitation facilities and arrangement for water. Electricity has been made available for the common areas, but many individuals have managed to take a connection for their homes illegally.

The living conditions in camps have been far from satisfactory (HRLN, 2007). The renovation of old houses and construction of new houses have been taken up by the state government and NGOs in some camps. New houses are being constructed on the same sites by demolishing the dilapidated old houses and by constructing new houses on the vacant lands available in the camps. Under renovation programs sponsored both by the state government and NGOs, asbestos roofs are being replaced by tiles so that the dwelling units remain cool in summer. The mud floors are being replaced with cement. Some of the old shelters have been converted into community centers. The RMC warehouses are being partitioned, ensuring the privacy of different families. To improve the basic amenities in camps, the government of Tamil Nadu proposes to spend 1,000,000,000 rupees ($25,000,000 US) for the repair and renovation of old houses and the construction of new ones, to repair or provide new bore wells and hand pumps, repair or install new overhead tanks, provide new water pipelines and extend other pipelines, repair existing toilets and construct new ones, repair drainage and construct new drainage, repair roads in the camps, provide electrical poles and street lights, and repair electrical wiring and fittings in the houses (OfERR, n.d.d).

Refugee families are provided subsidized rice in sufficient quantity at the rate of 0.57 rupees per kilogram (market price is about 14 rupees, or $0.35 US per kilogram) through fair price shops. Utensils and free clothing materials are also provided. Previously, a cash dole of about 1,000 rupees ($25 US) per month for a family of five was provided. This figure has doubled since 2006.

The movement of refugees in camps is restricted (SAHRDC, 1997). Officially the refugees are allowed to stay out of camps between 6:00 am and 8:00 pm, but the government has liberalized such restrictions by issuing individual identity cards. At first only one registration card was provided to each family, so that if one member of the family moved out with the family card, others could not stay out of camps beyond the designated hours. Individual identity cards have helped the free movement of refugees. As a result, refugee students are able to pursue their studies anywhere in Tamil Nadu, and their entitlements for cash dole and other benefits are made available to their parents in the camps.

About 400 families whose financial statuses have improved have moved out of camps and are living on their own. Families wishing to move out of camps have to apply for permission from the Department of Rehabilitation. Once this is granted, they have to register with the local police. About 500 refugee families who were previously living outside camps in rented accommodation have moved back into camps because of an increase in rental prices and improved living conditions in camps. The government has been liberal in allowing such willing families to move into the camps.

There also has been movement of refugees from one camp to another. The refugees prefer camps closer to big cities where educational and job opportunities are better. For instance, the Gummidipindi camp in Thiruvallur district, which is very close to the capital Chennai, once had 850 families residing in it, but now it has 1,020 families, and more and more request permission to move to this camp.

The Indian Tamils share common bonds of ethnicity and language with the Sri Lankan Tamils. For example, a substantial number of refugees are descendants of Tamil laborers who were taken from India to Ceylon in the 19th and 20th centuries to provide much-needed labor for the tea plantations. The refugee issue has always dominated state politics. As a result, successive state governments of Tamil Nadu have been sympathetic, by and large, to the cause of the refugees and have liberally extended various facilities to them. On a few occasions, however, the refugees have had to face serious hardships.

In 1984, M.G.Ramachandran of the All India Dravida Munetra Kazhagam (AIDMK) party was the Chief Minister of Tamil Nadu. He was very concerned about the welfare of refugees. During his regime, clear instructions were given to all District Collectors, the chief administrative officers in a district, to ensure admission of refugee students in schools and colleges (OfERR, n.d.c). They were made fully responsible for students' welfare. Students were admitted to schools without any documents as they did not have any (Valatheeswaran & Rajan, 2011). The teachers assessed their educational levels, and also took into consideration their age, and admitted them to different classes. The students seeking admission in class 10 and class 12 were assessed with rigor and often admitted to a lower class so that they could familiarize themselves with the syllabus and curriculum. Refugee students were admitted to colleges on the basis of their declaration, but they were asked to produce the mark sheet (transcript) later after obtaining a duplicate copy from the Sri Lankan Examination Board. Universities insisted that students should have studied English and other essential subjects in order to gain admission. In 1984, about 200 Tamil refugee students sought admission to colleges and were admitted because places were reserved specifically for Sri Lankan refugee students. In the event that few refugee students applied, other local students could be admitted to these places. Places were also reserved in professional colleges for refugee students: 10 seats in medical and 25 seats in engineering courses. Refugee students who were living outside the camps also benefited from this reservation policy.

Until 1990, Sri Lankan Tamil refugee students did not face any problem in educational matters. After the assassination of Rajiv Gandhi in May 1991, however, the situation changed (Valatheeswaran & Rajan, 2011). The infiltration of militants into the refugee population was a matter of concern. In the election held in 1991, the AIDMK party government came to power, and this government was hostile to the refugee cause. For example, admission of refugee students into class 10, class 12, and colleges was made difficult. From 1991 to 1996, refugee students were not able to gain admission to colleges, and the places once reserved for them in various courses were abolished. Even private colleges were reluctant to admit students because of the attitude of the state government, and refugee students were not admitted to them during this period.

In 1996, the Dravida Munetra Kazhagam (DMK) party came to power. This government restored quotas in the professional colleges for refugee students. However, in a 2002 writ petition in the High Court at Chennai, the overall reservation policy on admission into colleges was challenged, including the places reserved for the refugee students. The High Court *inter alia* set aside the reserved places for refugee students in the professional colleges (Saha, 2009). Admission in the general arts and sciences courses, however, has not suffered since 1996. Refugee students who become eligible for admission in colleges on merit are admitted straight away. Other refugee students are admitted depending on the vacancies available in the colleges after the closure of admissions for local students. Generally, students do manage to get admission in the government colleges in the arts and sciences courses where the fees are nominal. Sri Lankan refugee students who fail to get admission in government colleges in arts and sciences courses, and those who are interested in professional courses, try to get admission in private colleges, where the fees are very high.

Through its sustained educational programs the OfERR has supplemented the efforts of the state government. It is therefore important to consider its organization and then consider its education program.

ORGANIZATION OF OFERR

Given the changing nature of state support for Sri Lankan Tamil refugees, the creation of the OfERR program was a timely intervention that protected their interests. OfERR is an organization of Sri Lankan Tamil refugees committed to the principles of human development and sustainable livelihoods (UNHCR, 2011). Its mission is to improve and develop the lives and well-being of refugees in India and to prepare them for their eventual return to Sri Lanka. Its key objective is to build the capacity of refugees, empowering them to make a significant contribution to their social and economic development (OfERR, n.d.a). Its founder, Mr. S. C. Chandrahasan, who began his career as an advocate in the Supreme Court of Sri Lanka, comes from a renowned Sri Lankan political family and has dedicated his life to the welfare of refugees. He is assisted by a dedicated team of volunteers, many of whom are refugees themselves. Some of these volunteers have trained as qualified trainer/coordinators in areas such as human resource development, women's empowerment, camp management, education, or administration.

In 1984, the legal formalities for OfERR functioning as a non-profit organization were completed and it was registered as a society under the Tamil Nadu Societies Act. The organization has been afforded charitable status under Sec. 12(A) of the Income Tax Act. Any contribution by an individual or an organization to OfERR is eligible for tax exemption. OfERR is also registered with the Indian government Ministry of Home Affairs so it can receive foreign contributions under 6(1) (a) of the Foreign Contribution (Regulation) Act 1976 (OfERR, n.d.a). This is an important means of supplementing the funds made available from the government. The organization has also been permitted to clear in kind donations from abroad free of customs duty for distribution among the refugees.

OfERR comprises a general body, a management committee, the regional and district steering committees, and the camp management committees. The general body decides the policies and the programs of the organization and is made up of about 150 members who come from camps and other important persons amongst refugees who are living outside camps (Saha, 2009). The management committee is the principal decision-making body of the organization, and its office-bearers are elected at an annual general meeting (OfERR, n.d.d).

The regional steering committees are operational in three of the four regions in Tamil Nadu: Trichy, Erode, and Tirunelveli. The district steering committees provide forums for the camp management committee members to discuss issues affecting refugees across the camps. Office holders and members of the camp management committees decide the office holders of the district steering committee, who then elect the office bearers of the regional steering committee. The district committees discuss issues that need to be brought to the notice of the district level authorities, such as disruptions in water and electricity supplies; issues that cannot be sorted out at the district level are taken up with higher authorities by OfERR (OfERR, n.d.d).

The camp-level management committees are responsible for bringing the people together, identifying their needs, and presenting these needs to the higher levels in OfERR, the government, and other NGOs when necessary (OfERR, n.d.a). These committees are comprised of ten to twenty members, depending on the size of the camp. The president and the secretary of these committees are elected by consensus. Thirty to forty percent of the members of the camp committees are women who are active in self-help groups (SHGs). The tenure of the camp committee members is two years. The camp management committee meets once every month to discuss supply issues such as rations and water quality and social issues such as outsiders frequenting camps, disputes, education, and health matters. These meetings are held at night so that every member can participate after finishing their day's work (Saha, 2009).

Student forums also exist in all camps (OfERR, n.d.c). Sports events, cultural programs, and drama are among the activities organized by these groups. The student forums also perform social work such as cleaning the camps, repairing facilities, and running blood donation campaigns.

THE EDUCATION PROGRAM OF OFERR

Tamil refugees fleeing Sri Lanka have undergone great physical and mental suffering (OfERR, n.d.a). They have lost their belongings, their jobs, and, in many cases, family members. The trauma of escape and displacement, accompanied by the boredom, sense of worthlessness, and lack of privacy in the refugee camp situation often leads to depression, stress, and anxiety (Saha, 2009). The depressing family environment, the disruption of studies, and the difficulties of living conditions in the camps have had an adverse impact on refugee students. It is because of these conditions that OfERR developed a comprehensive approach to education that included counseling and other services (OfERR, n.d.c).

There are about 22,000 refugee students involved in the educational programs supported by OfERR (OfERR, n.d.c). They include students from early childhood through college. OfERR runs 87 nursery schools catering to about 3,000 children aged three to five (OfERR, n.d.c). These nursery schools also function as day-care centers and allow parents to seek work outside the camps. Children of primary school age are admitted into government schools in the vicinity of the camps. The same is the case for children in middle and high school. While the middle schools are located within a distance of one kilometer from the camps, students in high schools sometimes have to travel four to five kilometers. The Tamil Nadu government provides free bus passes to all students, and some go to schools by bicycle (Valatheeswaran & Rajan, 2011). In Tamil Nadu, almost all the government schools have a good infrastructure and good teaching staff.

The dispersal of refugees in various camps throughout the state facilitated the admission of refugee students by not severely increasing enrollments or adversely affecting the interests of local communities. The government's pro-refugee policy also helped secure their admission. There was thus no need for OfERR to start separate schools for Sri Lankan Tamil refugee students. Tamil, the common language, helped with the easy integration of refugees into the local student community. Most refugee students and their parents are highly committed to the pursuit of education. Some of the parents have also admitted their children to English-speaking private schools and to convent schools. The fees in these schools are high, and parents often meet them from the support they receive from their relatives abroad or their earnings from hard labor.

Government schools are free up to class twelve. OfERR provides notebooks to every student. The schools provide free textbooks and uniforms to all students (OfERR, n.d.c). As with local students, refugee students benefit from a free midday meal (Valatheeswaran & Rajan, 2011). In the beginning, fewer girls attended school than boys, as parents were reluctant to send them in their adolescence. Over the years, however, equal participation has developed. Although 100% enrollment in schools has been achieved, however, there is an approximately 12–13% dropout rate (Saha, 2009). The dropouts are mostly boys in classes 10 and 12. The main reasons for dropout are financial problems, family situations, and the camp environment. At the camp level, through the efforts of college students, OfERR encourages dropout students to acquire vocational training. Some of the students who do not attend school train as carpenters, painters, masons, automobile mechanics, and gem-cutters (OfERR, n.d.a).

OfERR monitors the progress of all students, collecting data annually in each region. OfERR also pays for extra tuition in math and English to help students prepare for important government exams that take place in years 10 and 12. Each year-10 student receives 300 rupees ($7.50 US) for this purpose, and each year-12 student receives 500 rupees ($12.50 US). Coaching classes are conducted for class 10 and class 12 students by trained OfERR teachers and refugee college students, who receive a small allowance for their work (OfERR, n.d.c).

In 2009–2010, 750 students took the class 10 examination, and 81% passed. Eighty two students received marks of 80% or above. The class 12 examination was taken by 510 students; thirteen secured marks of 80% or above. Some of the refugee students whose names were on the merit list of the board exams were rewarded in cash by the state authorities and NGOs (OfERR, n.d.a). Their results are all the more creditable as such excellent academic performance was achieved despite difficult living conditions in camps.

In December 2006, OfERR was able to conduct the Ceylon General Certificate of Education (Ordinary Level) [GCE (O/L)] examination, equivalent to class 10, in Tamil Nadu, for newly arrived refugee students whose studies in Sri Lanka had been interrupted (OfERR, n.d.a). Ninety six students participated in this exam. This was repeated in December 2007, when a further 50 students took the exam. The Sri Lankan High Commission in Chennai and the Government of Tamil Nadu worked together with OfERR to ensure the success of this program (OfERR, n.d.c).

OfERR accords ten refugee students every year the opportunity to pursue a one-year computer operating and program assistant course at Chennai (OfERR, n.d.d). Additionally, about 70 students have completed their vocational education, gaining the National Certificate for Vocational Training. Most have subsequently found employment in the private sector (Saha, 2009).

Soon after completion of class 12, students are encouraged to attend a regional meeting organized by OfERR's education committee, where advice and counseling are given on how to select a suitable course in college. Most refugee families do not have the resources to meet higher education expenses. OfERR assesses the level of assistance they require and gives priority to the most disadvantaged students.

To assist in the payment of fees, OfERR provides financial assistance of 9,500 rupees ($237.50 US) per student for medical and engineering and 6,000 rupees ($150 US) for arts and sciences students annually (OfERR, n.d.a). The amounts provided by OfERR more or less meet the tuition fees in government colleges. In the absence of a state government order to allow admission of refugee students to professional government colleges, refugee students have been forced to seek education in private colleges, where fees are often excessive and unmanageable. Students follow a variety of college programs, including medicine, engineering, agriculture, law, veterinary science, polytechnic, and art and science courses (OfERR, n.d.c).

The total budget of OfERR each year for assisting higher education students with college fees, travelling expenses, and book fees is around 55,000,000 rupees (approximately $137,500 US). A major part of this assistance is provided by the Ecumenical Scholarship Program (ESP), a German NGO (Saha, 2009). In addition, Sri Lankan expatriates and other well-wishers make crucial contributions.

The budget for OfERR's school education program, involving roughly 21,225 students from nursery/early childhood to class 12, is about 47,000,000 rupees ($117,500 US). The different types of expenditure are notebooks for all, including college students; tuition fees for extra classes in math and English for students in classes 10 and 12; student forum motivation activities; student drop-out encouragement programs and their enrollment in vocational courses; and the payment of salaries to 92 nursery teachers engaged by OfERR (OfERR, n.d.c) .

More than 20,000 Sri Lankan Tamil refugee students have completed their tertiary studies. Of these, more than 250 refugee students have completed medical courses and more than 1,000 have completed engineering courses. Students who are pursuing engineering courses in private colleges are required to pay fees up to 65,000 rupees ($1,625 US) annually. Fees for other professional courses vary from 15,000 to 50,000 rupees ($375 to $1,250 US) annually (OfERR, n.d.c). No concession in fees is granted to refugee students by private educational institutions. Many refugee parents educate two or three of their children in private professional educational institutions at one time, and it can well be imagined how difficult it must be to mobilize resources for the payment of such high fees. One refugee working as a tractor driver at Rameshwaram, a fishing port, has educated two of his sons in a diploma program in engineering through private colleges, and one daughter in biotechnology, again through a private college. His family lived in Salem but he lived away from them to earn a living and educate his children (Saha, 2009). There are numerous other similar situations.

The refugees who are detained in special camps for their alleged links to militants are also encouraged to pursue studies. They can enroll themselves through correspondence courses at universities and can attend special classes on Sundays under police escort.

IMPACT OF EDUCATION ON THE REFUGEE COMMUNITY

Women's Empowerment

Education has helped empower women. Refugee women continue to face many problems such as sexual abuse and domestic violence, male alcoholism, spiralling debt owed to local money lenders, illegal underage marriage and truncated education, lack of privacy in the crowded camp environment, and AIDS spread by infidelity (OfERR, n.d.b). The women mainly perform manual labor outside the camps, working in agriculture or rice mills. OfERR has facilitated the creation of self-help groups (SHGs) through a wide range of awareness programs among refugee women. SHGs consist of twelve to twenty members and initially focus on accumulating money for their future security (OfERR, n.d.b). Refugee families are now less reliant on unscrupulous money lenders because of SHGs.

Women's empowerment has helped improve general health in camps. OfERR supplements government health service care by organizing a range of awareness campaigns to improve community health. OfERR conducts regular screening of high-risk groups by its health workers, general medical services at camp levels, and specialist medical camps at the district level. Refugee mothers and children are given special care by OfERR. Ninety five percent of births are institutional deliveries. OfERR has attained 100% immunization coverage of children under five, with around 1,000 infants receiving BCG, measles, and DPT or oral polio vaccines. No epidemics have occurred in any of the 113 camps (OfERR, n.d.b).

MIOT (Medical Institute of Tamils), an organization of Sri Lankan doctors now living in the UK, supplies training to refugee health workers. Refugee medical students, whose education is supported by OfERR, visit the camps to treat chronically ill patients. NGOs such as the Indian Red Cross, the Tamil Nadu Volunteer Health Association (TNVHA), and Christian Mission Service India (CMSI) provide support for medical camps organized by OfERR (OfERR, n.d.b).

Advocacy

Education has helped the refugee community with advocacy. Because of advocacy, the Department of Rehabilitation has recently improved basic facilities in many camps through roof repairs, house repairs, and new toilets (Valatheeswaran & Rajan, 2011). The government also permitted NGOs such as OfERR, the Catholic Relief Services (CRS), and the Adventist Development and Relief Agency (ADRA) to utilize their resources in improving the water and sanitation facilities for refugees (OfERR, n.d.a).

Through sustained advocacy among the Indian political leaders and the public service authorities, OfERR convinced the authorities of the need for an individual Refugee Identity Certificate for each of the Sri Lanka Tamil refugees who remained in India. These cards were issued in 2006, when the district collectors were authorized to issue them to all Sri Lanka Tamil refugees in Tamil Nadu. Previously, one refugee card was issued to each family, which restricted their movements (OfERR, n.d.a).

It is known that Sri Lankan refugees were treated differently in every district, with no uniformity in the application of rules. Because of advocacy from OfERR, the Commissioner of Rehabilitation has prepared a guide in English and Tamil in order to help officials take uniform actions in respect to refugees (OfERR, n.d.a).

OfERR has also forged an agreement with the Bank of Ceylon, which allows refugees in India to open savings accounts in Sri Lanka. This will enable refugees to maintain and make use of these savings immediately on their return to Sri Lanka (OfERR, n.d.a).

Livelihood

Education has had a significant impact on the livelihood of refugees. Sri Lankan refugees are not entitled to work in the public sector in India. The refugees based in the camps seek whatever work they can find locally, usually low-paid laboring work in construction and in agriculture (Valatheeswaran & Rajan, 2011).

Sixty eight women's SHGs have secured bank loans to invest in small business ventures, including tailoring, dress shops and clothes repair, community canteens and sweet meat stalls, handicrafts such as candle and broomstick making, detergent powders and dye sales, gem-cutting, poultry rearing and sales, home gardens for vegetable sales, and spirulina and mushroom cultivation. Most SHG business is done within the camps, but many SHGs take their businesses outside as well (OfERR, n.d.b).

Small enterprises have been set up by OfERR; for example, a browsing center and a garment store in Chennai, and a grocery shop and telephone booth at Nallayan Research Center. These enterprises are managed by women and are yielding good profits from trade with the local community. Tailoring units in Chennai and Trichy also provide training for refugee women. OfERR has a training center for gem-cutting and marketing. Women working in gem-cutting, on construction sites, or in agriculture earn 2,000 to 3,000 rupees ($50 to $75 US) per month, and most of their earnings are spent in supporting the education of their children (Saha, 2009).

Sri Lankan skilled labor enjoys the reputation of being more professional and more hardworking than local skilled labour. Thus refugees easily find work as masons, painters, carpenters, and mechanics. Salaries in private sector jobs, however, are low, and as a result many students prefer to work as painters, carpenters, and masons, and are able to earn about 300 to 400 rupees ($7.50 to 10 US) per day (Valatheeswaran & Rajan, 2011).

The refugees who attain a high level of education have greater opportunities, and many of those who have graduated from Indian colleges have found work in the private sector. The students with technical qualifications also find better jobs (Saha, 2009).

Any private organization willing to recruit a Sri Lankan refugee has to request the Department of Rehabilitation for a "No objection certificate" (NOC), which is issued after obtaining clearance from the intelligence branch of the police. The district authorities have been authorized by the Rehabilitation Department to issue an NOC (Saha, 2009). If a refugee makes a request for an NOC for employment in any other state, no such permission is granted. But many refugees, particularly those near Hosur in Bangalore in the neighboring state of Karnataka, unofficially work in private companies. So far about 1,000 NOCs have been issued. It has been observed that qualified refugees working in the private sector receive less pay than local employees (Buscher, 2011). Some of the private sector businesses that provide employment are textile mills, biscuit factories, rice mills, IT companies, transport companies, and call centers. Refugee doctors find employment in the hospitals set up by Sri Lankan Tamils in cities, and also in other private hospitals.

Many refugee students who do not find suitable employment in the private sector work for OfERR as camp or district-level workers, or as counselors or nutrition assistants. They also find employment as office assistants in regional and head offices, as computer operators or as district-level volunteers.

LESSONS THAT MAY BE LEARNED FROM OFERR

From the accumulated experiences of OfERR, a number of lessons have been learned that may be useful to other organizations endeavoring to work with refugees. Some of the outcomes that seem most impressive are described in the following.

A Dedicated Refugee Organization

A dedicated refugee organization is desirable for managing the affairs of the refugees. It helps in articulating refugee needs. Such an organization can connect with and coordinate its activities with government agencies and is important in maintaining a dialogue with them on a regular basis. With a refugee organization in place, it becomes easier for government agencies to communicate about their programs. Such dialogue helps in developing good rapport and a proper understanding among all participants. This helps the refugee organization to understand the limitations of the government agencies, and for the government agencies in turn to understand the priorities of the refugees. The role and activities of the organization evolve over time. As the organization grows it is able to use the experience it has gained working with government agencies to mobilize different kinds of assistance from different agencies for the welfare of refugees.

Leadership in the Organization

In the initial phases, leadership must be in the hands of a team of persons who are the most acceptable (i.e., respected and honest) representatives from among the refugees. The team has to be built by choosing the most suitable members among the refugees by consensus from the refugees. Understanding among members is likely to be better with a team chosen by consensus. Further, if the tenure of members is fixed, it affords opportunities to others to serve the organization and thus assists with smooth transition of leadership.

Organization Committees at Different Levels

It has been seen that in the case of OfERR, the organization is built along committee lines with the committees at the camp level, the district level, and the regional level, each functioning within their respective domains and in coordination with each other. Each of these committees has a proper delegation of power. These committees can make decisions within their delegated powers and many issues relating to the improvement of living conditions in camps, such as health and education, can be resolved at the appropriate levels.

Cadre of Volunteers

It is always useful to develop a cadre of volunteers from among the refugees. It needs to be appreciated that refugees have tremendous potential. If they are given proper training and support, they can become trainers or coordinators for different programs. They understand their own people and can be very effective in contributing to and implementing the programs meant for the welfare of other refugees. Furthermore, utilizing volunteers is cost effective and ensures the optimum use of resources. It also ensures flexibility in program arrangements. The volunteers can be moved from one program/location to the other as program needs change.

Recipients' Payback to the Community

Refugees who benefit from the organization often feel an obligation to it and in return donate their services to the refugee community. This helps strengthen fellow-feeling among refugees. Such benefactors add to the strength of the volunteers of the organization. For example, refugee youth benefiting from educational support from OfERR often become tutors of younger students in their camp areas (Saha, 2009).

Mobilization of Resources

Every organization needs resources to carry out its activities. In the initial phases, it is difficult to mobilize resources. Refugee organizations should take maximum advantage of the programs of assistance of host countries. It is only when the credibility of a refugee organization is established that other NGOs will come forward with offers of specific program support. Over time, OfERR was able to mobilize support from multiple international donor agencies as well as garner resources provided by Sri Lankan Tamils settled in other countries (Saha, 2009). Through genuine appeal and innovative approaches, it is possible to enlist the support of individuals and organizations who can help according to their capacity. Proper documentation and dissemination of the activities of the refugee organization also helps with this.

Education as a Priority

Education should be a priority for all refugee organizations. They should particularly insist that host countries make suitable arrangements for the education of refugee students. To the extent possible, refugee students should be allowed to pursue education in existing local schools and colleges. Educational institutions may have to be started by the refugees themselves, such as when language barriers pose problems for communication. Education not only helps empower refugees but also makes them responsible. It also helps the host country in managing the affairs of refugees. Formal education may be difficult for many refugees; the option of vocational training should therefore receive priority.

Dispersal of Refugees

The dispersal of refugees is a necessity in case of a large influx. Dispersal helps the host country provide relief and assistance. Distributing refugees over a wide area ensures the education of refugee students without overburdening local schools or conflicting with the needs of the local communities. If suitable powers are delegated to district authorities, many issues relating to education can be resolved at the local level.

Counseling Program

Counseling should be part of the education program. In any refugee situation, the trauma that the refugees undergo can be reduced only with proper counseling. OfERR created a very effective counseling service by training its volunteers, and it has been effective with refugees and with victims of the Indian tsunami in 2006 (Ravindran, 2009).

Empowerment of Women

The empowerment of women should be an important activity of the education program. Empowered women can bring about change in their own lives and in the living conditions of refugee families. Empowered women are likely to ensure the education of their children, and with their own education, expand their ability to contribute to the life of their families and communities.

Advocacy

Advocacy is very important for securing assistance from the host country and improving the living conditions of the refugees. An empowered refugee community is in a better position for effective advocacy, and this can be achieved with strong refugee organizations. OfERR can protect the interests of the refugees and secure many benefits for them with its effective advocacy program with Indian political leaders, and with representatives of the Sri Lankan government.

Livelihood Options

The ultimate aim of any education program is to create livelihood options. These emerge through formal education and through skill development and vocational training. In the long run, the burden on the host country in maintaining refugee communities does not increase when the refugees are able to earn their own livelihoods.

Repatriation of Refugees

An educated and empowered refugee community is likely to be only too willing to repatriate once normalcy returns in the country of origin. A trained refugee community will be in a better position to rebuild their home country upon repatriation. With peace finally established, it is assumed that most refugees will return to Sri Lanka.

CONCLUSION

The significant contributions refugee communities make to local economies and communities are due, in no small measure, to continued support from state and federal governments. While India is not a signatory to the UN conventions governing the rights of refugees, Sri Lankan Tamil refugees have been only marginally been hindered by this due to the historic connection between Tamil Nadu and the Tamil populations in Sri Lanka. The willingness of both state and federal governments to provide humanitarian assistance for these refugees, and the advantage of sharing a common language and culture, meant that Sri Lankan Tamil refugees living in Tamil Nadu had opportunities for education and employment that other refugee groups do not enjoy. It is particularly important to note the strength of the refugee organization OfERR, which has been instrumental in organizing camp life, in providing educational support to Sri Lankan refugee students, and in acting as an advocate for refugee rights within the political context of Tamil Nadu. Without the combined efforts of government and refugees, the successful educational experiences of Sri Lankan refugee students would have been unlikely to occur.

REFERENCES

Bose, T. K. (200). *India: Policies and laws towards refugees.* Human Rights Solidarity. Retrieved from www.hrsolidarity.net/mainfile.php/2000vol10no10745

Buscher, D. (2011). *Bright lights, big city: Urban refugees struggle to make a living.* New York, NY: Women's Refugee Commission, New Delhi.

Human Rights Law Network. (2007). Report of refugee populations in India. Delhi, India: Author.

Organization for Eelam Refugees Rehabilitation (OfERR) (n.d.a). *Advocacy.* Available from www.oferr.org/content.php?id=95

Organization for Eelam Refugees Rehabilitation (OfERR) (n.d.b). *Women.* Available from www.oferr.org/content.php?id=224

Organization for Eelam Refugees Rehabilitation (OfERR) (n.d.c). *Education.* Available from www.oferr.org/content.php?id=234

Organization for Eelam Refugees Rehabilitation (OfERR) (n.d.d). *Camp.* Available from www.oferr.org/content.php?id=231

Organization for Eelam Refugees rehabilitation. (2006). *Database: Central government and Tamil Nadu government helping assistance. Camp population of Sri Lankan refugees at various camp communities in Tamil Nadu as of 1 December 2006.* Retrieved from http://www.oferr.org

Ravindran, I. P. (2009). Refugee resources: Sri Lankan Tamils in India. *Forced Migration Review, 33,* 38–39. Retrieved from http://www.fmreview.org/protracted.htm

Saha, K. C. (2004). Learning from empowerment of Sri Lankan refugees in India. *Forced Migration Review. 20,* 19–20. Retrieved from http://www.fmreview.org/forcedmigration.htm

Saha, K. C. (2009). Unpublished interview records available from the author.

South Asia Human Rights Documentation Centre. (2008). *Tibetan refugees in India: Declining sympathies, diminishing rights.* Retrieved from http://www.hrdc.net/sahrdc/hrfeatures/HRF183

South Asia Human Rights Documentation Centre. (n.d.). *Country report on the refugee situation in India.* Delhi, India: SAHRDC.

South Asian Human Rights Documentation Centre. (1997). *Refugee protection in India.* Retrieved from http://www.hrdc.net/sahrdc/resourcces/refugee_protection.htm

United Nations High Commissioner for Refugees. (2011). *Country operations profile: India.* Geneva, Switzerland: Author.

Valatheeswaran, C., & Rajan, S.I. (2011). Sri Lankan Tamil refugees in India: rehabilitation mechanisms, livelihood strategies, and last solutions. *Refugee Survey Quarterly, 30*(2), 24–44. doi: 10.1093/rsq/hdr005.

ABOUT THE CONTRIBUTORS

Susan Banki

Susan Banki is a Lecturer in Human Rights at the University of Sydney. Her research interests lie in the political, institutional, and legal contexts that explain the roots of and solutions to international human rights violations. In particular, she is interested in the ways that questions of sovereignty, citizenship/membership, and humanitarian principles have shaped our understanding of and reactions to the international human rights regime, international migration, and the provision of international aid. Susan's focus is the Asia-Pacific region, where she has conducted extensive field research in Thailand, Nepal, Bangladesh, and Japan on refugee/migrant protection, statelessness, and border control.

Timothy Brown

After obtaining his doctorate in London, Timothy Brown taught at universities in Southern Sudan and Kenya. He then joined UNHCR Uganda as UN Volunteer Education Adviser—first near the refugee camps in the north and then at the Branch Office in Kampala. He went on to UNHCR headquarters to help set up the independent Refugee Education Trust (RET) for post-primary education and write a chapter in a UNHCR book on refugee education. This was followed by a stint in Southern Sudan as Education Officer for the Sudanese repatriation. He subsequently worked for UNICEF in post-conflict West Africa helping Sierra Leone and Liberia with coordination of the education sector. His most recent assignments have been as Officer-In-Charge of UNESCO Liberia and Education Adviser for UNICEF in Nepal.

Refugee and Immigrant Students, pages 227–232
Copyright © 2012 by Information Age Publishing
227

Tracey Derwing

Tracey Derwing is a professor of TESL at the University of Alberta, and Co-Director of the Prairie Metropolis Centre for Research on Immigration, Integration and Diversity. She has carried out extensive research on second language learners' oral fluency and pronunciation. She has also conducted studies on the settlement experiences of refugees. Dr. Derwing's publications appear in journals such as *Language Learning, Studies in Second Language Acquisition,* and *TESOL Quarterly.* She has edited both the *TESL Canada Journal* and more recently the *Canadian Modern Language Review.* In 2008 she received a Killam professorship in recognition of her academic and public service contributions.

Karen Dooley

Karen Dooley is a literacy lecturer in the School of Cultural and Language Studies in Education, Queensland University of Technology (Australia). Her research uses sociological frameworks to investigate pedagogy in conditions of linguistic and cultural difference. In addition to the study of engagement of refugee students reported in this paper, Karen is currently undertaking a project on digital and print literacies in a linguistically and culturally diverse and low socio-economic primary school.

Jillian Ford

Jillian Ford is a Ph.D. Candidate in Educational Studies at Emory University. She received her B.A./M.T. from the University of Virginia and taught 10th and 11th grade history courses in East Point, GA. Ms. Ford co-founded/sponsored "Know Your History" clubs in Charlottesville, VA and Tri-Cities High in East Point. Both organizations were Afro-centric arenas for student growth. The aim of her research is to make change in traditional social studies education by advocating for alternative curriculum development. Her research interests include citizenship, human rights and social justice education. Jillian works with refugee students and communities in Atlanta.

Anna Kirova

Anna Kirova is professor of early childhood education, Department of Elementary Education, University of Alberta, Canada. Between 2005 and 2010 she was a Domain Leader of the Education Domain and a Domain Leader for the Family, Children and Youth Domain with the Prairie Metropolis Centre for Immigration and Integration.

The main focus of Dr. Kirova's work has been on understanding the peer relationships of culturally and linguistically diverse children and their experiences of loneliness and isolation at school. Her current research focuses on arts-based collaborative research with vulnerable children, and community-based participatory research.

Florence McCarthy

Florence McCarthy has extensive academic experience in educational and social development issues and programs, and is currently engaged in research focusing on educational issues for refugee students both in Australia and other parts of the world. She has been Professor of Economics and Business Management and Special Adviser in Service Learning at the International Christian University, Tokyo, Japan. She has considerable professional experience as a researcher, teacher, consultant, and policy adviser in the areas of development studies, gender, and education. She has taught at Cornell University and Teachers College, Columbia, and has been involved in international service-learning in the US since 1989, and since 2001 has been instrumental in the development of service-learning in tertiary institutions across Asia and Australia.

J. Lynn McBrien

J. Lynn McBrien, Ph.D., received her doctorate in Educational Studies from Emory University in 2005, where she was also awarded the university's Humanitarian Award for her work with refugee students. She is currently an Assistant Professor at the University of South Florida, Sarasota-Manatee, where she teaches undergraduate and graduate courses in social foundations, comparative education, and media education. She has researched and written about resettled refugees in the United States since 2002, and in 2010 she began work on-site with refugee students at Buduburam Refugee Camp in Ghana and former child soldiers and their teachers in northern Uganda.

Su-Ann Oh

Su-Ann Oh is a sociologist specialising in education and is currently a visiting research fellow at the Institute of Southeast Asian Studies, Singapore. She has been working on research on the education of refugees along the Thai-Burmese border since 2005. Her research to date has examined the educational experience of Burmese and Palestinian refugees and the needs of marginalised students in England and Singapore. She has recently published papers and reports on the education of Burmese refugees and the daily experiences of separated children in Thai refugee camps. She is a co-founder of the Room to Grow Foundation (roomtogrowfoundation.org), a charity based on the Thai-Burmese border, which provides basic necessities to migrant and refugee children living in camps and in migrant areas.

Marian Rossiter

Marian Rossiter is Associate Professor and Coordinator of the Teaching English as a Second Language Program, in the Department of Educational Psychology, University of Alberta. She has had over twenty years' experience teaching in and coordinating adult ESL programs. She is a refugee co-sponsor and Associate Editor of the *TESL Canada Journal*. In 2009 she received an Honourary Life Membership from TESL Canada and the Coutts-Clarke Research Fellowship from the Faculty of Education at the University of Alberta. Her primary research interests are in second language speaking fluency, strategy use, and the settlement of immigrant and refugee youth in Canada.

Jill Rutter

Jill Rutter is the Research Manager at Daycare Trust and an associate fellow in migration at the Institute for Public Policy Research (ippr), the UK's leading think tank. Previously Jill was a Senior Research Fellow in Migration at ippr, where she undertook work on migrant integration, public service responses to migration, public attitudes and changing migration flows in Europe. Jill has published extensively on all aspects of migration with well over 100 books, chapters, and papers on this subject, including *Refugee Children in the UK* (Open University Press, 2006). Prior to joining ippr, Jill was senior lecturer in education at London Metropolitan University. From 1988–2001 she was a Policy Advisor at the Refugee Council, London. She has also worked as a school teacher and on development projects in India.

K. C. Saha

K.C. Saha is Development Commissioner in Bihar, India. He has 36 years experience in Public Administration. He has worked in different sectors such as education, health, agriculture, industries, rural development, local government, social welfare, planning, rural livelihood, infrastructure development and conduct of elections for Parliament and Assemblies. His skills include design and implementation of schemes for the marginalized section of society. He has managed large portfolios of World Bank and ADB loans and DFID grants for the state. He is monitoring the Bill and Melinda Gates Foundation health program in Bihar. Saha has independently carried out research on refugee issues and irregular migration. He has published more than 15 research articles in national and international journals. He worked as a senior research consultant in the United Nations Office on Drugs and Crimes, India. Saha has a MSc in Physics and LLB from Delhi University. He also has a Diploma in Public Administration from Institut Internationale d'Administration Publique, Paris.

Linda Silka

Linda Silka directs the Margaret Chase Smith Policy Center at the University of Maine, USA, where she is a faculty member in the School of Economics. For many years Dr. Silka has worked with new refugee and immigrant families to create supportive community structures that assist people in building new lives in their new country. Many of these endeavors have involved bringing universities into partnerships with community entities such as schools, health care facilities, law enforcement agencies, and non-profit agencies that are on the front lines of the changing demographics of communities.

Margaret Vickers

Margaret Vickers is a Professor of Education at the University of Western Sydney. Her career includes senior appointments in the Australian Public Service and the Paris-based OECD. She has authored several studies on refugee education, on secondary schooling for socially and economically vulnerable populations, on early school leaving, and on youth in transition. Over the past three years she has developed and researched programs to support students from refugee backgrounds, including a UWS program through which beginning teachers learn to work as refugee tutors. She is currently leading a large research project funded by the Australian Research Council and the NSW Department of Education and Communities, located in areas of significant socio-economic disadvantage, examining the impact of the new school leaving-age on schools and young people in these areas.

Printed in Great Britain
by Amazon